Economic Change and Rural Resistance in Southern Bolivia, 1880-1930

ERICK D. LANGER

ECONOMIC CHANGE AND
RURAL RESISTANCE IN

SOUTHERN BOLIVIA

1880-1930

Stanford University Press, Stanford, California 1989

Stanford University Press, Stanford, California
© 1989 by the Board of Trustees of the Leland Stanford Junior University
Printed in the United States of America
CIP data appear at the end of the book

Published with the assistance of a special grant
from the Stanford University Faculty Publication Fund to help support
nonfaculty work originating at Stanford.

To the memory of

CARL E. SOLBERG

Acknowledgments

This enterprise owes much to many people. In a sense, this book was in the making from the first time I set foot in Sucre, in 1972, as a Rotary Club high school foreign exchange student. The family of Dr. Luis Sanchez Ch. took me in with open arms and in many ways helped stimulate my interest in Bolivia. They, the Sucre and Lake City (Seattle) Clubs, and Rotary International are largely to blame for my subsequent career. Carl Solberg's enthusiasm for Latin American history was a decisive influence during my undergraduate years and gave me the impetus to go into the field. The present book began as a dissertation: I owe much to the training that my adviser, Richard M. Morse, and Frederick P. Bowser, John D. Wirth, and John J. Johnson provided at Stanford. I am particularly indebted to the first two and to Don E. Fehrenbacher, who served on my dissertation committee and improved the work with many useful suggestions. In Bolivia, Tristan Platt was instrumental in teaching me to ask the right questions and kindly shared information from his findings. Likewise, Xavier Albó, René Arze, Ramiro Condarco Morales, Daniel Gade, Lynn Meisch, Silvia Rivera, and Ann Zulawski were extremely helpful. In North America, Jeffery Cole, Carlos del Castillo, Erwin P. Grieshaber, Donna Guy, Tulio Halperin Donghi, Inge Harman, Kevin Healy, Herbert Klein, Roger Rasnake, and John Rowe contributed important information. Two of my colleagues at Carnegie-Mellon, David W. Miller and Peter N. Stearns, made valuable comments on the manuscript. The lively presentations and discussions in the graduate seminar on Comparative Rural History, which I co-taught with

David Miller, were extremely helpful in defining many issues I had been mulling over.

A study of this kind, which relies extensively on document collections in private hands, interviews, and archives that are generally not open to researchers, owes much to the unselfish help and support of many people. The list of people who helped me in finding my material is long. Don Gunnar Mendoza, director of the Archivo Nacional de Bolivia, aided me in all aspects of my research and opened many doors. I am also grateful to Dr. María del Carmen Rua de Tirado, director of the Centro Bibliográfico Documental Histórico of the University of San Francisco Xavier in Sucre, and Alberto Crespo R., director of the Biblioteca Universitaria in La Paz. Walter Pérez Chacon, executive secretary to the prefect; Dr. Carlos Arce Brown and Dr. Hugo Lora, presidents of the Superior Court of Chuquisaca; and Colonel Rómulo Mercado, Colonel Gustavo Ribera C., Lieutenant Colonel Mario Mendez M., and Lieutenant Colonel Julio Loayza V., prefects during 1981–82, provided me with essential recommendations. Acción Cultural Loyola, under the directorship of Father Jorge Trías, S.J., and the Centro de Investigaciones Sociales sponsored me in Bolivia in 1981–82. I also express my heartfelt thanks to all those who agreed to be interviewed, as well as to those who opened up their private archives. At the Sociedad Agrícola, Ganadera e Industrial de Cinti, Carlos Calvo and Mario Cortes were extremely supportive of my project. I owe much to the judges, court clerks, notaries, and government and church officials who put up with the disturbance of a historian working in their midst, particularly Dr. Antonio Cosulich, Dr. Ana María Palacios de Valda, Dr. María del Carmen Baldivieso, Zenón Vacaflores, Jaime Barron, Esteban Arancibia, Dr. Edgar Torres, Eliodoro Alarcón, René Aceytuno I., Miguel López Avila, Dr. Luis Subirana Hurtado, Dr. Hugo Subieta D., Guillermo Sensano Pericon, Dr. Tomás Tudela Tapia (twice over!), Mariano Civera, Dr. Armando Vargas Rojas, and Dr. Julio Vega Belaúnde.

A number of others provided essential help. My greatest thanks go to Pilar Giménez D., my friend and research assistant in 1981–82. Holger and Alejandra Schuett, Rolando Urioste and family, Tomás Daroca, P. Otto, Gaston Cavero, Ronald Poppe, Luis and Sandra Rodríguez, Carlos Querejazu and family, Jorge Arduz, Emilio Barrientos, Alberto Guzman, Gerardo Maldini, O.F.M., Julio Entrasambaguas, William Lofstrom, Joaquin Gantier V., Cecilia Córdova, Antonio Rojas, and Thom Whigham also aided in different ways in the completion of this book.

Financial support was crucial. A Stanford Summer Research grant, administered by the Latin American Center, helped me define research issues in 1979. The Social Science Research Council and the American Council of Learned Societies, the Inter-American Foundation, and the Fulbright-Hays Fellowship program (IEE) provided funds for doctoral research in 1981–82. Generous support from the College of Humanities and Social Science at Carnegie-Mellon, through Falk Fund Faculty Development Grants, made it possible for me to return to Bolivia and finish my research.

Some of the material in this book has appeared in two papers: "Andean Banditry and Peasant Community Organization, 1882–1930," in Richard W. Slatta, ed., *Bandidos: The Varieties of Latin American Banditry* (Westport, Conn., 1987), pp. 113–30, and "Labor Strikes and Reciprocity on Chuquisaca Haciendas," *Hispanic American Historical Review*, 65.2 (1985), pp. 255–77. I thank the respective publishers, Greenwood Press and Duke University Press, for permission to draw freely on this material.

I owe most of all to my family—my wife, Laurie, and my children, Jimmy, Naomi, Rafael, and Elizabeth—who have had to put up with many things, including living for fourteen months in another country, making do during my extended absences on field trips, and too often taking second place to this book as I researched and wrote it.

E.D.L.

Contents

Maps and Tables

Economic Change and Rural Resistance in Southern Bolivia, 1880-1930

CHAPTER ONE

Introduction

Rural non-elites only recently have begun to receive the attention they deserve as independent actors in their own right. As historians, rural sociologists, and anthropologists delve deeper into new kinds of sources, they find that, in the countryside, resistance to change, particularly in labor systems and patterns of land tenure, has been much more widespread and more effective than previously realized. Peasants, agricultural laborers, and tribal peoples exercised a number of choices that to a large extent determined the subsequent shape of rural society. The transformation of local economies was especially apparent in Latin America in the late nineteenth and early twentieth centuries when, as a result of the worldwide demand for raw materials such as tin, much of the region became tightly integrated into the burgeoning world economy. This study concentrates on the department of Chuquisaca, in southern Bolivia, to show how rural peoples, by resisting and accommodating, greatly affected the outcome of the changes that swept the countryside during this period.

The process of economic change in Latin America during the late nineteenth and early twentieth centuries has been studied extensively, but the emphasis, especially as the dependency model briefly gained ascendancy in the 1970's, has been mainly on the export sector.[1] Recently, however, a new generation has begun to look at the implications of export-led development on regional systems not directly involved in the production for foreign markets. Florencia Mallon, for example, has shown how local elites in the Central Highlands of Peru, in both villages and cities, accommodated themselves to the presence of the enormous foreign-owned Cerro de Pasco Corporation. These elites found it possible to thrive on the new economic opportunities in the revived internal markets that the corporation provided, although they did so by exploiting village communal traditions for their own financial gain. According to Mallon, the introduction of foreign capital into local economies eventually led to a differentiation between prosperous farmers and a large mass of proletarianized peasant villagers.[2]

This pattern of internal differentiation within the villages, as well as an increasing income gap between regional elites and the rural masses, appears to have been a common phenomenon throughout Latin America during this period—in Mexico, for example, under the Porfiriato.[3] New national elites, imbued with liberal and positivist ideals, emerged after a long period of civil wars and *caudillismo*, and consolidated their countries into nations under central political control. As part of their reorganization of society on an oligarchical model, they enacted laws designed to exploit more efficiently the resources of the countryside, especially labor and land.[4]

One of the most important causes of the increasing disequilibrium in wealth was the expansion of the large estate at the expense of Indian communities and smallholders. Only the period of the establishment of landed estates in the seventeenth century rivals the late nineteenth and early twentieth centuries in the amount of land that came under the control of haciendas and plantations.[5] In areas such as the Andes and Mesoamerica, where large concentrations of Indians survived in communities dating back to the early colonial period, the elites realized that they first had to destroy the Indians' land base to obtain their labor. David McCreery has documented the extent to which, in Guatemala in the late nineteenth century, village lands were incorporated into latifundios on a massive scale as a way of getting workers for coffee cultivation. The expanding plantations left minifundios, that is, plots of land too small for subsistence, and unemployed agricultural workers were hereupon arrested under vagrancy laws and put to work as cheap labor on the coffee plantations.[6] François Chevalier and Jean Piel have estimated that in southern Peru large estates reached their full extent at the expense of Indian communities only in the nineteenth and twentieth centuries; research by Ramiro Condarco Morales and Silvia Rivera suggests that this was also the case for the *altiplano* in northern Bolivia.[7]

The consequences for Indians who were incorporated into the

hacienda labor force were not always drastic. Effects varied from region to region, depending to a large degree on previous conditions; but it has become increasingly apparent that integration into haciendas did not necessarily bring about the destruction of native modes of organization. According to Erwin Grieshaber, the ability to resist the impact of Spanish culture depended not only on the density of the Indian population and the strength of the Indian communal organization, but also on the type of agricultural production, the proximity to a large Spanish city, and the number of non-Indians living in the countryside.[8] Nonetheless, although the emphasis on continuities holds much promise for examining the densely populated "core" areas of Mesoamerica and the highland Andes, there is no doubt that during the late nineteenth and early twentieth centuries, frontier areas, where native populations had not been well integrated into the dominant society, suffered great changes. Witness, for example, the often brutal conditions that accompanied the incorporation of Indian land and labor in the Yaqui valley in northern Mexico and in Yucatán.[9]

Although there is still much to be learned about the economic and social organization among the Indians of the frontier region, recent scholarship, particularly that of the ethnohistorian John V. Murra, has provided a detailed view of the peculiar characteristics of Andean agricultural organization. In a series of important articles Murra unraveled land-tenure patterns, economic activities, and political control among the Inca and a variety of other Andean ethnic groups at the time of the Spanish Conquest. Murra believes that the mechanisms of reciprocity and redistribution were central to the Inca society and economy. The Inca state provided raw materials for textile production, for example, which the Indian women made into cloth and returned to the state. The state then distributed the cloth to its subject population in a show of largesse and as a way of bringing the various Andean ethnic groups more closely into the state. This relationship of subject to state in a pattern of piecework for finished goods constituted an effective mechanism of Inca rule throughout the Andean world, and it was crucial in cementing social relations in a region that had no market economy.[10]

Tristan Platt and other scholars believe that these mechanisms of reciprocity and redistribution continue to the present day. Platt's case study of the Indian communities, or *ayllus*, of northern Potosí shows how the Andean ideals not only were the basis for smooth relations within the ayllus themselves but also were essential elements in the relationship between the Bolivian state and the communities, at least as perceived by the Indians. In his important book *Estado boliviano y ayllu andino* (1982), Platt describes how, up until the late nineteenth century, the Indians of northern Potosí paid tribute and fulfilled various other obligations for local officials in the expectation that the state would protect the territorial integrity of their communities. After the state reneged on this reciprocal pact by abolishing the communities and distributing the land among individual community members, the ayllus rebelled in certain ways that were designed to reestablish the earlier arrangement.[11] Although Platt carefully limits his conclusions to the highly traditional northern Potosí communities, Grieshaber's insight that native cultural norms continued to persist even after the Indians had been absorbed into haciendas makes it necessary to test whether Andean concepts permeated relations on the highland estates as well.

We cannot fully understand the nature of rural society in areas where large haciendas predominated without knowing something about how labor was organized, what the benefits were for the landlord, and—not least but frequently overlooked—how estate workers accommodated themselves to the labor system. Often, the alternatives available to hacienda laborers, as Friedrich Katz has shown in the case of Porfirian Mexico, were just as important as the power of the landlord. The pendulum of scholarly opinion, which until the 1970's assumed that the landlord possessed virtually all power, has gradually begun to swing the other way, examining more critically the relationship between hacendados and their workers. Arnold Bauer, in his discussion of debt peonage in Spanish America in the nineteenth and twentieth centuries, especially stimulated a rethinking of the relative power between the two sides. He argued that debt peonage often benefited the worker more than the hacendado. The hacendado had to sink large amounts of capital into his labor force, because workers insisted on a cash advance, and hacendado attempts to retrieve debts often were not completely successful. In effect, it appears that systems of debt peonage worked to the hacendado's advantage primarily in marginal frontier areas where the landowner had overwhelming power and could administer swift justice without interference by the state.[12]

The increasing use of estate records has given historians a much more detailed and precise view of how Spanish American haciendas functioned. Much of the recent work on debt peonage and the profitability of rural properties has resulted from the study of estate records, and it has been extremely valuable in clearing up important and fundamental questions about the nature of the hacienda regime. Only lately have scholars attempted to go beyond these obvious uses of estate records to show how the hacienda functioned and was able to survive for centuries. If the hacendado did not rule simply by fiat and the peon was not in most cases a hapless, overexploited victim with no recourse whatsoever, then, obviously, the characteristics of the hacienda labor regime cannot be ascribed solely to what the landowners needed. Instead, accommodation and reciprocity between landlord and peon appear to have played a much greater role than we had thought.[13] One of the most useful ways of examining this problem is to analyze how both landlords and peons manipulated paternalistic ideology for their own purposes.[14] This approach is particularly relevant in the Andean region, where the concepts of reciprocity and redistribution as methods of rule remained vigorous from before the Spanish Conquest to the present. In a sense, this traditional Andean culture served as the foundation for what Herbert Gutman has called for first-generation industrial workers in nineteenth-century North America the "working-class subculture," which helped define workers' lives and determined the modes of resistance to changes that hacienda laborers felt were detrimental to their interests.[15]

Highland hacienda workers were not the only ones who resisted the wrenching changes of the late nineteenth and early twentieth centuries. It is becoming increasingly clear that smallholders, community Indians, and other countryfolk also reacted, often violently, to the restructuring of the national economies. The British historian E. P. Thompson, upon whose work Gutman relied heavily, defined the basis upon which "pre-political" peoples felt compelled quite literally to take the law into their own hands. Thompson's influential study of the bread riots that followed the imposition of the Corn Laws in eighteenth-century England revealed what he terms the "moral economy of the crowd." The crowd, when protesting certain abuses, engaged in specific actions grounded in the "traditional view of social norms and obligations of the proper economic functioning of several parties in the community."[16] The authorities, moreover, fostered this view by their paternalism toward the poor. James C. Scott applied the same concept of the moral economy of the crowd to peasant revolts that occurred early in the twentieth century in Southeast Asia and postulated that for the peasant, the moral economy was based on the right to a subsistence. He suggested that peasants relied on reciprocal relations among themselves and the moral obligation of the elites to redistribute their gains in bad times. When market forces and a more powerful state threatened these traditional arrangements, the peasants rose in rebellion to assert the rights that ensured their livelihood.[17]

Scott's paradigm for Southeast Asia assumed that all peasants are organized in more or less the same way, among themselves and also in certain worker-client bonds with other elements of society such as merchants and landlords. This is not necessarily the case in all peasant societies. Howard Handelman, in an examination of the hacienda land invasions in Peru in the 1960's, posited that only "transitional" communities having some communal organization but also numerous ties to outside actors were likely to mobilize effectively. In contrast, communities that were fully traditional did not mobilize, nor did villages that were completely integrated into the national political and economic system. The traditional societies were too conservative and had too few contacts with regional and national institutions, and the integrated villages lacked the internal solidarity that was needed for mobilization on the community level.[18] To some extent Handelman's conclusions would seem to ignore the long history of social conflict between Indian communities and haciendas even while the villages were presumably fully traditional, but in emphasizing the importance of community organization in peasant resistance, Handelman's approach has interesting implications. Indeed, much of the recent debate on whether certain types of peasants are more revolutionary than others has often at least implicitly focused on this very point.[19]

A number of researchers have recognized that resistance to changes in the rural economy was not restricted to strikes, rebellions, or outright insurrection; opposition could also take the form of court challenges, banditry, or simply flight from oppressive conditions.[20] It seems clear that the range of possible resistance, and the reasons why a group would engage in one or several forms of resistance but not others, are related to some extent to how the particular peasant society is organized. However, the type of organization must be placed in the context of the relative power of peasants, landlords, and the state if we are to determine just what possibilities were in fact open to rural peoples who wanted to ameliorate their condition during the tremendous economic changes of the late nineteenth and early twentieth centuries.[21]

The great diversity of geographic, economic, and social conditions in the Andean countryside has led to very distinct ways in which the rural inhabitants have perceived and acted on their environment. Nowhere is this more evident than in the department of Chuquisaca, located in the southern half of Bolivia. The department encompasses a broad range of conditions, from the wide-open, windswept highlands, where there are clusters of peasant households divided among former haciendas and Indian communities, to the steaming subtropical jungle of the rugged Andean foothills, where the only inhabitants are isolated tribes of Indians. Ethnic and linguistic boundaries bisect the department. In the west, sedentary Indians speaking Quechua, the language of the Inca empire, predominate. In the central portion, the rural population is mostly Spanish-speaking mestizos and descendants of Spaniards. To the east, the Guaraní-speaking Chiriguanos, who practice slash-and-burn agriculture, until recently outnumbered Spanish speakers and the more primitive hunters and gatherers of the harsh Chaco desert.

This at times bewildering variety of peoples and geography can be broken down into four principal zones, which correspond roughly to the provincial boundaries that existed around 1900—that is, Yamparaez, Cinti, Tomina, and Azero (see Map 1).[22] Yamparaez province, in northwestern Chuquisaca, contains the capital city, Sucre, the traditional residence of the elite silver-mine owners and their descendants. Quechua-speaking Indians predominated in Yamparaez, living not only in the many small communities that dotted the mountainous countryside but also on the haciendas owned by wealthy townspeople. Cinti, a province of narrow, fertile valleys, having no significant urban center, was populated mainly by people descended from highland Indians, Spaniards, Chiriguanos, and black slaves. They cultivated grapes, fruit, and sugarcane, which were made into wines and liquors for export to the mining centers in the adjacent department of Potosí.

During the colonial and early republican period, Tomina and Azero were a single political unit. This region was long a disputed frontier at times under the control of the warrior-like Chiriguanos, but by the eighteenth century the Spaniards had completely colonized Tomina. Many Chiriguanos fled eastward to Azero, into the predominantly mestizo rural population; those who remained

Map 1. Department of Chuquisaca, ca. 1900. Sucre is both the legal national capital and the departmental capital.

were absorbed into the cattle-based Spanish society. In the dense jungles of the Andean foothills in Azero, the Chiriguanos were able to remain relatively untouched by Spanish influence until the late nineteenth century. As in Tomina, cattle raising was the chief activity of the sparse Spanish and mestizo population, but the Chiriguanos supplied most of the laborers on the huge land grants parceled out among colonists.

Not surprisingly, in view of the distinctive conditions and history of the four zones, the inhabitants reacted differently to changing historical forces. This was certainly true in the critical period from roughly 1890 to the Great Depression of the 1930's, when Latin America integrated itself firmly into the world economy as a principal exporter of raw materials. Although Chuquisaca did not participate in this export led process of economic growth, the changes that occurred in the structure of the Bolivian and Argentine economies brought important changes also to the department's rural societies. To the extent that the four provinces of Chuquisaca are representative of types of regions common throughout Latin America, an examination of these changes is relevant beyond the narrow confines of southern Bolivia. Yamparaez was one of the traditional heavily populated peasant "core" areas in Latin America, in which haciendas and Indian communities competed for land and labor; Cinti was a highly commercialized region in which large estates clearly predominated; Azero was a frontier region where settlers, relatively unrestrained by state control, subdued and then forced the recalcitrant natives into debt servitude on their rural properties; and Tomina was a region in which a numerous mestizo smallholding peasantry fluctuated between a commercial orientation and mere subsistence.

The transformation of the central Andean economy manifested itself on the local level in three different but closely interrelated areas: reorientation of interregional commercial ties and changes in the types of products commercialized; the creation or expansion in many areas of large estates; and a general worsening of social conditions, apparent in declining labor conditions and the impoverishment of the peasantry. We are gradually coming to realize that the rural peoples who were exposed to these large and impersonal historical forces were not mere passive victims, but instead reacted in many different ways to alter or at least ameliorate their fate. How and why rural peoples adapted to and resisted the changes in their lives was determined primarily by the specific historical circumstances and the various opportunities available to them. Nevertheless, in the reactions to change in the different types of region, whether they contained traditional village-based Indian communities, mestizo smallholders, or loosely organized tribal peoples, one sees certain common characteristics that transcend the particular region and can be discerned also in other parts of Latin America. In this work, the four provinces of Chuquisaca will serve as case studies, representative to some degree of resistance elsewhere in Latin America during the same period.[23]

So far as it can be done, this study endeavors to examine the fundamental changes that took place in rural southern Bolivia during the crucial period of the late nineteenth and early twentieth centuries from the perspectives both of the elites and of the vast majority of the members of rural society. The salient characteristics of the process of change, though not present equally in all areas, were the increasing internal differentiation within Chuquisaca society, land concentration at the expense of indigenous groups, and worsening labor conditions. The reactions of the rural inhabitants, ranging from adaptation to rebellion, show clearly the kind of society that had evolved in these regions and also how these countryfolk helped to shape their own destiny. A knowledge of how and why Chuquisaca's peoples resisted these new forces helps us to understand in a comparative manner the process of rural conflict in the rest of Latin America and other parts of the world.

Diverse though the four zones in Chuquisaca were in economic and social organization, all were affected by one major economic event of the late nineteenth century—the disintegration of the silver-mining economic complex, which had survived, albeit in modified form, since the colonial period. Chapter 2 examines the context of the great economic and political transformations that occurred in the region as a result of the decline of silver as Bolivia's major export, foremost of which was the increasing marginalization of southern Bolivia. Chapter 3 delineates the reactions of the oligarchy based in the capital city. The Sucre elites had relied heavily on income from the silver-mining companies, and after this source of income vanished, they attempted to regain their preeminent financial and political position by a number of different strategies, many of which had profound effects on the surrounding countryside. Chapter 4 analyzes the conflict between the expanding haciendas and the Indian communities of Yamparaez province, as well as the effects of changing labor conditions on provincial haciendas and the peons' reactions to these changes. Chapter 5 examines the grape-growing Cinti region and its decline as a result of the loss of highland urban markets, and it investigates in detail the subsequent creation of a number of enormous agro-industrial estates and their attendant labor problems to determine the constraints to modernization in the Andean context. Chapter 6 describes the gradual subjugation of the tribal Chiriguanos and the colonization of Azero province as a result of changing commercial impulses. The crushing of armed resistance and the integration of the Chiriguanos into the hacienda system through debt peonage, and their attempts to escape these conditions by migrating or by joining Franciscan missions, are detailed. Chapter 7 deals with the peculiar social and commercial relations of Tomina province and the rise of banditry as the provincial economy declined. The final chapter compares and contrasts the various types of resistance and their social, economic, political, and cultural foundations as evidenced by the case studies of each province. Also, the Agrarian Reform of 1953 and its effects on Chuquisaca society are discussed as the results of the long process of historical change in which the rural people of the department have participated in important ways.

CHAPTER TWO

The Southern Bolivian
Mining Economy

From an early date, the proximity of the rich silver deposits of Potosí tied the rural economy of Chuquisaca as a supplier of agricultural goods to that of the mines. Indeed, from the early sixteenth century on, much of the Spanish South American economy during the colonial period revolved around the silver mines in the southern Bolivian highlands, and it was only toward the end of the nineteenth century that this regional economy based on the southern Bolivian silver mines broke down. As the mining of silver in Potosí became less and less profitable, the rise of other exports and the reorientation of the economies of central South America toward exports other than silver left southern Bolivia in an economically marginal position. Also, as a result of its economic decline, the region lost its former political preeminence within Bolivia. For the countryside, the demise of the silver mines had such important consequences that a full understanding of the evolution of the rural society in Chuquisaca can only be arrived at within the framework of the rise and decline of the colonial regional economic network centered on the Potosí silver-mining complex.

The city of Potosí, lying at the foot of an imposing and silver-rich mountain called the *cerro rico*, was founded in 1546, one year after an Indian discovered the rich veins of silver ore. The boom town grew quickly. At its founding, the city counted 14,000 settlers. By 1600 it contained almost half of the male Indian population of central and southern Peru; forty years later, it reached its maximum size, with 160,000 inhabitants, making it by far the largest city in the Western Hemisphere.[1] Feeding and otherwise supplying these large numbers in the city and the surrounding areas presented great problems, since Potosí as well as most of the other nearby mining centers were located in the barren and cold highlands above 4,000 meters altitude, where most agriculture was impracticable.

To fill the mining markets' demand, an enormous trade network covering much of Spanish South America grew up. As Gwendolin Cobb has shown, this network extended from Ecuador, where sweatshops manufactured rough textile to clothe the Potosí mine workers, to Tucumán in northern Argentina and farther south, where mules were bred as pack animals to transport goods to the mines. Carlos Sempat Assadourian defined the characteristics that governed the Potosí trade. He showed that the Potosí mining economy created what he called the "Peruvian economic space." Because of the remote location of the mines, much of the silver extracted necessarily circulated throughout the Viceroyalty of Peru before being exported in one form or another, and it stimulated the production of a large variety of goods. Thus a regional distribution of labor evolved; this regional specialization encouraged the development of a complex web of exchange within the Peruvian economic space, which in time became virtually self-sufficient.[2]

The Jesuits, for example, developed intricate commercial circuits in South America to take advantage of the high prices in the mining centers. Despite a prohibition to buy for the purpose of re-selling, the Jesuits collected *yerba mate*, leaves that make a tea-like beverage, from their extensive missions in Paraguay, and sold them to the Jesuit college in Córdoba (Argentina) for transshipment to Peru. In the seventeenth century, the Argentine colleges maintained representatives in Salta and Potosí to keep them posted on economic conditions in these markets. Similar arrangements were made for the sale of cloth from Ecuador, sugar from the Peruvian coastal valleys, and cattle hides from Argentina.[3]

This trade network survived into the republican period in spite of the disruptions caused by the partition of the Viceroyalty of Peru in 1776 and the wars for independence in the first quarter of the nineteenth century. After the declaration of independence in 1825, however, the conditions of the mines were deplorable. The richest shafts had flooded as a result of the neglect during the fifteen years of revolution and the little silver extracted came mainly from slag heaps discarded during the more prosperous colonial period. But even though silver production stagnated for fifty years following the declaration of Bolivian independence, the mining economy still dominated a large area.[4] Bolivia remained relatively inaccessible to commerce, since foreign merchants had to traverse either the water-scarce deserts of the Pacific coast or travel over a thousand kilometers from Buenos Aires. In the absence of foreign goods in the highlands, silver produced in the department of Potosí continued to circulate throughout the central Andes, stimulating native production for the mining centers. In effect, the core area of the Peruvian economic space, which included southern Peru, Bolivia, and northern Argentina, did not participate to the same extent in the early-nineteenth-century trade boom generated by massive imports of primarily British goods into the new South American republics.[5]

The central Andean region, as during the colonial period, continued to specialize in various products for sale in the mines. In Bolivia, the Cochabamba sweatshops (*obrajes*) still manufactured cotton cloth. Chuquisaca sold its wheat, corn, and wines in Potosí in return for silver, coca, and manufactured goods from other areas within the Potosí regional economic complex. Beyond the largely artificial national boundaries of Bolivia, the wines and spirits of the Moquegua and Tambo valleys in southern Peru were marketed in the southern Bolivian mining centers. Rough wool cloth from Cuzco, Huamanga, and Andahuaillas, as well as rugs and ponchos from Puno and Lampa, were also exported almost exclusively to Bolivia. Although in Argentina British textiles replaced the rougher cloth from Cochabamba, the trade in northern Argentine mules, donkeys, horses, and tanned leather goods to the mining areas of Potosí continued.[6]

Trade circuits were not the only colonial legacy. Government policies, after a brief period of reform in the first years of independence, reverted to colonial modes. Among the most important policies were those concerning Indian tribute and monetary matters. Simón Bolívar abolished Indian tribute payments in 1825, but two years later the state's continuous fiscal demands made it necessary to reimpose them, and until the 1860's tribute remained the single most important item in the national budget, constituting between one-fourth and one-half of total state income.[7] The terminology was changed, from tribute to *contribución indigenal*, but the tax exclusively on Indians perpetuated the racial divisions that had been imposed by the Spanish Conquest. It also made the state take a direct interest in preserving Indian land. The govern-

TABLE I

Emission of Pesos Febles, 1830–1859

Period	Undebased coins	Pesos febles	Percent feble
1830–34	8,109,636	1,347,750	14%
1835–39	8,357,518	2,072,749	20
1840–44	6,786,059	4,694,626	41
1845–49	4,425,912	4,482,097	50
1850–54	2,301,928	9,681,676	81
1855–59	1,186,051	11,568,535	91

SOURCE: Antonio Mitre, *Los patriarcas de la plata* (Lima, 1981), p. 48.

ment recognized that the communities needed land to earn money to pay the tax; without land, tribute payments would cease. In 1842, the legislature declared that community land belonged to the state and tribute was a type of rent. Although this measure laid the legal groundwork for later attempts to expropriate Indian lands, its immediate effect was to underscore the state's interest in preserving the Indians' holdings and preventing the encroachment of haciendas.[8]

The new Bolivian state also maintained the colonial mining policies. Miners had to take all silver to *bancos de rescate*, or governmental mining banks, to sell at a lower price than they might have earned on the open market. In 1830, President Andrés de Santa Cruz started emitting debased coins, called *pesos febles*, to pay for his wide-ranging military ventures. Although this was meant to be only a temporary measure, the constant lack of fiscal resources led subsequent governments to continue the practice, to the point where debased coins constituted over 90 percent of all money emitted (see Table 1). What with government taxes on minting and payment in debased coins, the miners suffered greatly. For entrepreneurs, the conversion from ore to coin at the *bancos de rescate* cost up to 28 percent of the original value of the ore.[9]

Bolivian manufacturers and artisans, on the other hand, gained a good deal from the government's mining and minting policies. Since the devaluation of Bolivian currency made local goods cheaper than imported goods, produced outside the zone dominated by the Bolivian peso, manufacturers and artisans were able to compete effectively with foreign manufactures. The statistician José María Dalence estimated in 1846 that the commerce in domestic manufactures was worth almost 16,000,000 pesos, whereas

European imports amounted to only half that sum. A large amount of *pesos febles* also accumulated in southern Peru and northern Argentina, showing that these regions remained inside the Potosí mining markets' sphere of influence.[10]

By the 1850's, a new group of miners emerged who were not tied to the old colonial economy. With the liberalization of commerce following independence, a large number of small-scale merchants brought foreign goods from the Pacific coast to the interior. As the first flush of enthusiasm abated and the difficulties of competing with native industries became apparent, most small traders went out of business. Only the large commercial houses with foreign, especially Chilean, backing survived. These large-scale merchants, with access to credit in Valparaíso, became the intermediaries to the Bolivian mining companies for loans, or invested their own money in mining enterprises. In some cases, the mining companies proceeded to build costly and long-term infrastructure necessary for sustained operations. But interest rates remained high, and silver production stagnated; beginning in the 1850's, many miners were forced to sell out to the merchants or let new administrators tied to Chilean mercantile interests take over management. The new administrators modernized production methods, hired European mining experts, and actively solicited foreign capital for their expansion plans.[11]

The new breed of miners, many of them former merchants, were primarily from southern Bolivia and usually resided in Sucre or Potosí. José Avelino Aramayo, one of the foremost silver barons of the country, started out as a trader who, among other things, imported mercury for silver refining. Gregorio Pacheco, another prominent miner, who was president of Bolivia from 1884 to 1888, was also a former merchant.[12] From the scant biographical information available, it appears that the new mining entrepreneurs belonged to relatively impoverished families from the social elite of the country but did not belong to the families of the colonial mining aristocracy.[13] The new generation of miners bought landed estates as their wealth grew, and by the second half of the nineteenth century, they were active in commerce and rural and urban real estate, as well as in mining. They were also politically inclined, and during the second half of the nineteenth century, they and their allies formulated a reform program based on classic liberal principles to throw off the last vestiges of colonial society and reshape the country's economy. These reforms were to have a tremendous impact on Bolivian rural society as well.

One of the chief aims of the new miners and large import-export merchants was to open Bolivia to foreign trade. Almost since the establishment of the republic a debate had raged over the merits of internal trade versus a liberal trade policy favoring foreign commerce. The aims of the new miner-merchant coalition obviously posed a threat to the manufacturing sector that had survived from the colonial period, and domestic manufacturers and artisans opposed any move to free-trade policies. By the late 1840's and the 1850's, as silver production finally increased and the mining sector revived, the debate sharpened, and the advocates of free trade this time spoke with more financial and political authority. Nevertheless, the protectionists also had important support. Their most systematic spokesman was José María Dalence, president of the Supreme Court in the 1840's and later head of the Board of Statistics. The result of Dalence's labor, published in 1851 as the *Bosquejo estadístico de Bolivia (Statistical Study of Bolivia)* showed the enormous resources of the country and their potential for internal economic development. Dalence used his figures to argue that governmental policy should concentrate on promoting internal trade and so aid the development of native industry. For example, he argued that the state followed an unwise tariff policy, exempting many products from the exterior from import duties while at the same time taxing locally produced items. This policy, Dalence said, was rapidly destroying the manufacturing sector and was detrimental to the country's economy.[14]

Dalence's eloquence and mastery of statistics proved no match for the new economic forces tied to the reviving mining sector, and as the century wore on, a number of circumstances improved the miners' financial position vis-à-vis the other sectors of the Bolivian economy. After 1850, the full-scale production of the mercury mines of California, discovered in 1845, caused a drop in the price of mercury, essential in the silver-refining process. Capital expenditures in mining equipment made possible by the infusion of Chilean capital paid off almost immediately: in the second half of the nineteenth century, the ore that was mined contained high concentrations of silver.[15] By the 1870's, the increasingly prosperous miners were in a position to influence the government and push through the legislature a reform program that attempted to remake the country according to their own political and economic visions.

The measures that had greatest direct effect on the national economy were the changes in the mining code. In 1872, the legislature approved a law that allowed the free export of silver; the following year the minting of *pesos febles* was prohibited.[16] By allowing the free export of silver without the governmental *bancos de rescate*, the miners took advantage of the higher free market prices and also avoided the direct and indirect taxes on silver production. The prohibition on minting new *pesos febles* made the importation of modern machinery less expensive. Its major effect, however, was to increase the demand in Bolivia for foreign goods, since native manufacturers no longer maintained their price advantage. The destruction of the colonial economic system was a lengthy process, and large quantities of debased coins continued to circulate for decades despite stipulations that the Banco Nacional de Bolivia buy up all *pesos febles*.[17] Nevertheless, although gradual in their effects, the new mining and coining laws ended the era of colonial economic policies and also helped precipitate the loss of southern Peru and northern Argentina to their respective national economies.

Another part of the miners' program concerned the transformation of the agricultural sector. In the most important reform, the legislature abolished the Indian communities. As early as 1866, President Mariano Melgarejo had decreed the abolition of all Indian communal property. Melgarejo's law required that all Indians buy their plots within 60 days; if they failed to do so, the government reserved the right to sell the land at public auction. Now, in 1868, following the precedent of a similar 1842 law, the Constituent Assembly declared that all communal land was the property of the state. Although based on liberal ideas popular in Latin America at that time, these measures were dictated by Melgarejo's desperate fiscal plight, which persisted throughout his chaotic years as head of state. Since most purchases of land were made with devalued government bonds, little money was actually raised. Furthermore, as anticipated, the impossibly short time given the Indians to pay for their land meant that many communities were sold to urban speculators, often military cronies and relatives of the president. And inevitably, the laws raised the ire of the Indians, especially around La Paz, where most community land was sold. An Indian revolt in 1870–71 on the altiplano was instrumental in finally bringing down the turbulent Melgarejo regime.[18]

The new Constituent Assembly of 1871 voided all laws passed during the Melgarejo interlude, in part to placate the rebellious Indian masses. Most land that had been usurped was returned to the communities, at least on the altiplano around La Paz, where Indian resistance had been strongest.[19] The 1871 Assembly contained many representatives of the new commercial and mining elites, and although most abhorred the corrupt caudillismo and arbitrary military rule under Melgarejo, they were sympathetic to the liberal ideas obstensibly behind the 1866 and 1868 laws.[20] The rich pamphlet literature of the period shows that even those who favored the return of Indian land immediately after the overthrow of Melgarejo did not recognize the Indian communities as legitimate corporate entities. Rather, they argued that Melgarejo had sold land that did not belong to the state, since the Bolivarian decree of 1825 and subsequent laws gave property rights to Indians as individuals.[21] Those who had bought community lands under Melgarejo vehemently denied this legal point; they also argued that large estates were economically more efficient, and that Indians living in communities would be much better off as hacienda peons because their masters would protect them from abuses perpetrated by local officials and corrupt priests.[22]

In the spirit of this argument and in response to substantial pressure from the purchasers of community land during the Melgarejo years, the Assembly passed a law in 1874 that, while conceding the right of landownership to the Indians, again abolished the Indian community as a juridical entity. The law, the *ley de exvinculación*, provided for the parceling of community land among community members based on surveys made by a commission appointed by the prefects, the heads of the departments. After the commission had distributed land titles to each Indian, the plots could then be sold with the intervention of the public prosecutor in the departmental capital. The law also converted the old Indian tribute from a head tax to an assessment on the holding. The land tax was to be paid in the new bolivianos rather than in the old, debased *pesos febles*—a stipulation that effectively increased the tax by 20 percent.[23]

Some of the most idealistic legislators hoped that in abolishing the Indian communities they would turn the Indians into yeomen who would produce a surplus to be marketed in the towns. This, they argued, would create many benefits as the Indians were assimilated into national life. One pamphleteer described the benefits in this typically Eurocentric liberal view:

The frank and free possession of wealth [i.e. land], however little it would be, would waken him [the Indian] to new necessities and new pleasures, and take him out of his present indolence and apathy; it would open to him that world of brilliant illusions, of satisfactions without end, that is only given to the educated and civilized man. [The Indian] would then join the other classes of society, would mix with them, and bring an end to that engulfing power of class distinctions that erodes the foundations of our nationhood.[24]

In 1876, before the agrarian reform program could be implemented, another general, Hilarión Daza, overthrew the government. In 1879, the War of the Pacific, with Bolivia and Peru allied against Chile, broke out. After a series of rapid and disastrous defeats at the hands of the Chilean forces, Bolivia lost its Littoral department, which had been its sole access to the Pacific. The military, now thoroughly discredited, lost the overwhelming influence in political affairs it had exercised since independence. A coup led by General Narciso Campero, the cousin of silver miner Gregorio Pacheco, finally put the ascendant silver-mining oligarchy firmly into power.[25]

During Campero's term (1880–84), the miners organized the Conservative Party, initially formed to pressure the government into suing for peace with Chile. Campero favored the continuation of the war effort, but the Conservatives believed that the war was detrimental to Bolivia's economy and to the important business links they had formed with Chilean capitalists. Conservative ideology stressed dedication to civilian political rule and the implementation of laissez-faire economic policies designed to develop the export sector of the Bolivian economy. Though fervently pro-Church in its rhetoric, the policies of the Conservative Party in other respects closely followed liberal economic and social policies, implementing the reforms passed by the legislature in the 1870's. Except for the war issue, the opposition Liberal Party, founded in 1883 by pro-war, anti-Chile factions, espoused a fundamentally similar program.[26]

To consolidate their power and implement their vision of Bolivian society, the mining interests organized under the banners of the Conservative Party complemented their agrarian reforms with modifications to the *ley de exvinculación*, buttressed by a series of new laws aimed at rationalizing the land-tax structure. By the 1880's, the purposes of the 1874 law were reinterpreted more in line with the wave of Positivism that swept the country's intelligentsia during this period. In effect, the position espoused by the purchasers of community land during the Melgarejo regime had triumphed. Ladislao Cabrera, the minister of state, declared to the

National Convention of 1880 that the *ley de exvinculación* was meant to result in the sale of community lands. According to Cabrera, once these lands were put on the market, they would fall under the control of "intelligent landowners and capitalists," who would increase agricultural production, thereby also filling the state's coffers. This argument assumed, following the Social Darwinist strain particularly strong in the Bolivian version of Positivism, that the Indian race was so backward that it had to be guided by the strong hand of the superior white race.[27]

Cabrera also insisted that the country adopt a unitary land-tax system that would abolish the dual tax structure of one tax for Indians and another for non-Indians. The 1880 convention placed a tax, called the *impuesto predial rústico* or *catastro*, on the annual income of all rural properties; initially, the tax amounted to 5 percent of a property's income. The first tax census, also called *catastro*, was conducted soon after, but the findings were not used because in 1882 the government, suffering financially from the war with Chile, was forced to reinstitute the tribute, now called *contribución territorial*. It was another decade before the catastros were compiled on a regular basis and the tax collected. During this decade, the Indian tribute was collected regularly, but from 1885 on, the monies from this impost filled departmental coffers rather than the national treasury.[28]

During their years in power, the Conservatives also passed a series of public-land laws aimed at settling the sparsely populated tropical lowlands of the east. These laws were designed to establish full national sovereignty in the tropical lowland areas so that national territory would not be lost, as the Littoral department had been lost during the War of the Pacific. Although some frontier areas had been adjudicated during previous governments, the disposal of public lands had been unsystematic; most often, tracts had been granted in the eastern section of the country to reward people for services rendered to the government. The laws of 1886 and 1890 established a coherent policy by creating an Office of Public Lands and Colonies and a uniform procedure for the sale of vacant tracts. This legislation permitted the sale of lands that lay at least 60 kilometers beyond cantonal capitals in tracts of one to ten square leagues (25 sq. km), with a limit of ten tracts per person or company. In areas closer to these towns, no more than three 25-hectare plots could be sold to the same person. Land claims were to be registered in the departmental prefectures, and the colonist had to cultivate at least one-tenth of his land within four years of registering his claim. By coincidence, these new laws came into effect just as the rubber boom transformed the tropical forests in the Bolivian Amazon basin. To deal with these new circumstances, new legislation was simply appended to the existing framework. Only in 1905 was a new and comprehensive law passed that, while reforming substantial sections of the ordinances dealing with rubber tree stands, left the basic procedure for other lands intact.[29]

Despite the zeal with which the miners promoted the settling of Bolivia's eastern frontiers, their policies did not change the population distribution of the country. The economic center of the country remained solidly in the mineral-rich highlands, where the vast majority of the population resided. Moreover, as in the case of Chuquisaca's frontiers, the colonization laws led to much unproductive speculation in public lands, made worse by the fact that colonists disregarded stipulations on the cultivation of land; these regulations proved unenforceable in the poorly administered frontier areas. As a result, in the twentieth century, Bolivia suffered a series of further territorial dismemberments at the hands of Brazil and Paraguay.

In a superficial sense, the situation in the late nineteenth century resembled that of the sixteenth and seventeenth centuries, when the Potosí silver mines were the economic motors of the Bolivian economy. Many of the richest miners still lived in Sucre, giving weight to the city's claim of being the political, cultural, and financial center of the country, and the combined political and economic power of the Sucre–Potosí axis dominated not only southern Bolivia but also the commercially more dynamic and more populous La Paz. The nineteenth-century silver boom, however, was quite different from its colonial counterpart. Instead of contributing to the strength of the regional economy, the mining oligarchy's actions strengthened the export sector at the expense of internal trade. This laid the foundations for the demise of the remnants of the colonial "Peruvian economic space" that had sustained the economic and political preeminence of the Sucre–Potosí axis. By the twentieth century, southern Bolivia had entered a protracted period of decline from which it has never fully recovered. Essentially, this decline was a result of three factors: the inability of the silver boom to stimulate economic growth outside the mining sector, the impact of foreign investments on the mining industry, and the advent of the rail network.

Even in Potosí, the increase in mining in the late nineteenth century did not create an urban market as large as that of the colonial boom period. From its peak population of 160,000 in 1641, the city shrank to 25,600 inhabitants in 1854 and only 20,900 in 1900. Although there are no reliable statistics for the 46-year period between these last dates, Potosí apparently did not experience a large increase in population as a result of the silver boom. The relatively small effect of the nineteenth-century mining upswing on the city's population is also reflected in the fact that even during this period the city did not reach its former seventeenth-century boundaries.[30]

Potosí had been founded at the foot of the *cerro rico* to exploit its rich silver veins, and in the nineteenth century, this mountain still dominated the city's economy, but the richest silver mines were now located elsewhere—still mostly within the department of Potosí, but far from the city of Potosí. The growth that occurred was in provincial towns that lay close to the principal mines. The population of the town of Pulacayo, over a hundred kilometers southwest of Potosí, where the mines of the largest mining enterprise, the Huanchaca Mining Company, were located, more than tripled, rising from some 2,000 in 1870 to 6,512 in 1900. In the northern Potosí mining district, the town of Colquechaca, founded only in 1871, rapidly became the most populous urban center in the area. By 1900 Colquechaca boasted a population of almost 5,000 inhabitants.[31]

For several reasons, however, the number of miners, even during the boom, was much less than it had been in the colonial period. In the colonial period, a large proportion (theoretically one-sixth) of the Indian males from as far away as Cuzco were forced to leave their communities to work in the Potosí mines. This forced labor in the mines, the *mita*, was abolished soon after independence. No large numbers of workers migrated to the mining centers during the silver boom of the late nineteenth century. Rather, the mine workers were recruited among the local population or from the heavily populated valleys of Cochabamba.[32] Antonio Mitre, in his recent book on nineteenth-century silver mining in Bolivia, calculated that the industry did not employ more than 20,000 workers, or about 1 percent of the country's total population; nevertheless, production was higher than during any other period in the history of the Potosí mines because of the extremely high concentrations of silver in the ore. Modern machinery also helped keep the demand for labor down.[33] By the 1870's, the Huanchaca company was using the most advanced machinery available, and a technology fully equal to that used in European and North American mines.[34]

Before the War of the Pacific, Chilean participation in Bolivian mining enterprises was heavy, acting as an important stimulus for the accumulation of capital for the Bolivian mines. Not only did Chile have a much better developed credit market, but a new group of Chilean entrepreneurs willing to invest in the risky mining business emerged by the middle of the nineteenth century. This made the Chileans ideal partners for Bolivian silver miners searching for capital.[35] However, most Chilean capitalists preferred to invest in the Littoral department, where by the 1870's they owned virtually all mining companies with little or no Bolivian participation. These enterprises included all nitrate concessions as well as the important silver mines at Caracoles.[36]

Chilean capital was invested to a lesser degree in the silver mines of the department of Potosí, and these mines were all under Bolivian control. Throughout the boom, the largest and most profitable company, the Huanchaca Company of Bolivia, was the particular target of Chilean as well as other foreign investors. In 1878, Chileans owned 1,260 of the company's 6,000 shares, or 21 percent of the total stock; all the rest belonged to Bolivians.[37] By 1886, Chileans controlled 1,783 shares, or almost one-third, and French investors 1,574. Nevertheless, Bolivians continued to hold the largest block of shares, with 1,851, and the company was administered by Aniceto Arce, the Bolivian silver magnate and later president of the country (1888–92). Reflecting the importance of both Bolivian and Chilean capital, the company's directorate was registered in Sucre and Valparaíso.[38]

Access to sources of credit for the expensive silver-mining operations was crucial to the success of the new mining companies. In this area, Chilean investment was also very important. The National Bank of Bolivia, which became the prime lending institution of the silver-mining companies, benefited from the presence of Chilean investors. A group of Valparaíso bankers and merchants founded the bank in 1871 to take advantage of the financial activity generated by the exploitation of guano and nitrate in the Bolivian coastal area. Legal domicile was in both Cobija (at the time capital of the Littoral department) and Valparaíso. Of the 3,000 shares that went on the market, 1,673 were bought by people residing in Bolivia (though not necessarily Bolivian citizens).[39] Agustín Edwards, the Chilean nitrate magnate and founder of the Antofagasta Nitrate and Railway Company, was named president of the new bank. Its first branch office was opened in Sucre in 1872, where the need for capital to fund the silver-mining industry was great. By 1873, other branches had been installed in La Paz, Cochabamba, and Potosí, as well as Cobija.[40]

In 1876, owing to the different financial needs of the nitrate and silver-mining industries, the bank was divided into two separate entities. The Chilean portion, with rights to a branch in the Bolivian port of Antofagasta, became the Consolidated Bank of Chile. The reorganized National Bank, with the directorship meeting in Sucre under the presidency of Gregorio Pacheco, now was fully under the control of the Bolivian silver miners. Until 1884, the National Bank had no rival in the country save for the Real Estate Credit Bank, which as its name suggests, restricted itself to real estate financing. Even after the founding of the Bank of Potosí and other banks after 1884, the National Bank remained the most important financial institution in the country, a position it held until the second decade of the twentieth century.[41]

Chilean financing established the precedent for the penetration of foreign capital into the Bolivian mining sector. Although Chilean investors usually concentrated their efforts in well-defined areas of the Bolivian economy and never played a preponderant role during the nineteenth century, later foreign investments on a much more massive scale led to the destruction of the old economic circuits centering on the Potosí mining markets. The railroad-building program, initiated during the silver boom, also contributed heavily to the breakdown of the old commercial circuits. Even railroads built in neighboring countries a bit earlier than the ones in Bolivia contributed to this problem. The railroad from Mollendo, on the Peruvian coast, had a great effect on commercial routes in Bolivia. This line, built by Henry Meiggs, the intrepid North American capitalist, reached Puno by 1874. The merchants of La Paz, only 60 kilometers away on the other side of Lake Titicaca, took full advantage of this inexpensive link to the coast, with the result that the city enjoyed a resurgence in foreign trade and firmly established its position as the commercial center of Bolivia and port of entry for foreign goods.[42]

Of greater importance for the fate of the southern Bolivian economy was the extension of the Antofagasta railroad to Uyuni in 1889. Originally conceived as merely a rail link to the nitrate fields behind Antofagasta on the coast, the line continued into the interior as a joint venture of the Chilean-owned Antofagasta Nitrate and Railroad Company and the Huanchaca Company. In 1886, the Antofagasta Company sold out to Huanchaca, which in turn sold its concession to the London-based Antofagasta and Boli-

Map 2.   The Bolivian rail network, 1925. The years in parentheses are the dates of completion. Source: Herbert S. Klein, *Bolivia* (New York, 1982).

vian Railroad Company. That company then leased the railroad back to Huanchaca for fifteen years. Huanchaca also built feeder lines to its mines and processing mills in Pulacayo and Huanchaca. The railroad reached Oruro in 1892 and La Paz in 1908 (see Map 2).[43]

The construction of the railroad was partly aimed at cutting operating expenses in an attempt to remain competitive as international market forces drove down the price of silver. From the late 1860's, after gold strikes in California, Arizona, and Australia, the price of silver dropped steadily. Then, in 1892, the price fell precipitously, and when it leveled off in 1897, the figure was lower than the prevailing rate in 1860. The increased supply of gold made it possible to base the world's economy on gold rather than silver. Germany led the way, switching to the gold standard as early as 1873. Increased silver production in Mexico and at Nevada's Comstock Lode, together with Bolivia's own silver boom, further depressed silver prices (see Table 2).[44]

Falling silver prices forced the silver-mining companies to lower costs by making economies of scale. Before the construction of the railroad, transportation was slow and costly. Llamas and mules usually took twenty-five days to reach the coast, compared with twenty-four hours by rail, and the cost of transporting goods from, for example, Colquechaca to Challapata by pack animal cost as much as the Challapata-Antofagasta railroad trip, which was ten times as long.[45] Obviously, proximity to the railroad became extremely important to the continued profitability of the mines as the price of silver continued to drop. Mines located far from the line were at a severe disadvantage compared with companies like Huanchaca or Real Socavón de la Virgen in Oruro, which enjoyed easy access to the rail network.

Moreover, the railroad destroyed the regional commercial networks and economies that were based on supplying the mines with foodstuffs and other goods. Once the railroad reached the mining centers, it was often cheaper to buy foreign goods. The case of sugar is instructive. Transport costs for 100 kilograms of

TABLE 2

London Silver Prices, 1855–1914

(Pence per ounce; 5-year averages)

Period	Price	Period	Price
1855–1859	61.55	1885–1889	44.82
1860–1864	61.33	1890–1894	39.41
1865–1869	60.74	1895–1899	28.51
1870–1874	59.82	1900–1904	26.18
1875–1878[a]	54.15	1905–1909[b]	26.59
1880–1884	51.35	1910–1914	26.01

SOURCE: Antonio Mitre, *Los patriarcas de la plata* (Lima, 1981), p. 194.
[a] 4-year average; omits 1879.
[b] 4-year average; omits 1907.

sugar from Santa Cruz in the eastern tropical lowlands, a traditional supplier of the mining markets, were twenty-nine in the
late 1890's,* but it cost only 12 Bs to bring the same amount of
Peruvian sugar from Antofagasta.⁴⁶ The situation was just as lop-
sided in the case of wheat flour. Cochabamba, Tarija, northern
Potosí, and Chuquisaca, the traditional wheat producers of Bolivia, were unable to compete with imported Chilean flour, which,
thanks to modern mills and better winnowing procedures and
strains of wheat, was superior in quality to the Bolivian product
and well worth its usually slightly higher price. Bolivian producers
found it difficult to sell domestic flour in a saturated market; only
in abundant years, when prices were extremely low, was it possible to market Cochabamba flour in the mining areas.⁴⁷ Even in
the wheat-producing areas, Chilean competition kept prices low.
In 1894, in a report on the haciendas of the miner Gregorio
Pacheco, Pacheco's secretary related in disgust: "The agricultural
year has been good and would be better with the prospect of good
prices, except that [Chilean] competition makes them decline, and
especially the [Antofagasta] railroad, which with every train vomits
quintals of wheat flour for each one of ours, dominating the market over what our mills produce. In Sucre no bread is bought except that produced with Chilean flour mixed with a little of the
local product."⁴⁸

The silver crisis in the 1890's destroyed the economic ascendancy of the Sucre oligarchy. The miners who owned haciendas
saw their income melt away because of Chilean competition. To
make matters worse, the Bank of Potosí, the country's second-
largest bank, capitalized at 2,000,000 Bs, failed in 1895. The bank
had expanded its loan program just before the steep decline in
silver prices, and as more and more mining companies, unable to
make a profit after 1892, postponed their loan payments, the bank
was forced into liquidation.⁴⁹ With other sources of income drying
up as well, the bankruptcy put the silver miners in a serious pre-
dicament. One of the miners hard hit by the twin calamities of the
falling price of silver and the bank's failure was Pacheco. His
Guadalupe Company in southern Potosí made a big strike in July
1893, but just as the happy news reached Sucre, there was a report
of another fall in silver prices on the European market. Nevertheless, the company paid out dividends until April 1894. At that

*Henceforth, I use the standard abbreviation "Bs" for the Bolivian currency.
In 1894, one boliviano = U.S.$ 0.531.

TABLE 3

Silver Production of the Guadalupe Company, 1895–1902

Year	Marcos	Approximate value (bolivianos)	Year	Marcos	Approximate value (bolivianos)
1895	48,923	513,691	1899	21,115	221,707
1896	42,745	448,822	1900	30,619	321,499
1897	42,263	443,716	1901	26,022	273,531
1898	32,523	386,491	1902	23,019	251,699

SOURCE: International Bureau of American Republics, *Bolivia: Geographical Sketch, Natural Resources, Laws, Economic Condition, Actual Development, Prospects of Future Growth* (Washington, D.C., 1904), p. 103.

point, Pacheco began putting the profits back into the mine and to take out loans from both the National Bank and the Bank of Potosí to cover his costs. In July 1895, Guadalupe again paid out dividends, in part to increase its credit rating to procure more loans for an ambitious expansion of operations. It was in that month that the Bank of Potosí, where Pacheco had outstanding loans of 27,745 Bs, went into liquidation. Pacheco also owed the National Bank 220,415 Bs. As a result of the Bank of Potosí's failure, the National Bank reduced Pacheco's credit limit 25 percent, which meant, in effect, that he had to pay the bank 26,615 Bs within twenty days. Pacheco was forced to sell one of his houses and a printing press, and he tried to sell his shares in the Ytos and Gallofa silver-mining companies. He also had to drop his plan to expand the Guadalupe mine. New machinery bought during the 1893–94 period made it possible to maintain silver production until 1897, but production dropped off after that and never again reached previous levels (see Table 3).[50]

In an effort to counteract the effects of the silver crisis, a number of mining companies merged, hoping that by concentrating their capital they could make economies of scale. The largest company to emerge from this process was the United Company of Colquechaca, formed out of the five largest mining enterprises in northern Potosí. Even this tactic failed to halt the decline. The new companies still had to borrow heavily, often from foreign mining concerns and mineral purchasing and exporting agencies. When returns did not cover interest payments, the companies dissolved or fell into the hands of their creditors. Such was the case with the Colquechaca and Guadalupe companies. By 1906, Chileans had purchased Guadalupe's once-prosperous holdings and re-organized it as the Oploca Mining and Agricultural Company of Bolivia, with its main offices located in Santiago.[51]

As the silver crisis worsened, the economic center of gravity shifted from the declining south to the more dynamic north, especially La Paz. La Paz's easy access to the Pacific coast made it the commercial hub of the country, and at the turn of the century, its population of 60,000 made it by far the largest city in the country, exceeding all the others combined.[52] The trip to Oruro, the railhead of the Antofagasta line by 1892, was relatively inexpensive and easy over the flat altiplano. The Mollendo–Puno railway also made La Paz accessible to foreign commerce through Peru. Surprisingly, the Arica–La Paz route, with only 65 kilometers of railroad to Tacna, successfully competed with the two railroads because of an easy trail and a substantial volume of llama traffic.[53]

As the financial resources of the silver barons waned, so did their political power. The municipal elections in 1897 gave the victory to the Liberal Party. A blatant effort to cover up the results of the elections precipitated a wave of riots in La Paz. When Conservative President Severo Fernández Alonso attempted to move the government to La Paz to placate that city's sentiments, the delegates from southern Bolivia countered by passing a law in the Congress establishing Sucre as the permanent site of government.

The Liberals took advantage of this crisis, skillfully exploiting the *paceños'* resentment of the south's political domination to start a revolt. After the delegates from La Paz left Sucre in protest, the Liberal Party leaders fomented paceño regionalist sympathies. They were finally able to unite both La Paz Liberals and Conservatives under the common cause of federalism. Fernández Alonso, who had been minister of war in the previous Conservative government, marched his army from Sucre to Oruro, but his troops were defeated in 1899, owing in part to his perpetual indecision and not least to the massive participation of the Aymara Indians on the Liberal side. The Liberals had wooed the Indians into their camp by promising to return the lands they had lost as a result of the *ley de exvinculación*. Once the Liberals gained power under the leadership of General José Manuel Pando, they ignored the federalism issue, as well as all promises made to the Indians. To forestall the Conservatives based in Sucre, the new rulers moved the capital to La Paz but maintained a centralist government. With their cause betrayed, the Indians began fighting the Liberals, threatening to turn the struggle into a race war. Pando led the remnants of the regular army against the Indian rebels, defeated them, and had their leaders executed.[54]

During their twenty-year reign, the Liberals continued most of the Conservative policies they had decried during their years as opposition party. The liberal, laissez-faire attitude toward mining remained unchanged. The assault on Indian communities increased. In 1904, the government signed a peace treaty with Chile without gaining any territorial concessions, thereby reneging on the major ideological issue that had distinguished the Liberals from the Conservatives during the 1880's.[55]

Coincidentally, the turn of the century marked the beginning of the tin era in Bolivia. In the last years of the nineteenth century, the industrialized countries discovered new uses for tin, such as the now ubiquitous tin can. As a result, the metal, commonly found in conjunction with silver and largely ignored till now, suddenly became a valuable commodity. As the price of tin zoomed upward, Bolivian production increased by leaps and bounds. Between 1887 and 1889, output doubled. By 1902, tin represented 30 percent of the total value of Bolivia's exports; in 1904, the figure jumped to 43 percent; and by the 1920's, over 70 percent of Bolivia's export income came from tin.[56] Although rubber also contributed a large portion of Bolivia's export earnings around the turn of the century, the rubber boom faded by 1912 as cheap rubber from Malayan plantations flooded the market. The location of Bolivia's rubber trees in the sparsely populated and inaccessible Amazon River basin meant that latex production never occupied a large share of the Bolivian labor force or contributed much to economic development.[57]

The development of tin mining confirmed northern Bolivia, with its rail connections, as the economic center of the country. Since the volume of ore required to make tin mining profitable far exceeded that of silver, a rail network was essential. Oruro, the railhead of the Antofagasta line until 1908, developed into the primary market for tin and became the center from which the mines were provisioned. The richest tin mines were situated in the northern part of Potosí department, but the mines were much closer to Oruro than to the city of Potosí. The Llallagua-area mines, the richest in the country, were only 60 kilometers from the nearest railway station (in Challapata, Oruro department), and they were only 90 kilometers from the city of Oruro, or almost twice as close as Potosí by road.[58] Thus, the tin boom relegated Potosí to a peripheral position in the mining economy for the first time in its long history. Sucre, with close ties to Potosí and even farther from the railroads, inevitably shared Potosí's fate. La Paz, too, gained from the commercial activity generated by the tin boom. Although La Paz department had almost no silver mines, it proved to have exploitable tin deposits. La Paz's role as de facto capital and its relatively easy connections with the outside world made it the logical site for the headquarters of the many new tin-mining companies.[59] The city's communications further improved in 1908, when the Antofagasta railroad reached the city. The Arica–La Paz railroad, one of the few concessions wrung from the Chileans in the 1904 peace treaty, was completed in 1913 and further solidified La Paz's predominant role.

The establishment of the tin-mining companies' Bolivian head-quarters in La Paz, the city with the best connections to the outside world, also reflected the dominant character of foreign capital in the extraction of the metal. Even more than silver, tin required enormous investments in machinery and technology because of the amount of ore necessary to make operations profitable. At the peak of Huanchaca's production in the early 1890's, the amount of silver extracted never surpassed 400 tons a year; in 1910, by contrast, the richest tin mine, La Salvadora, produced 9,000 tons of tin refined to 65 percent purity.[60] But because native capital was simply insufficient to exploit Bolivia's tin resources fully, large foreign corporations dominated from early on and capitalized all successful tin enterprises.[61]

Even Simón I. Patiño, the Bolivian tin king and eventually the largest producer of the metal, relied heavily on U.S. and British capital to finance his operations. His company, the Patiño Mines and Enterprises Consolidated, was incorporated in Delaware, and a large portion of the company's shares were owned by National Lead, a U.S. company based in New Jersey. Patiño also used the British firms Penny and Duncan and the Anglo–South American Bank to buy out Chilean interests in Llallagua.[62] Patiño's financial empire encompassed many other foreign companies, such as the largest tin smelter in the world, Harvey, Williams in Liverpool. Patiño was Bolivian-born, but he eventually moved to Paris, from where he directed his worldwide network of enterprises. He made his last trip ever to Bolivia in 1920. Patiño's alliance with British and North American capitalists and his residence abroad meant that a great part of the earnings of his Bolivian companies left the country in the form of profits and stock dividends, and therefore

Bolivia shared only a small fraction of the tremendous wealth accumulated by its native son.[63]

Patiño controlled about half of total Bolivian tin production; Mauricio Hochschild and Félix Avelino Aramayo (son of the silver baron José Avelino) between them shared the other half. The role of foreign investments in their companies was similarily strong. Even though both directed their holdings from Bolivia, the companies they headed were financed primarily by European capital.[64] The Aramayo firm, Aramayo, Francke Company, was registered in London and had heavy foreign participation.

The Aramayo family was the only silver-mining family that was able to make the transition to tin. The other Sucre-based silver miners, especially in the years just before the crash, had put all their financial resources into improving silver production to beat the constantly declining prices, so that when the crash came in the 1890's they had no capital left to change from silver to tin production. And because they were restricted primarily to the local credit market, they could not negotiate the necessary loans after the bankruptcy of the Bank of Potosí. Indeed, most Sucre capitalists, who had so successfully revived the traditional silver mining, did not even consider switching to tin mining: they were simply not interested in exploiting a metal seen as inferior to the more valuable and aristocratic silver. Even the Huanchaca Company, despite its preponderance of foreign shareholders, attempted to continue extracting silver, thanks to its direction by Sucre-based miners. In 1904, the company brought in new machinery to improve production, but this only led it closer to bankruptcy. Finally, after many years of abandonment, Hochschild leased the once-great Huanchaca mines.[65]

Only one *chuquisaqueño*, the lawyer Pastor Sainz, profited directly as mine owner during the tin boom, and he, significantly, was something of an outsider in Sucre's elite mining society. Sainz's father had left his wife after he discovered that she was having an affair with José Ballivián, then president of Bolivia. Cast out from polite society, Sainz's mother continued her scandalous affairs and had two illegitimate children by different fathers. Beyond all this, Pastor Sainz was a Liberal in an overwhelming Conservative city. He went to northern Potosí in the 1880's, because of his party affiliations, and became a partner in a few mining concessions in return for working them as well as defending them from legal attack. Although by 1896 he was 60,000 Bs in debt to the

Aramayo, Francke Company, he bought out his partner, and after more loans from Aramayo, finally hit a rich tin vein. He paid off his debtors and by 1899 was making a net profit of 50,000 Bs a month, even though production methods on his claim remained extremely primitive. Finally, in 1906, Sainz, over sixty years of age and ready to retire, sold his mine to Chilean capitalists for 350,000 pounds sterling and returned to Sucre.[66]

Despite the Sucre miners' lack of participation in the tin boom (Sainz being the exception that proves the rule), Sucre's decline was not immediate. The city maintained its position as the country's banking center; the only two general-service banks in Bolivia after 1895, the Francisco Argandoña Bank and the National Bank, both had their headquarters in Sucre and were dominated by Sucre money. The Argandoña family, which had made its wealth in silver mining, owned the Argandoña Bank. The National Bank was a public corporation; in 1913, Sucre residents owned almost 50,000 of its 80,000 shares, or 62 percent of the total. In contrast, La Paz capitalists owned only 12,533 shares, or about 16 percent.[67]

La Paz did not challenge Sucre's predominance as the financial capital until well after the silver boom had ended. In 1911, the national government in La Paz created the Banco de la Nación. Three years later, the new bank gained the exclusive privilege of issuing bank notes. According to one foreign observer, the bank was created "largely as a protest of La Paz interests against the predominance of Sucre banks in the financial system of the country."[68] Even though the Francisco Argandoña Bank merged with the National Bank in 1919, the new prohibition against issuing bank notes, combined with the immensely larger financial resources of the government-backed Banco de la Nación, finally shifted the financial impetus to La Paz. Simón Patiño also founded a bank, the Mercantile Bank, in La Paz, further consolidating the northern city's financial predominance.

By the second decade of the twentieth century, La Paz's hegemony over national politics and the Bolivian economy was complete, and Sucre faded in importance. Without silver mining, southern Bolivia for the first time since the Spanish Conquest lost its role as the country's primary exporting region. With insufficient financial resources and bereft of economic dynamism, the south became a marginal backwater.

The decline of the silver-mining economy also meant the end of the old Potosí economic space that had encompassed areas outside the national boundaries. As the Potosí silver production declined and a vigorous Argentine coastal economy began to expand into the interior, southern Bolivia was split between the highland economy linked to northern Bolivia and the Pacific and the Buenos Aires–led Atlantic commercial network. The northward extension of the Argentine railways in the 1890's brought northern Argentina more and more into the Argentine national economy, and as trade connections between Buenos Aires and the interior provinces improved, the peripheral areas of Bolivia, such as the department of Tarija, the Chaco, and even Santa Cruz, were drawn into the Argentine economic orbit. In the first few decades of the twentieth century, many of the southern Bolivian border regions developed closer economic ties with Argentina than with the rest of Bolivia. Argentine and European goods introduced from Buenos Aires dominated the markets in these areas, and Chaco cattle and Indians from southeastern Bolivia descended into Argentina, creating new commercial links.

The Potosí-centered commercial structure was able to maintain its relative importance only in areas closest to the mining regions, and even there not at the level of earlier years. When the railroad finally reached Potosí in 1911, the city regained some of its commercial significance. However, most goods transported from the countryside to Potosí were not consumed there but were transferred to the railroad to be sold in La Paz or in the tin-mining centers north of Potosí. Therefore, while some trade circuits continued to function, the great commercial network based on the southern Bolivian mining economy had ceased to exist. In its place, the railway system opened up the Bolivian economy to the outside world; it was a system designed for the export of minerals, and it did not function as a link between regions within the country. Transport by rail was so much cheaper than hauling goods with pack animals over Bolivia's rugged terrain that many foreign goods, even basic foodstuffs such as wheat flour and sugar, were cheaper than goods produced within the country but far from a rail link. Thus the liberal policies put into effect by the silver miners destroyed the internal economic space that had endured since colonial times. What was begun by the silver miners of southern Bolivia was brought to its logical conclusion by the La Paz interests and tin miners. Ironically, the result was the economic and political marginalization of the initiators of this program, the southern Bolivian elites.

CHAPTER THREE

The Rise and Fall
of the Sucre Oligarchy

Sucre, called La Plata during the colonial period, was founded in 1538. After the discovery of silver in nearby Potosí, many of its residents were drawn to the new boom town. Nevertheless, because of its mild climate and lower altitude, La Plata remained vital as the chosen residence of the Audiencia de Charcas, the combined judicial and administrative body that ruled over an enormous territory encompassing what is now Bolivia, Argentina, Paraguay, and Uruguay. La Plata's position as an important Spanish colonial administrative center, with its attendant population of wealthy government functionaries and wealthy mine owners, made it the political and social hub of the region.

Sucre (renamed in 1839 in honor of the revolutionary leader Antonio José de Sucre) remained the principal residence of the country's elites throughout the nineteenth century. Although it did not increase in size, it continued to dominate the life of the nation and, even more so, as the departmental capital, the affairs of Chuquisaca.[1] Sucre's domination over the surrounding countryside not only continued well beyond the city's decline as a national center after the turn of the century, but in fact increased considerably. This apparent paradox—the strengthening of Sucre's grip over the surrounding rural areas precisely as it was becoming a marginal political, social, and economic center—can only be explained by the reactions of the Sucre elites as they attempted to adjust to the silver crisis beginning in the 1890's.

Hard pressed though they were, many of the silver barons still had money to invest—not enough to embark on tin mining, even had they wished to do so, but enough to look for other likely ventures. In the end, they spent much of their remaining resources on land, especially in Yamparaez province.* The flow of capital into the countryside changed not only land-tenure patterns that had prevailed since colonial times, but eventually also rural work patterns and social relations. The switch from silver mining to land may seem in retrospect to have been the major effect of the Sucre elites' decline, but it was not a retreat into self-sufficiency, as Chevalier describes for northern Mexico in the seventeenth century.[2] Rather, the Sucre oligarchs put their money into land because it offered potentially the best investment among a limited number of opportunities and because it was in a sense a last resort. Land was a commodity—a useful, if only temporary, way to maintain their financial and social position. Land that was bought as an investment could always be sold.

Sucre's old colonial mining elite had been added to in the course of the nineteenth-century silver boom as self-made men who had started out in commerce and then bought mines with the help of Chilean money moved to the city after striking it rich. They were attracted by Sucre's benign climate, proximity to the mining areas, and position as the nation's political and cultural center. Gregorio Pacheco moved there in 1863 for the climate after three of his children died in quick succession in Tupiza (Potosí).[3] Like other miners before him, he quickly joined the city's old elite.

During the unsettled period of the first half of the nineteenth century, the older elite had maintained itself by controlling many of the positions in the government bureaucracy and, more important, by owning a multitude of haciendas that dotted the countryside of Yamparaez province. Once established in Sucre, the new mining entrepreneurs began buying haciendas from the old elite, displacing the colonial aristocracy from the land just as they had displaced them from the mines some years earlier. Other than a few properties close to Sucre, the silver barons bought the bulk of haciendas as money-making ventures. The old elite also participated in the joint stock companies that had been essential in making available enough native capital for the feverish mining activity in the second half of the nineteenth century, but the new miners kept the largest share of the stocks and so reaped most of

*Yamparaez province was split into two provinces in 1912; Tarabuco, Paccha, and Yamparaez cantons retained the old name, and the rest of the province became Oropeza. In this chapter all references to Yamparaez are to the pre-1912 unit.

the profits. Much of the income that was not reinvested in the mines went into the purchase of land. Investments in land did not yield nearly so high a return as mining did—perhaps 3 percent to 10 percent a year in Yamparaez—but they were much less risky.[4]

Gregorio Pacheco's papers show just how useful land could be. Besides Ñucchu, his palatial summer estate in the Cachimayo valley just beyond the outskirts of Sucre, Pacheco owned haciendas in Yamparaez canton, forty kilometers east of Sucre, in Cochabamba, and in Potosí. These more distant haciendas were administered by agents, and Pacheco rarely visited them. It is clear in his correspondence with his hacienda administrator that he bought the haciendas in Yamparaez for the barley crop, which he could always sell at a handsome profit to the government establishment in Sucre, which included large contingents of cavalry.[5] Pacheco marketed the crops from his properties in Potosí and Cochabamba in the mines; at times he obtained contracts to supply the Huanchaca Company with barley for fodder, and all his haciendas sent products to the Guadalupe mines, in which he had a controlling interest.[6] This union of agriculture and mining reached its fullest expression in the huge estate of the Condado de Oploca in southern Potosí, which Pacheco bought in 1881. Oploca had rich silver mines as well as a huge hacienda, which could supply the mining camp with both peon labor and many foodstuffs and animals.[7]

Most major stockholders of the mining companies engaged in many economic activities besides their main ones of mining and agriculture, although the largest part of their capital was in mining. Juan de Mata Melgarejo and his wife, Manuela Arteche, are a case in point. In the 1880's, the Melgarejos owned stock in six different mining companies worth more than 300,000 Bs. In Chuquisaca, they owned nine haciendas worth a total of 133,649 Bs. One of these was the most valuable estate in all Yamparaez, Potolo, later to become a canton in itself; in 1881, it was valued at 79,760 Bs. The Melgarejos also owned several houses in Sucre and Tacna (Peru), as well as some stock of undisclosed value in South American steamship lines. Juan de Mata also successfully bid for the post of municipal leather tax collector in 1884 and three years later he became the tithe collector for Potolo; for this privilege he bid 522 Bs and mortgaged one of his houses in Sucre as security.[8]

Having diversified activities proved to be of some help to the silver miners in the silver crisis of the 1890's, but it was the land that went first. Pacheco and a few others were able to invest large quantities of capital in the mines in an effort to increase productivity, but this often took most of their assets, including the land they had accumulated. In 1892, Juan de Mata Melgarejo was forced to sell Surima, his hacienda north of Sucre, to pay his debts. All but 1,707 Bs of the sale price of 10,400 Bs went to pay his overdue accounts. That same year, Melgarejo also sold his Potolo estate, for 202,397 Bs. He sold his stocks in two mining companies to a consortium of other silver miners, including Gregorio Pacheco and Aniceto Arce, and he even called in his debts, such as the 30,000 Bs he was owed on the sale of an estate in Potosí. Despite all this, Melgarejo was in such bad financial straits by 1894 that he had to pay a carpenter's bill by ceding the man a small plot of land on the outskirts of Sucre. In 1895, Melgarejo's wife sold another suburban plot to make ends meet. Thereafter, the Melgarejos disappeared completely from the land tax rolls.[9]

Some Sucre merchants also lost their lands during the silver crisis, but most survived the 1890's in much better financial shape than the miners. Since most traders supplied various urban markets as well as the mines, the diversity of their interests and their greater liquidity made them less vulnerable to the vagaries of the mining economy. Those who had also invested part of their money in mining stocks were caught short when dividend payments ceased, and some were unable to pay off the credit they had received from foreign merchant firms. For example, the merchant family headed by Corina Morena v. de Harriague had invested part of its capital in the Consolidada and Flamenca mining companies, which by the 1890's were in serious financial trouble. In 1892, the Harriagues had to give up their property, Bellavista, located in the Cachimayo valley south of Sucre and valued at 22,000 Bs, to A. Désprez and Company of Paris. This prominent merchant house with many branches on the Pacific coast of South America had no interest in Chuquisaca real estate and promptly sold the hacienda to recoup its investment.[10] Even so, the Harriagues as well as most other Sucre-based import-export firms managed to survive the silver crisis.[11]

Legal maneuvers were one way of trying to preserve assets during the silver crash. In 1893, Mariano Lora, a miner-merchant who had heavy investments in the northern Potosí silver mines and was president of two mining companies there, saved his properties from his creditors by transferring them to his wife in a *partición voluntaria*, or living will.[12] Mariano's brother, Nicolas, did not fare as well; although he used a similar procedure, signing his Hacienda Aranjuez over to his children in 1892, in 1895 and 1897 he was forced to sell two estates in Tomina province for 32,000 Bs to creditors.[13]

Among the Sucre elite with large investments in mining, a few were fortunate enough to own stock in companies such as the Huanchaca Company that remained financially sound into the 1890's. As investments in silver became increasingly unprofitable, they transferred part of their money out of mining into other enterprises, especially land. They were the ones who bought most of the land that was put up for sale during the silver crash. They also invested in bank stocks, urban real estate, and even shops and small factories. Candelaria Argandoña de Rodríguez, a shrewd widow, is representative of this more fortunate group. Her account books spanning the period 1893–1900 give a detailed picture of her clever investments during this crucial period.[14] In 1893, Señora Rodríguez owned 823,000 Bs worth of mining stocks in seven different companies, including 180 shares in Huanchaca valued at 720,000 Bs. Her second-largest assets were in land. Among various properties, she owned Hacienda Aranjuez, worth 30,000 Bs. This estate, which was located within a few kilometers of Sucre and served as her summer residence, contained a handsome and spacious *casa de hacienda* surrounded by orchards, flower beds, and vegetable gardens. The other estates were clearly profit-making investments. Five of them, valued at 186,094 Bs, were located between 40 and 60 kilometers east of Sucre, in the cantons of Yamparaez and Tarabuco. Señora Rodríguez also owned an estate in the *"frontera"* (presumably in the low Andean foothills in the eastern part of Tomina or in Azero). In addition, she had 81,060 Bs in bank accounts or bank stock at three different institutions and 4,600 Bs in letters of credit. Of the total amount, 78,960 Bs was in the National Bank and 300 Bs in the Bank of Potosí. She also owned seven other houses: in Sucre (3), Potosí (2), Tarabuco (1), and Yamparaez (1).

The value of Señora Rodríguez's different investments changed little until 1896, when there was a sudden jump in all categories (see Table 4). Although the source of income that made this possible is not mentioned, it was probably her Huanchaca stocks, since the value of her investments in the company jumped 150,000 Bs, to 870,000 Bs. The effects of the silver crisis first hit Señora Rodríguez in 1896, though only in a minor way, when the Ancona Mining Company was liquidated and she lost 54,544 Bs. Between 1894 and 1896 she sold one of her houses in Potosí for 2,000 Bs and bought another in Sucre for 10,000 Bs. Because she

TABLE 4

Assets of Candelaria Argandoña v. de Rodríguez, 1893–1900
(Bolivianos)

Item	1893	1894	1896	1897	1898	1900
Banks	85,660	86,360	104,433	102,771	119,445	97,900
Merchants	—	—	—	—	57,751	139,336
Mines	823,000	826,883	978,495	924,684	923,400	138,994
Haciendas	186,094	189,653	203,138	215,360	221,221	323,000
Houses	68,000	77,117	86,030	79,375	85,917	96,200
Misc.[a]		160	4,459	15,190	15,062	12,080
TOTAL	1,162,754	1,180,013	1,376,555	1,337,380	1,422,796	807,510

SOURCE: Archivo José Rodríguez, "Libro de cuentas de Candelaria Argandoña v. de Rodríguez."
[a]Includes cigar factory, shop, and loans to Nestor Rojas E.

had only 300 Bs in the Bank of Potosí, its bankruptcy in 1895 did not affect her financial position greatly.

In 1897, Señora Rodríguez invested in a cigar factory, spending 11,775 Bs to set up shop. However, the largest changes in her portfolio came between 1898 and 1900, a period in which she gave up the cigar factory, sold her smallest rural properties for 16,571 Bs, and let one of her houses in Sucre go for 13,450 Bs. More important, her assets in the Huanchaca Company plummeted from 870,000 Bs to only 131,452 Bs. With the proceeds of the sale of properties, houses, and mining stock, Señora Rodríguez bought a cattle ranch in Tomina (6,000 Bs) and a large grain-growing hacienda, La Candelaria, 85 kilometers from Sucre. La Candelaria, for which Señora Rodríguez paid 45,000 Bs, had previously belonged to Fulgencio Arce, a prominent member of the Sucre elite; he lost the hacienda when he defaulted on a loan from the National Bank in 1899.[15] Señora Rodríguez also funneled 139,336 Bs into French and British trading companies, such as A. Désprez and Anthony Gibbs and Company, up from 57,751 Bs in 1898.

By 1900, Señora Rodríguez's holdings had undergone dramatic changes. In 1893, she had 70 percent of her money in mining and only 16 percent in rural properties. At the turn of the century her assets were much more evenly distributed—40 percent in haciendas and 17 percent each in mining companies and foreign mercantile houses. Because of the sale and devaluation of her Huanchaca stocks, Señora Rodríguez lost over 600,000 Bs between 1898 and 1900, or 43 percent of her assets, but she moved just in time to

TABLE 5

Aniceto Arce's Rural Property Acquisitions in Chuquisaca,
1893–1897

(Total value: 92,175 bolivianos)

Year	Hacienda	Canton	Province	Value
1893	El Puente/La Calera	Huaillas	Yamparaez	12,000
1894	Mayca	Huaillas	Yamparaez	4,000
1894	Obejería (part)	Chuquichuquí	Yamparaez	4,000
1894	Pilcomayo	Tuero	Yamparaez	3,200
1895	Santa Isabel	Mojocoya	Tomina	2,880
1895	Seripona	Mojocoya	Tomina	16,200[a]
1896	Liquinas	Rodeo	Yamparaez	592
1896	Casa Pulqui	Yamparaez	Yamparaez	20,000
1896	Pomanasa	Copavilque	Yamparaez	28,337
1897	Obejería (part)	Chuquichuquí	Yamparaez	966

SOURCES: Archivo de la Corte Superior de Chuquisaca, Derechos Reales, Sucre y su Cercado, 1893: 119, 1894: 83, 87, 1897: 4; Tomina, 1895: 39, 58, 1896: 3, 4, 13, 34.
[a]Includes the redemption of 2,600 Bs worth of censos, or Church loans.

preserve most of her wealth by investing in land and foreign trading companies.

Even Aniceto Arce, probably the richest silver miner in the country and a major stockholder in the Huanchaca Company, followed this strategy. In the 1880's, Arce owned eight large haciendas worth 222,999 Bs in Chuquisaca. Six of these estates were located in Yamparaez and were valued at 122,999 Bs; the other two were in western Tomina, just outside the border of Yamparaez.[16] Between 1889 and 1892, Arce did not invest any money in Chuquisaca land, but after 1892 he began buying land again, adding ten more properties to his already extensive holdings and so increasing by almost half his investments in land (see Table 5). Seven of these properties were in Yamparaez and were worth 72,503 Bs. Between 1892 and 1895, he also acquired six properties, of unknown value, in Azero province.[17]

It was the legislation abolishing the Indian communities, which many of the silver miners had strongly supported, that made these lands available for purchase to the desperate Sucre elite. For the first time since the 1874 law was passed there was an incentive to buy this often marginal land on a large scale.* Mostly, the former

---

*Although in cash terms, the Indian properties represented only a small portion of total land sales in the province, their value was not as low as the sale documents indicate. As will be shown, because of the way Indian land was acquired, its true value cannot be calculated.

silver miners bought community lands in Yamparaez province, but they occasionally branched out into Tomina province and even into northern Potosí. The expansion of the hacienda in northern Potosí was noticeable in the cantons adjacent to Chuquisaca and, as was the case in Yamparaez as well, occurred primarily after the Federalist War of 1898–99.[18]

Some Sucre residents heavily involved in silver mining carved whole haciendas out of the communities, or ayllus. Such was the case with Eulogio Téllez, originally from Turuchipa in the department of Potosí, who moved to Sucre in the 1880's. Téllez owned stocks in the Flamenca Mining Company and was almost certainly a member of the important merchant house of Téllez Hermanos.[19] He already owned a fairly large hacienda in Tuero canton, which he had bought in 1872. In the two years 1895–96, in seventeen different transactions, he acquired a large area of Indian land in Tarabuco canton. He consolidated these lands into an hacienda named El Carmen and then, probably because of his difficulties with his mining interests, sold the estate to his son-in-law for 13,000 Bs.[20] The hacienda later became the focal point of a dispute between hacendados and the surrounding Indian communities in the Tarabuco area. In another case, in 1897–98, Santiago Rivera Aillon, scion of one of Sucre's most important mining families, acquired, again in seventeen different transactions, a large portion of Indian community land in the cantons of Huaillas and Quilaquila, creating Hacienda Tipoyo. Only three years later, however, in a trial contesting the validity of one of the transactions, Aillon stated that he had already sold the property to Pastor Sainz, the tin magnate.[21]

Beyond land and foreign mercantile firms, the last refuge for the silver miners' money was the Sucre banks. Two families related by marriage, the Argandoñas and the Uriostes, had founded the Francisco Argandoña Bank in 1893 to diversify their assets and so diminish their dependence on mining. But after the failure of the Bank of Potosí in 1895, other miners were nervous about investing in the seemingly risky banking business. Only after the turn of the century, when the banking system stabilized, did the Sucre elite put much of their remaining capital into bank stocks.

By 1900, most silver mines had been abandoned, leaving it up to small-scale operators, called *ccachas*, to exploit the silver veins as best they could, using the most rudimentary of techniques. Pedro Aniceto Blanco, in his important book describing mining conditions in Bolivia, estimated that in 1910, 10,000 silver mines lay deserted "because of the lack of capital or the lack of means to extract water and other inconveniences, never because of a lack of metal."[22] The crisis of the 1890's and the continued low prices of silver had effectively wiped out large-scale silver mining upon which the Sucre oligarchy had been dependent for much of its income. Some wealth remained in Sucre, to be sure, but on a much-diminished scale. As the tin boom in the twentieth century propelled La Paz and northern Bolivia into prosperity, southern Bolivia and with it the Sucre oligarchy became marginal to the politics and the economic affairs of the country.

Even the few Sucrenses who made a fortune in tin mining dropped out soon after the turn of the century as the industry fell into the hands of capital-rich foreign companies. Among the former tin miners was Anselmo Hernández, who gave up mining in 1914 to devote himself to farming. Already an important hacendado by inheritance in the department of Potosí, Hernández bought three large haciendas and one small property in Yamparaez; the largest, La Calera, which he acquired in 1908 for 85,000 Bs, had formerly belonged to Aniceto Arce.[23] Pastor Sainz quit tin mining in 1903 and bought at least four haciendas in Yamparaez before 1907, worth over 180,000 Bs. Sainz also acquired Indian land adjacent to his hacienda in Huaillas canton south of Sucre; he made a total of eighteen purchases between 1899 and 1905.[24] Just as had occurred with the silver miners, the few local tin magnates, once they had been squeezed out of mining, invested their money in land.

After the turn of the century, the Sucre elite attempted to maintain the traditions of the more prosperous past. Foreign travelers who passed through the city noted how tenaciously the elite families clung to their aristocratic pretensions and to their belief in Sucre's superiority over other Bolivian cities, including La Paz, for all its far greater commercial importance.[25] The strict residential pattern within Sucre reflected the social levels. Those families that lived within a one-block radius of the central plaza were considered most prestigious. The rest of the city proper was inhabited by poorer relations of the few and powerful elite families. The urban fringes, as usual in Latin American cities, were left to artisans, servants, *chicha* makers, and other members of the lower classes. Within the elite itself, social clubs defined their members' prominence. At the apex stood the Union Club, which in 1900 boasted among its members such distinguished residents as Pastor Sainz, Francisco Argandoña, Carlos Arce (son of Aniceto), and José María Linares.[26]

Even after the loss of income from silver mining, the Sucre elite maintained its patterns of conspicuous consumption. After seeing the poverty of the countryside, a pair of British missionaries were surprised to find that "the gentlemen of Sucre are as particular to wear their tall black hats and black clothes as the most exacting Londoner or Parisian, while the ladies are as well dressed as those in any part of the world."[27] At the *tertulias*, the social gatherings in the salons of the wealthiest residents, with the attendant dances, music, and conversations, the dames of Sucre high society attempted to outshine each other in modeling the latest fashions. Many elite Sucrenses accepted this emphasis on elegance and exaggerated courtesy as a sign of the city's progress and rightful place as the center of civilization in Bolivia. Appearances, however, were increasingly hard to maintain once the government moved to La Paz, a painful fact that the lavish parties could not hide.[28]

Part of the fortunes saved from the silver crisis went into the remodeling of the oligarchy's houses, and in the early twentieth century, the appearance of the city changed as colonial-era facades, with simple whitewashed adobe walls and wooden balconies, were transformed into elaborate neoclassical buildings in the Parisian style.[29] The interest in emulating the French, in architecture as in everything else, was brought about by the newly fashionable practice of packing the whole family off to Europe for vacation. Whereas earlier generations had traveled to Europe primarily for business purposes or to learn the practical skills necessary for mining, Sucre's elite now traveled for pleasure and culture.[30] Sons were sent to the best academies of Europe and, to a lesser extent, the United States.

This ostentatious spending and indulgent lifestyle led the occasional foreign visitors to assume that the wealthiest people in Bolivia lived in Sucre. Hiram Bingham, who passed through Sucre on his way from Buenos Aires to Lima in the early 1900's, concluded that the city's elite were the wealthiest in the country because "the great landowners have established here the headquarters of the most important banks of the country."[31] In this phrase, Bingham succinctly summarized the economic foundations of the Sucre elite after the end of the silver boom: land and banks. However, this wealth was not founded on the dynamic mining economy as in the previous century, but on far less profitable enterprises in an increasingly marginal and economically stagnant region.

The new generation that came of age in Sucre after 1910, nurtured on the tales of luck, wealth, and dynamism of nineteenth-century Sucre, tried to recoup the position that their parents had occupied. Like their forebears, most tried to make their fortunes in mining. Even for those with a fair share of business acumen, the times were not right: the structure of the Bolivian economy had changed too much. The days when a determined and lucky entrepreneur with limited resources could eventually build a business empire were over. New efforts came to naught as enterprises failed or, when successful, were rapidly absorbed by the new foreign companies.

Most speculation was on a small scale—a partnership with two or perhaps as many as ten members. Like many of the mid-nineteenth-century silver-mining companies, most of the new companies were started with only a small amount of capital. The shareholders tended to be large hacendados. Sebastian García, for example, a Sucre lawyer who owned Hacienda Humaca west of Sucre, worth 54,000 Bs, organized the mining company Nazareno de Ocurí to mine tin and silver in northern Potosí. His partners were six merchants, all but one of whom owned considerable amounts of land.[32] Notarial records do not show whether García's claim turned a profit, but most such ventures were abandoned after a few years.

A platinum mine claimed in the late 1920's demonstrated clearly the problems that led to the failure of many of these enterprises. In 1928, Georges Rouma, a Belgian anthropologist and educator who had spent many years in Bolivia, formed a company called the Platinum Syndicate with six associates, including Félix de Argandoña, Luis Arana Urioste, and Clovis Urioste Argandoña, all descendants of old silver-mining families. They intended to exploit platinum ores in Paccha canton (Yamparaez) and the adjacent canton of Presto, in Tomina province. The project, launched in the dry season, went well at first: the ore found was of good quality and the hastily improved trail was able to accommodate the mule trains that carried the ore to Sucre for refining. But when the rainy season started, the trail broke down, and it was impossible to transport the heavy loads of ore. Although the company's resources were considerable, it did not have enough capital to build an all-weather road. Since mining only part of the year was clearly unprofitable, the syndicate had to abandon the claim.[33] Descendants of the tin miner Pastor Sainz also attempted to get back into mining in the twentieth century. In 1913, Néstor Sainz, one of Pastor's sons, laid claim to a tin-mining concession in the rich Llallagua district in northern Potosí. Sainz's coinvestor, with a 50 percent share, was his brother-in-law Cayetano Llobet, a schoolteacher who had emigrated from Spain.[34] In 1922, another of Pastor's sons, José, joined a Syrian merchant-miner and five members of established Sucre families in a tin-mining venture in Linares province in Potosí. The enterprise probably absorbed too much capital, for later that year, the partners sold out to a Chilean company, just as José Sainz's father had done in 1905 with his much larger company.[35] José tried again in 1927, this time with a company called Romero, Sainz, and Santander (Romero was a large merchant and landowner from Cinti, and Santander a small-scale miner from Sucre). The purpose was to exploit lead and silver in Oruro, but, like other efforts of Pastor Sainz's descendants to reenter mining, this one failed.[36]

In 1918, the Sucre elite mounted a last, gargantuan effort to reconquer its former position in the mining sector. The effort was spearheaded by the newly formed tin-mining company Gallofa Consolidated of Colquechaca, capitalized at 1,275,000 Bs. Most of the heirs of the Sucre silver miners invested heavily in this enterprise—names such as Urioste, Argandoña, and Arce were prominently represented in the list of stockholders—and the company's home offices were located in Sucre. In the late nineteenth century, at the height of the silver boom, Gallofa Consolidated, worth over 1,000,000 Bs, would have ranked among the ten richest companies in Bolivia. But the mining industry had changed, and Gallofa was competing with giant foreign firms that had access to huge amounts of capital, such as the Guggenheim Mining Company of New York and Patiño Enterprises. By 1922, Gallofa's initial funding was exhausted, and the board of directors sold the company to Simón Patiño, who added it to his already immense holdings.[37]

Members of the Sucre elite also speculated in petroleum, but here, too, their successes were limited—at least in the long run. Oil had been discovered in 1895 by Manual Cuéllar during a surveying trip for a road between Azero and the Paraguay River. Cuéllar, a Sucre resident and shareholder in various silver-mining companies, joined with Ernesto Reyes, also from Sucre, member of a family that owned extensive haciendas in eastern Tomina, in the Lagunillas Petroleum Company to exploit this find. The discovery of substantial quantities of black gold electrified the city. Petroleum fever reached its peak in Sucre between 1912 and 1916, as many of the city's moneyed residents staked claims to petroleum concessions throughout the Bolivian Oriente. One of the more important concessionaires was Mamerto Urriolagoitia, a prominent Sucre merchant and landowner, who in 1913 staked claims to two petroleum concessions in Azero totaling 6,036 hectares.[38] Most of the grants on petroleum lands went to experienced members of the Sucre elite, men who had already done prospecting in the oil-bearing Andean foothills. Perhaps the most famous of these prospectors was Adolfo Costa du Rels, who, after spending years searching for oil, went on to a distinguished career as writer and diplomat. In 1914, he became secretary of the Incahuasi Petroleum Syndicate, and by 1916 he had claims totaling 500,000 hectares in his name. He later published a novel, *Tierras hechizadas*, based partly on his experiences prospecting in the province of Azero.[39]

Those of the Sucre elite who were personally unable to supervise the surveying of claims hired experienced foreign prospectors to do the work in return for part of the concession. Mamerto Urriolagoitia worked with Ernest F. Moore, an accountant from Great Britain, in the Sucre Syndicate. Néstor Sainz and Graciano Guzman, a Sucre lawyer and son-in-law of the silver miner Eulogio Téllez, went into partnership with John Burman, a mining engineer from the United States, to claim a concession of 80,000 hectares named Pioneer.[40]

In 1916, the Bolivian government, worried about runaway speculation, prohibited any further petroleum concessions, and issued new regulations and increased the tax on the existing ones.[41] According to the prefect of Chuquisaca, many people had acquired rights to concessions only to sell them later at a profit.[42] The truth was that most claimants lacked the capital to put the fields into production, and even after the new regulations, which encouraged the consolidation of claims, were unable to find sufficient capital to exploit the finds.

In 1920, the government resumed the granting of concessions because the native speculators, most of whom were Sucre residents, had not started production.[43] Almost immediately, capitalists from the United States moved in and offered those holding promising grants fantastically high prices. Most of the original concessionaires sold out. Néstor Sainz, who had bought his one-third share in

Pioneer in 1914 for 150 pounds sterling, sold it in 1920 to the New York–based Richmond Levering Company for 25,000 pounds. The William Braden interests bought four petroleum syndicates with concessions totaling 2,145,000 hectares in Azero and Tarija for 750,000 pounds.[44] Both U.S. companies may have been fronts for Standard Oil of New Jersey, which in 1921 acquired both the Richmond Levering and the Braden concession for over $5,500,000. Standard Oil started surveying and exploiting its holdings soon after it signed an agreement with the Bolivian government accepting the takeover. By 1928, after having invested almost $11,500,000, the company had at least eight producing wells, pumping 6,000 tons of crude oil annually.[45] Despite the windfall profits gained from speculation in oil, the Sucre elite again had failed to regain its preeminent position within the country.

After their frustrated attempts at finding wealth in extractive industries, the Sucre oligarchs hoarded the last remains of their fortunes in very conservative investments. Many members of the post–silver crash generation bought bank stocks; others in turn took this money out in the form of loans so that they could maintain their opulent lifestyles. The collateral for loans was often land—haciendas either owned before or bought in the wake of the silver crash. Land was the only form of wealth the Sucre elite still controlled. Consider, for example, Jorge Calvo, whose family included prominent landowners, miners, and politicians. In 1911, Calvo and his wife, Lucrecia Linares, from another of Sucre's oldest families, borrowed 80,000 Bs from the National Bank, using their vineyard in Cinti province as collateral. Similarily, Calvo's aunt, Alcira Linares v. de Romero, between 1916 and 1924 accumulated debts of 200,000 Bs, with the enormous Hacienda Incahuasi in southeastern Cinti as security.[46]

Although there is evidence that Señora Romero, at least, spent a small portion of the borrowed money on mine claims and agricultural improvements, the vast majority of these loans were essentially unproductive and contributed very little to the economic revival of the region. A vicious circle had been created, whereby the purchase of bank stocks provided the cash for loans to maintain lifestyles beyond the means of some of the now-impoverished Sucre aristocracy. As a prominent Sucre intellectual, Alfredo Jáuregui Rosquellas, complained, this strategy was self-defeating: "There is an absolute lack of industry in this locality [Sucre], either because of the difficult conditions that exist or because of the natural timidity of the capitalists, but there is no doubt that the bank vaults are full of money, the interest from which they live on. . . . If that wealth were put into circulation in the form of transportation, agricultural, ranching, or extractive enterprises, it would have enormous yields and would intensify the [commercial] life of Sucre."[47]

The fall of silver prices in the last decade of the nineteenth century resulted in the political, economic, and cultural decadence of Sucre. The Sucre oligarchy, which had based its political and financial preeminence on silver mining, failed to adjust to the new economic circumstances and went into a period of prolonged decline. Three different phases of this decline can be detected. The first entailed the transfer of funds from mining to other investments, especially land, after it became clear that further investment in silver would only lead to financial ruin. Why invest in safe but not very profitable rural estates? Perhaps part of the answer lies in the age of the most successful silver barons, who had spent their youth and middle age building up their fortunes only to see everything come down around their heads at the end of their lives. Aniceto Arce and Gregorio Pacheco, for example, were, respectively, seventy-one and seventy-two years of age in 1895, when the silver crisis was at its worst. They were too old to start over. This was true also of the few people who benefited from the upsurge of tin, such as Pastor Sainz and Anselmo Hernández. Old land-tenure patterns also changed, as haciendas, especially in Chuquisaca, were transferred from owners who lost everything in the crisis to buyers who had been able to cut their losses in time. And with the strong financial motive to ignore Indian resistance and incorporate ayllu land into expanding haciendas, Indian communities, especially in Yamparaez province and on the fringes of northern Potosí, lost a significant portions of their lands.

The second phase, from the last years of the nineteenth century to about 1910, was a period of decadence. As the last silver barons finally went to their graves, the Sucre elite seemed paralyzed and unable to shake off the habits of the good old days. Many seemed to confuse opulence with progress. Luxurious ostentation, in the form of extravagant parties and the wholesale renovation of houses in the city's core on a Parisian model, were indicative of the backward-looking nature of the elites during this period.

But even the efforts of the new generation that came to prominence around 1910, the descendants of the old silver miners, failed to rebuild Sucre's fortunes. This new generation, motivated by a desire to restore old times, invested in the same types of small-scale mining projects that their ancestors had started with. Realizing that the days of silver were over, they staked claims to mines containing other metals, such as gold, platinum, copper, and especially tin. Even petroleum, a new and unconventional natural resource in the context of the Bolivian economy, became the object of many investors. But at best these investors, for all their dynamism, were simply speculators who risked their own limited fortunes in head-to-head competition with large foreign companies, firm's that bought the luckiest of them out when their funds were exhausted.

It soon became clear that it was no longer possible for a well-connected and moderately wealthy person to strike it rich after a few years of hard work and a bit of luck. Any mining enterprise, however modest, required the sort of financial resources that no individual Sucrense, even the wealthiest, possessed. Apparently the Sucre elite realized this by 1918. Even the well-financed Gallofa Consolidated of Colquechaca was no more successful than less-ambitious ventures had proved to be. Direct competition with the huge foreign companies ended in failure, and the Sucre elite finally gave up its quest to emerge from its marginal position in the economic life of the nation. In the Central Highlands of Peru, local elites were able to maintain most of their prosperity by complementing the large Cerro de Pasco mining concern; but in Bolivia the takeover of large-scale mining by foreign enterprises spelled the end of the days of prosperity for the Sucre oligarchy.[48] The city's poor geographical position, too far away from the nation's borders to control the export trade and without access to the railroad and thus the highland mines, meant that, once eliminated from mining, the Sucre elite became superfluous to the country's export economy. After the establishment of the state bank in La Paz, even the Sucre banks, which had continued the hegemony of the city at least in the financial sphere, were eclipsed. Thereafter, they existed mainly to pay dividends—and to make generous loans to the Sucre aristocrats to help them maintain their accustomed expensive lifestyle.

CHAPTER FOUR

Yamparaez Province

A series of Indian rebellions punctuated the Yamparaez country-side from 1918 onward, culminating in a massive uprising in 1927 that moved out of the northern Potosí highlands to sweep through the entire province. To understand this movement, we need to look at the history of Yamparaez province from four perspectives: the comparative strengths of the Indian communities and the hacienda before 1900; the labor system prevailing on the estates during the silver-mining boom; the process of alienation of Indian community lands; and the changes in the hacienda regime after the silver crash.

Haciendas and Communities Before 1900

The climate of Yamparaez is generally more benign than that of neighboring Potosí, and the climate was one of the reasons why many Potosí miners settled their families in Sucre and the surrounding countryside. Located to the east of the highest Andean ranges, the province is usually described as *valle*, or valley, but that designation masks the great variety of geographical features in Yamparaez. The province is extremely mountainous, with peaks 3,500 meters high; it also has deep subtropical valleys, carved out by the Río Grande on the northern border and the Pilcomayo River in the south. Within this area there are other, shallower valleys cut by small streams and rivers, like the Cachimayo, which almost disappear in the dry season. This rugged terrain only gives way to the cold, windswept plains near the towns of Yamparaez and Tarabuco to the east. Because of the great variations in altitude, the province produces all sorts of agricultural goods, ranging from tropical fruits, sugarcane, and corn to such cold-weather crops as potatoes, wheat, and barley.[1]

The first years of the republican era were a period of stagnation in the Yamparaez countryside. Alcides D'Orbigny, a French adventurer and naturalist who traveled through the province in the 1830's, described the important town of Tarabuco, razed during the wars of independence, as still in ruins, though Yamparaez, thirty kilometers to the west, was a "large town." According to D'Orbigny, the province had a wheat surplus that went primarily to the small market of Santa Cruz de la Sierra, in the eastern lowlands.[2] By 1846, just before the new silver boom, José María Dalence estimated that Chuquisaca produced 60,400 *fanegas* of wheat, 242,266 fanegas of corn, and 89,310 *cargas* of potatoes. Despite its apparent stagnation, this made Chuquisaca one of the largest producers of these crops in the country.*

According to Erwin Grieshaber, who has studied the Bolivian tribute records, the number of community Indians in Yamparaez remained stable during the nineteenth century. In contrast, the number of tribute-paying members of haciendas in the province dropped 35 percent between 1828 and 1877, bringing the number to the same level as the community Indians.[3] Grieshaber assumed that this drop meant a drop in the size of the hacienda labor force, which could be attributed to the decline of the population of Sucre during the period and the subsequent diminishing importance of the urban market.[4] But this hypothesis is unsatisfactory, on two counts. First, where did the tribute payers go if they did not remain on the haciendas (note that the urban population dropped in this period)? And second, why should the hacendado have dismissed part of his labor force when the number of laborers to a large extent determined the value of the landholding?[5] Part of the problem is that Grieshaber assumes—wrongly—that all hacienda laborers, or at least the vast majority, paid tribute. By the late nineteenth century, in fact, many workers on the estates either were mestizos or successfully passed themselves off as such, thereby avoiding payment of tribute. Especially by the 1870's, when the

---

*Dalence, *Bosquejo*, p. 238. The measurements used for agricultural products in Bolivia are extremely diverse and vary over time, area, and type of crop. Usually, a fanega equals about 250 kg, a carga between 100 and 125 kg, and a quintal 46 kg.

TABLE 6

Communal, Hacienda, and Urban Tribute Payers in Yamparaez, 1833–1877

Tribute payers	1833	1856	1877
Total[a]	2,110	2,065	1,679
Communal			
Number	768	871	782
Percent	36%	42%	47%
Hacienda			
Number	1,212	1,058	784
Percent	57%	51%	47%
Urban			
Number	130	136	113
Percent	6%	7%	7%

SOURCE: Erwin P. Grieshaber, "Survival of Indian Communities in Nineteenth-Century Bolivia," Ph.D. dissertation, University of North Carolina, 1977, pp. 132–37.
NOTE: Percentages do not add to 100 because of rounding.
[a]Excludes Tarabuco canton, which was not part of Yamparaez until 1880.

silver miners already wielded considerable power, they probably used their influence to convert some of their labor force to mestizo status. This would obviously not show up on paper. Nevertheless, it is perhaps indicative of the hacendados' strength in these matters that in the 1880's and 1890's they successfully opposed military conscription for their workers or their use for transporting mail, which had traditionally been the obligation of all tribute payers.[6] Therefore, although the *padrón*, or tribute list, might be a fairly accurate estimate of the size of the Indian communities, it does not necessarily show accurately the total number of workers on the haciendas (see Table 6).

More detailed information on haciendas in the province is available for the years after 1880, when the first rural tax census, the catastro, was compiled. This census listed all private properties, their owners, and the value, annual income, and production on each. Since the 1880's were the most prosperous decade of the silver boom, the list is extremely useful in understanding land-tenure patterns during this period. The catastro of 1881 listed 581 properties belonging to private individuals. Church-controlled lands were negligible in number and importance. Only five properties belonged to the Church; only one was a large hacienda. Four large landholdings belonged to Indian ayllus from the departments of Oruro and Potosí. The 586 non-Indian estates can be classified

TABLE 7

Agricultural Production on Non-Indian Lands in Yamparaez, 1881

| Commodity | Total production | Large haciendas[a] | |
		Production	Percent of total
Wheat (fanegas)	28,144	15,607	55%
Corn (cargas)	40,811	18,736	46
Potatoes (cargas)	22,221	11,163	50
Alfalfa (cargas)	18,990	13,690	72
Barley (quintals)	58,763	31,580	54

SOURCE: Centro Bibliográfico Documental Histórico, Universidad Mayor, Real y Pontificia de San Francisco Xavier de Chuquisaca (Sucre), Tesoro Departamental, "Catastro de la provincia de Yamparaez: propriedades rústicas (1881)."
[a] Value of at least 10,000 Bs.

into three categories: 238 small properties worth 1,000 Bs or less, 264 medium-sized properties worth more than 1,000 Bs and less than 10,000 Bs, and 84 haciendas worth 10,000 Bs or more. This categorization roughly corresponds to the different levels of production of the properties and their marketable surplus. Small properties were only sufficient to cover the subsistence needs of the resident families; the medium-sized landholdings usually produced a slight surplus; and the large haciendas, constituting 15 percent of the total and mostly owned by the Sucre elite, produced a considerable cash crop and employed a dependent resident labor force.[7]

The 1881 catastro does not list the size of the resident labor forces on haciendas, but the annual production figures clearly show the dominance of the large haciendas. Around half of the total wheat, corn, and potato crop produced on non-Indian land came from these properties (see Table 7). Large estates also controlled almost all the irrigated bottom land in the subtropical valleys and so monopolized the cultivation of fruits—bananas, chirimoyas, oranges, and others. More important, virtually all grain mills were located on large properties. This gave the hacendados a substantial amount of control over the commercialization of wheat and corn flour (the latter very important for making chicha, the Andean corn beer), since the smaller producers had to have their grain milled at the prices set by the large landowners.

The large estates were not evenly distributed in the province. Some cantons consisted mainly of large haciendas; others had almost none. As Map 3 shows, one area where large haciendas (val-

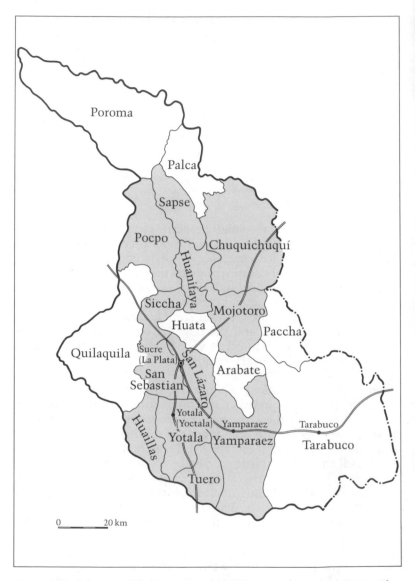

Map 3. Distribution of large haciendas in Yamparaez by canton, 1881. The tone area indicates the canton was predominantly made up of large haciendas. On this and subsequent maps, the double lines show the main roads.

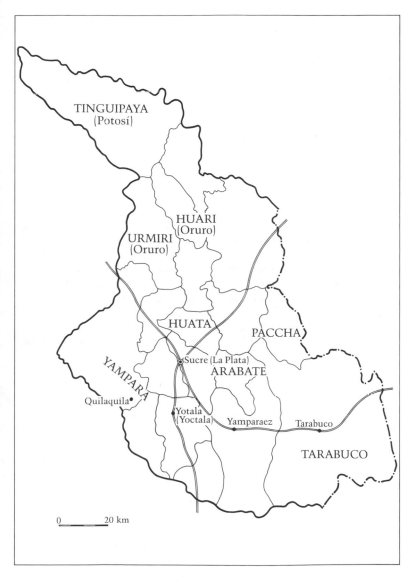

Map 4. Distribution of major Indian groups in Yamparaez, 1877. Source: TD, Matrículas de indígenas: Tomina 1877, Yamparaez, 1878.

ued at over 5,000 Bs) predominated was in the vicinity of Sucre, particularly the Cachimayo River Valley in Yotala and Tuero, where many members of the Sucre oligarchy maintained estates as summer retreats. This had been true since the eighteenth century, as noted by Concolorcorvo, who compared the houses La Plata's (Sucre's) elite in the Cachimayo Valley favorably with the manors of Cantabria in Spain.[8] In the 1880's and 1890's, the silver barons built sumptuous palaces there, such as Aniceto Arce's La Florida, making the area the "Versailles of Sucre."[9] To a lesser extent, there were similar estates in the subtropical Mojotoro Valley and in Huaillas, where the hot mineral springs made it a popular bathing area for the urban elites.

It is sometimes difficult to distinguish between the haciendas that were used for recreation and those that served only as money-making enterprises. Some were obviously not meant to produce many foodstuffs, such as Francisco Argandoña's La Glorieta, in the Cachimayo Valley. On this estate, Argandoña built a gaudy castle, mixing an Arabian minaret with a Gothic tower, among other architectural peculiarities. In 1881, the property produced only 12 cargas of corn, 200 cargas of alfalfa, and 70 cargas of husked barley, worth in all only 396 Bs.[10] On the other hand, Gregorio Pacheco's Ñucchu, not far from La Glorieta, was a producing hacienda as well as a retreat. Besides a palatial building and carefully landscaped gardens, it had fruit orchards, a vineyard, five grain mills, and extensive fields of corn, potatoes, and alfalfa. The total annual income from the landholding (in 1881) was 6,240 Bs, of which 4,000 Bs came from the mills. This was the highest annual income recorded for a single property in the 1881 catastro.[11]

In other areas, far from Sucre, and less attractive, haciendas were used exclusively for farming. This was true of the haciendas in the cantons of Yamparaez, Chuquichuqui, Huanifaya, Pocpo, and Siccha. Most of them had a *casa de hacienda* to accommodate the owner when he or she visited the estate during the sowing or harvest season, but these buildings were not elaborate like the ones in the Cachimayo Valley, and for most of the year only the hacienda administrator, often a relative of the owner, lived there. The administrator's job was to supervise the farming and to see that the crops were sent to market and that the requisite number of hacienda peons were sent to Sucre to work in the landlord's house as *semaneros*, or temporary house servants. Hacienda Alcantarí, for example, located thirty-one kilometers southeast of Sucre on the prime wheat-growing plains of Yamparaez, was owned in the

1880's by the prominent miner Mariano Lora, who lived in Sucre and only occasionally visited the estate. Since the main trail from Potosí to the lowlands to the east passed through the hacienda, it also served as a *tambo*, or roadway inn, but its main purpose was farming. Alcantarí encompassed some of the scarce level land in the province, and it was one of the largest wheat, potato, and barley producers of the area, netting its owner at least 1,440 Bs annually.[12]

Like Lora's Hacienda Alcantarí, most large haciendas were clustered around the main roads, which gave them year-round access to the urban and mining markets. This also reduced transport costs considerably because of easy transport and the large number of muleteers who frequented the road. As Map 3 shows, virtually all the cantons that contained a major highway were dominated by large haciendas. It is not clear what arrangements were made to market the crops; in many cases, the hacendado simply sold his produce from his house in the city. Also, since most of the large landowners in Yamparaez province were important stockholders in the mining companies, they often received preference in providing agricultural goods to these enterprises. This was the case, for example, in 1880, when Gregorio Pacheco sold all of that year's barley crop to the Huanchaca Company in advance at the highest rate other suppliers would get.[13]

While the silver boom lasted, most of the large landowners, who were almost without exception mining company stockholders, preferred to live in an urban environment where they could keep abreast of the latest silver-price quotations in London and manage their various business interests. Income from the mines still far exceeded that of the haciendas, and though many of the administrators received a percentage of the net profit on the most important crops as an incentive to maintain production, they usually did not have enough influence to dictate any significant changes in the management of the estates.[14] Rather, most landowners were content to receive their profits and their supply of semaneros regularly without attempting to change the way the hacienda was administered. Properties remained relatively neglected, and the obligations of the hacienda peons—*arrenderos* or *colonos*—were not too severe.

These obligations consisted of a variety of goods and services in return for a small plot of land, sufficient to provide for the subsistence of the peon's family. Usually they included work on certain critical days in the agricultural cycle, such as sowing, weeding, and harvesting, as well as transporting crops to Sucre or the nearest town. In addition, peons were required to stand duty as house servants in town and to pay a rent in kind, usually chickens, eggs, sheep, and firewood. They also paid a small cash rent.

During most of the nineteenth century, the state exacted of all producers payments called *diezmos* and *primicias*, that is, the tithe and first fruits. These taxes, originally collected to support the Catholic Church, were farmed out to the highest bidder in each department and were an important component of departmental income until 1896, when they were abolished in Chuquisaca. Sometimes the landowner bid on the collection of the diezmos and primicias of his canton as a way of avoiding the excessive exploitation of his own peons by other, more profit-minded collectors who might try to squeeze the arrenderos for as much as possible. Eulogio Téllez, the owner of the largest estate in Tuero, consistently was the tithe collector in that canton.[15] There was no apparent safeguard against landowners' making a profit in these collections on estates owned by others in the canton.

The obligations that the arrenderos were expected to fulfill were counterbalanced by reciprocal obligations on the part of the hacendado or his representative. Sowing and harvesting were invariably accompanied by a fiesta, called *mink'a*, at which the landowner distributed chicha, coca, and food to the workers and sometimes even hired a band of musicians. As Charles Erasmus pointed out, festive labor was especially important in areas where cash was short. The peons valued food and the usufruct of land over meager money wages. These fiestas also were essential as a goodwill measure: they satisfied a deeply ingrained Andean tradition from pre-Conquest times that required some form of redistribution for services rendered. One foreign traveler in the late nineteenth century remarked: "There is a prevalent custom of giving alcohol to the Indian on all feast days, on the breaking-in of animals, at commencement of sowing, reaping, etc. Failing this the Indian simply refuses to work. I remember one who quietly informed us that without alcohol no bullock was ever known to plough!"[16]

When the hacendado came to visit his estate, the head of each arrendero household appeared before him in turn, kissed his hand, and presented him with a chicken or other small item. To an outsider, this act appeared to indicate the total submission of the peon to his master, but in fact it reconfirmed the colono's subservience conditional on the hacendado's recognition of his obligations to the worker. This was demonstrated symbolically and in concrete terms by the fiesta that began immediately following this ceremony, when the patron responded by demonstrating his largesse. To the urban-oriented and Eurocentric landowner this custom seemed a quaint but effective paternalistic way of making sure that the workers did his bidding, but the peons saw this ceremonial exchange of goods as affirming an unwritten pact that ensured their livelihood in exchange for their labor and other goods.[17]

This unwritten pact meant that the hacendado could not easily dismiss workers from his estate, and when there was a bad crop year, he usually lowered or forgave the rent payments and provided new seed. During the silver boom, these actions were clearly to the landowner's advantage, since maintaining a large number of workers in a labor-intensive agricultural system raised the value of the land and ensured that the crops were harvested on time. During the whole of the nineteenth century, landowners rarely, if ever, challenged this system by attempting to modernize labor relations or introduce new machinery. The system provided steady though not spectacular profits and worked well enough without improvements. Besides, most hacendados were primarily concerned with their mining stocks and other such matters, and were content to leave the countryside in a state of benign neglect.[18]

After independence and during the course of the nineteenth century, the Indian communities achieved a tenuous equilibrium with the haciendas. Besides the legal problems inherent in obtaining Indian land before 1866, there were few economic motivations to convert communities into haciendas. The legal problems were especially great in Sucre, for the national government frequently resided in the city during the first 75 years of independence (even then the government had periodically moved to La Paz and other cities). Until 1874, the state had a vested interest in preventing the usurpation of Indian lands, since the loss of land meant a loss in tribute income, a very important item in the national budget.[19] Nevertheless, in consequence of historical development, the distribution of ayllu lands and the relative strengths of the various ethnic groups were by no means uniform in Yamparaez.

As the name of the province suggests, the Yampara Indians were the largest ethnic group in the area. By the first third of the seventeenth century, according to the monk Antonio de la Calancha, the Yamparas had been reduced to three towns, Yoctala (Yotala), Quilaquila, and Tarabuco.[20] As had occurred in many other regions of the Spanish empire, the principal *kurakas*, or ethnic lords, rapidly assimilated into Spanish society, but unlike other ethnic groups, which were rapidly shunted to the margins of the new Spanish cities, the Yampara lords, who had allied themselves with the Spaniards during the Conquest, lived on the plaza in the center of La Plata until at least 1620. Even in 1639, when Juan Aymoro, the principal Yampara kuraka, moved to an Indian *ranchería* on the outskirts, he maintained a seigneurial house with a tower, a garden, a fountain, and a small plaza in front.[21]

Another important settlement, the town of Tarabuco, was originally populated by *mitimaes*, or Inca-period agricultural and military colonists who came from Cuzco and the altiplano around Lake Titicaca to protect the Inca empire from the fierce lowland Chiriguano tribes. These mitimaes also cultivated coca in the lower valleys of the region. Only during Viceroy Toledo's tenure in the late sixteenth century were Yamparas also settled in the town itself. Tarabuco parish records going back to the early eighteenth century show ayllu names such as Pacaja, Pucarani, and Lupaca, suggesting that some Indians originally came from the Lake Titicaca region.[22] Calancha also noted two areas, Huata and Paccha, where Incas of royal blood lived. Another ethnic group, called Yanaguaras or Condes Arabates, lived a few kilometers northeast of La Plata in Arabate. According to Teresa Gisbert and José de Mesa, this group consisted of mitimaes from Arequipa (Peru). In addition, on the road to Mizque close to the Río Grande lived the Churumatas and Moyo ethnic groups.[23]

More than two centuries later, all but the Churumatas and Moyos still lived as separate groups, and in most cases they controlled much of the land in the cantons named after them. The 1877 tribute lists show that community Indians predominated in Quilaquila, where there were 120 *originarios* and 77 *forasteros* organized into five ayllus. A smaller presence of the same ethnic group was also noted in Tuero and Yotala. These groups were probably descendants of the Yamparas.[24]

The ayllus in the Tarabuco area had apparently lost their connections to their places of origin by the nineteenth century and had coalesced into one large administrative unit. They controlled more land and were more numerous than those in the Quilaquila area. The 363 originarios owned most of Tarabuco canton from the altiplano (over 3,000 meters) to the subtropical Pilcomayo Valley, as well as large tracts of land in the adjacent canton of Tacopaya in Tomina province. Furthermore, these ayllus maintained an "ecological island" in Sopachuy (Tomina), 90 kilometers to the southeast. Departing from the Andean pattern in the uplands, where each ayllu's plots were contiguous, the plots of the ayllus in the subtropical Sopachuy Valley were interspersed. By the nineteenth century, the Tarabuco ayllus no longer cultivated coca in the valleys but instead grew subsistence crops, chiefly corn.[25]

This control of different ecological levels, sometimes far from the main area in the highlands, was a traditional Andean strategy to maximize self-sufficiency and minimize the damage from localized crop failures. As the revisitas make clear in their lists of the Indians' properties, this pattern was duplicated on the household level as well. Most Indians owned widely dispersed lands at different altitudes to provide them with crops from both puna and valley. For example, in the 1898 revisita, Petrona Guarayo, from the ayllu Tercer Poco in Tarabuco, owned six plots upon which she cultivated wheat, barley, and corn.[26]

The ayllus of Paccha and Huata, composed of Incan descendants, were virtually extinguished by the late nineteenth century. In 1877, they contained a mere twenty-eight originarios and nine forasteros. Melgarejo's assault on community lands left its mark on Huata, where almost one-half of the *origenes* were sold and never returned to their original owners. This occurred only because by then the Huata ayllu was already too weak to defend its property rights.[27] The community in Arabate had also lost its links with the original ayllus in Peru. Though it was only a shadow of its former self, the community nevertheless had a total of seventy-five tributaries, including thirty-three originarios, four "sons of originarios who pay as forasteros," and thirty-three "forasteros without lands." This was not a large number, but the ayllu controlled most of the land in this small and sparsely populated canton (see Map 4).[28]

In addition to these ethnic groups, Indian ayllus from other departments controlled lands in the relatively warm northwest corner of Yamparaez. In all cases, communities from the cold altiplano owned these lands so as to have access to the agricultural products that could be grown in a milder climate. The ayllu of Tinguipaya from Potosí held two large *parcialidades*, called Soicoco and Colquebamba, in Poroma. These lands had been given to them during the colonial period "in compensation for the sterility of the [lands] they had in Tinguipaya."[29] Both Soicoco and Colquebamba were subtropical valley lands, and were mostly visited by the Indian owners only during the sowing and harvest seasons. The refusal of the Potosí Indians to pay tribute on their Chuquisaca lands to local officials or provide traditional services for Poroma officials had led to a long-standing dispute between the Potosí and Chuquisaca prefectures.[30]

Two other ayllus, both in Oruro close to Lake Poopó on the altiplano, maintained large tracts of land in Yamparaez. The community of Huari owned San Juan de Horca in Sapse. Apparently the Indians paid the *impuesto catastral*, the land tax imposed on non-Indian lands, since the holding appears in the 1881 catastro's list of haciendas. Horca was valued at 16,000 Bs, the second-highest value in the canton, and produced 500 fanegas of wheat, 300 cargas of corn, 300 cargas of potatoes, and 400 cargas of unhusked barley, as well as *ocas*, *papa lisa*, and beans.[31] Three properties of the Aymara-speaking Urmiri de Quillacas community were also listed in the 1881 catastro. With these lands valued at 21,000 Bs, the community was the third-largest landowner in Pocpo canton. These properties produced 630 fanegas of wheat, 400 cargas of corn, and 100 cargas of potatoes, as well as barley and ocas.[32] A murder trial involving members of the Quillacas ayllu with lands in Pocpo suggests a residence pattern similar to that of the Tinguipaya Indians. One of the accused testified that he usually came down to Pocpo only for the sowing season; he spent the rest of the year in the uplands, near Quillacas. His parents, however, had resided in Pocpo for the past two years.[33]

Although it is difficult to characterize the social organization of the Yamparaez ayllus because of a dearth of contemporary accounts and serious ethnographic research, we know in a general way how the late-nineteenth-century communities functioned. At the apex of the ayllu stood the kuraka, who was also the main link between the community and government.[34] In Yamparaez, as in most of the Andes, the kuraka was in charge of collecting the tribute and paying it to the local government official. If he did not pass on the assigned amount, he could be thrown into jail.[35] In addition, the kuraka handled most disputes between ayllu members, especially concerning land rights. He was also responsible for redistributing community land and guarding it against encroachment from outsiders.

Each household had usufruct rights to certain plots of agricultural lands and worked them with the aid of neighbors and relatives in complex reciprocal arrangements.[36] Most grazing land was held in common; fields lying fallow could also be used for pasture by all members of the community. Agricultural parcels not held in usufruct by a community household reverted back to the ayllu.

The kuraka had the right to redistribute these fields when the need arose. Members of the ayllu had access to different amounts of land based not only on its relative fertility but on the member's social position in the community. The different means of obtaining access to land and the reasons for the wide variety in the amounts of land held by different members are complex matters that fall beyond the scope of this work, but certainly a high degree of social stratification based largely on access to land existed within the communities. This stratification was mirrored partially in the fiscal categories of originario, *agregado*, and forastero. The originario, presumably a descendant of the original ayllu, usually had access to more land than forasteros and agregados who, in seventeenth-century terminology, were outsiders who had migrated to the community.[37]

Alienation of Indian Community Lands

George McBride, a U.S. geographer, wrote in 1921 that Indian communities in Bolivia had been reduced by half since the turn of the century, and that in Yamparaez Indians now controlled only the uplands. Although McBride's methodology is problematical, he correctly emphasized the expansion of haciendas at the expense of Indian communities as the major change in rural society in the Bolivian highlands in the late nineteenth century. His categorical statement about the extinction of Yamparaez's communities in the valleys is only partly correct, however. Not all areas of the province became dominated by haciendas; for a number of reasons, including the commercial potential of the land and the intensity of the Indian communities' resistance, many areas remained under Indian control.[38] The alienation of community lands in Yamparaez province was a multifaceted process that affected each major ayllu differently.

When the liberal reformers finally sent out the *mesas revisitadores* to measure the communities' lands and parcel them out to individual Indians, they met great resistance. The first surveying in Yamparaez was done in Tarabuco between 1881 and 1883. The rest of the province was not surveyed until the 1890's. Constant resistance by the Indians made the commission's work extremely difficult and ultimately unsuccessful in some parts because not all Indian lands were included. Ayllu members used the judicial system effectively to foil the commission; this was the case in the

1895 revisita in Quilaquila, where the Indians filed so many complaints against the revisitador that he had to suspend operations to answer the charges. This tactic was so successful that in 1896 the prefect complained in his annual report that after more than two years of work the commission had finished only cantons Quilaquila and part of Huaillas, a small portion of its task.[39]

Perhaps the most common method of avoiding inscription into the *matrícula* was simply not to appear before the commission. This tactic dragged out the proceedings, for witnesses had to be found who knew what fields the absent Indian controlled. And because of the dispersed nature of the holdings, it was often impossible to estimate correctly the extent of each person's property and so prepare an accurate title or assess the corresponding land tax.[40] Consequently, every few years new revisitas had to be conducted to complete the job of the previous one. Eventually, by the 1920's, all areas in Yamparaez except certain portions in Tarabuco had been duly covered.[41]

Despite the resistance, more and more Indian land was surveyed and so became eligible for purchase by outsiders. Two phases stand out in the sale of Indian lands, one before 1900, the other from then on. As Table 8 shows, there were only a few land sales in the 1880's, a period in which only one canton, Tarabuco, had been surveyed by the revisita, and then began to increase as the government made a concerted effort to complete the revisita process. The highest volume of Indian land sales during the whole period under examination occurred between 1895 and 1898 as a direct result of the falling price of silver, along with the perceived insecurity of bank investments after the failure of the Bank of Potosí. The 1898–99 civil war, when the Liberals gained power with the help of Indian allies, briefly depressed sales. In the second phase, 1900 and after, sales picked up to about half of the 1897 level, and then continued at a more or less constant pace except for a brief decline in 1906 and 1907, probably because of the financial scare of those years when suddenly falling tin prices virtually shut down the Bolivian economy. A new law passed in 1916 strictly regulating the acquisition of Indian lands and, finally, a 1920 decree prohibiting sales because of debts or without a judicial order, put an almost complete stop to the alienation of ayllu lands.

Of all land sales where the purchaser's residence was listed, 60 percent were from Sucre. During the pre-1900 phase, the predominance of Sucre residents was even more marked, constituting 70

TABLE 8

Indian Land Sales in Yamparaez by Year, 1880–1930

Year	Number	Year	Number	Year	Number
1882	12	1900	21	1913	37
1883	2	1901	29	1914	17
1885	2	1902	25	1915	14
1887	2	1903	32	1916	18
1891	3	1904	23	1917	3
1892	2	1905	31	1918	9
1893	3	1906	13	1919	9
1894	6	1907	10	1920	4
1895	15	1908	19	1923	3
1896	26	1909	30	1924	1
1897	63	1910	16	1928	1
1898	43	1911	14		
1899	26	1912	43		

SOURCES: Centro Bibliográfico Documental Histórico, Universidad Mayor, Real y Pontificia de San Francisco Xavier de Chuquisaca (Sucre), Fondo Prefectural: Notaría de Hacienda y Minas, 1887–1930; Archivos de la Corte Superior de Chuquisaca (Sucre), Derechos Reales, "Libros de propriedades de la Capital y su Cercado, no. 2, 1893–1899"; Julio L. Jaimes, Cuadros y trabajos de la mesa estadística, dirección de Julio L. Jaimes (La Paz, 1885), cuadro no. IV.
NOTE: Years of no sales are omitted.

percent of all purchasers; 86 percent of these Sucre residents belonged to the elite.[42] Only thirty-eight transactions out of a total of 636 involved the sale of land by one ayllu member to another; the largest number of these purchases, six, were made by one Quilaquila Indian, Pedro Pacheco, an agregado who with his acquisitions moved up to originario status.[43]

Even in the first phase, a third of all purchasers were people who lived in the small towns that dotted the Yamparaez countryside. After 1900, the figure rose to 40 percent, an increase that reflects the economic growth of the small towns in the Chuquisaca highlands after the turn of the century. This trend in fact began after 1880, when the tumultuous conditions in the country inherent in the incessant rebellions of the caudillo period began to abate, and it gained strength after the revisitas finally made expansion possible. Many of the towns in Yamparaez had been Toledan reducciones de indios and so were surrounded by ayllu land that remained largely outside their economies. Before the revisitas, town residents owned only small properties on the outskirts of town, often with titles of dubious legal validity, or rented Indian land to complement their income.

After individual titles had been distributed to the Indians, towns-people bought up much of the surrounding countryside and so were able to increase their earnings by the sale of crops. Pío León Daza, a small landowner and local notable in the town of Tarabuco, rented Indian lands until 1913, when he bought five fields in the pampa surrounding the town.[44] César Taboada, of Quilaquila, owned a small property, La Majada, worth 2,066 Bs in 1881 and rented some parcels from the ayllus. Between 1896 and 1911, he bought Indian land in thirty-two different transactions. According to the 1923 catastro, he owned eight properties worth a total of 47,640 Bs. This included only one other hacienda, Chaunaca Baja, that had existed before 1880, worth 10,000 Bs. In his acquisitions he apparently added considerably to La Majada, because the catastro commission estimated its value in 1923 at 24,000 Bs, more than ten times its 1881 value. One may allow for some inflation between 1881 and 1923, but the jump in value must have come primarily from the community land he bought. If one doubles the value of La Majada's 1881 assessment to calculate the 1923 value, a reasonable assumption, and subtracts the 10,000 Bs for Chaunaca Baja, the 1923 value of the former ayllu lands totaled 33,649 Bs. Taboada had bought these from the Indians for only 5,735 Bs. He was so successful that in 1901 he was able to move from the hamlet of Quilaquila to a newly purchased house in Sucre.[45]

While some townspeople like Taboada moved to the capital, many members of the Sucre elite, left with virtually only their lands, bought houses in towns close to their properties. For example, José Rodríguez, one of the sons of Candelaria Argandoña de Rodríguez, bought a house in Tarabuco in 1903. He owned Hacienda Talisco a few miles out of town and Hacienda La Mendoza in adjacent Yamparaez canton.[46] Since the large landowners inevitably brought along an entourage of family and servants, the Sucre oligarchy's move into the countryside not only strengthened the economic life of the towns, but also helped them to consolidate their hold over the surrounding rural areas.

Within Yamparaez especially, the town of Tarabuco enjoyed an economic revival that lasted well beyond the turn of the century. As will be detailed in Chapter 6, the frontier areas of Azero province were finally conquered in the last decades of the nineteenth century. Once free from the depredations of the Chiriguano Indians, the *cristianos*, as the settlers called themselves, pushed out into the Chaco and established a thriving ranching industry. Since Tarabuco was located on the main road linking the former frontier with the highlands, the hogs and cattle produced in Azero passed through the town. As a result, Tarabuco's Sunday market took on importance as a center for the sale and purchase of cattle and fodder (primarily barley). Barley was one of the main products of the high pampas close to town and therefore landowners and community Indians benefited from the trading boom in cattle. At the same time, however, outsiders began to pressure the ayllu Indians to sell their barley fields; half of all Indian lands sold in the canton fell in this category.[47]

The Indians rarely gave up their land voluntarily. In Yamparaez as a whole, where the reasons for sale are stated, 54 percent of the Indians sold their plots because of debts. This was especially the case in the Quilaquila region, to the west of Sucre, where the communities were unable to retain their lands. A favorite means of acquiring ayllu land was to lend money to Indians who later were unable to repay the debt. One merchant couple from Sucre, Manuel Rasguido and his wife, Susana Ríos, were especially adept at this practice. After the revisita, the Indians were told to pay the catastro instead of the tribute. When the catastro tax was assessed—a sum usually much higher than the tribute—Rasguido and his wife lent the Indians money with the understanding that they were to repay them within a year or forfeit their land. As often happened, the Indians were unable to pay, and the merchants took over the fields. In this manner the couple acquired fourteen *terrenos de origen* between 1898 and 1902.[48]

Frequent recourse to the courts to resolve disputes also led to the loss of lands; 34 percent of all Indians who sold their land did so to pay for court costs. Certain landowners financed the Indians' court challenges or defenses, and when the ayllu members were unable to pay back the court costs, they had to give up their land to their sponsors. César Taboada acquired some of his land in this fashion. He lent forty-two Bs to Nicolas Amaya, an Indian who had lost a suit against an hacendado over land rights, to pay the court costs. The loan was backed by a plot worth 190 Bs. When Amaya did not repay the loan after a year, Taboada took possession of the field. On another occasion, Taboada filed suit against three Indians who, unable to pay for their defense, sold the disputed land to one of his rivals.[49] Seven percent of the Indian owners in Yamparaez sold their land because they were too old to continue farming and had no heirs. This was certainly an example of the disruption of traditional ayllu procedures, for unclaimed fields traditionally returned to the ayllu for later distribution. Of the reasons given for selling, the remaining 5 percent ranged from migration to Sucre to paying for a fiesta.

Do the excessive reliance on courts to resolve disputes, the sale of land because of age, and migration to Sucre indicate a break- down of communal traditions? It is difficult to measure whether Indians used the courts any more often in the late nineteenth and early twentieth centuries than they had done previously. Cer- tainly, during the colonial period the Spanish Crown encouraged the Indians to litigate by setting up special courts and subsidizing some of the associated expenses.[50] In any case, filing suit against non-Indians was probably the most prudent thing for the Indians to do, even during the republican period, for any violent actions might well have brought the whole repressive apparatus of the state down on their heads. This does not account, however, for the very frequent suits brought by one Indian against another. To a certain extent, the recourse to courts does indicate a breakdown of ayllu structure, but perhaps primarily of the larger, ethnic group- ings rather than of the smaller, village-based units, which re- mained firmly embedded in Andean society. Within the smaller units, the local kuraka probably was able to resolve most disputes, whereas in disputes between members of different ayllus, no In- dian authorities existed that were recognized as supreme authori- ties and thus seen as legitimate by both sides. This was one of the consequences of the "destructurization" (in Nathan Wachtel's term) of Andean society.[51] Generally speaking, the Indian commu- nities in Yamparaez temporarily lost much of their internal cohe- sion during the late nineteenth and early twentieth centuries, as evidenced by the sale of land because of age or migration. Only after 1916 did the ayllus regain some cohesion in response to the haciendas' continued assaults on community lands.

It was very rare in Yamparaez for an Indian to sell all his parcels at once, though in the La Paz area, many of the Indian land sales included whole communities.[52] Of those in Yamparaez who men- tioned what proportion of the whole *terreno de orígen* was sold, only 19 percent said they were selling all their lands.[53] This particular pat- tern emerged in Chuquisaca because of the way in which the lands were acquired. Usually any debt was not worth all of the Indian's hold- ings, so he could sell off a parcel to pay back the loan and try to subsist on what he had left. And because of the dispersal of the plots, land disputes often only involved one or two parts out of many. These were at times sold either to the opponent or to another interested party. Eventually, however, many Indians were obliged to sell all their land because they found it impossible to live on a diminished land base.

TABLE 9

Indian Land Sales in Yamparaez by Canton, 1880–1930

Canton	Number	Canton	Number
Palca	3	San Sebastian	3
Sapse	1	Arabate	38
Pocpo	10	Huaillas	31
Quilaquila	259	Yotala	8
Huata	5	Yamparaez	11
Mojotoro	2	Tarabuco	242
Paccha	18		

SOURCES: Same as Table 8.
NOTE: Cantons with no sales are omitted.

A regional breakdown helps to show the impact of Indian land sales on individual ayllus (Table 9). In the Yampara area, which encompassed the cantons of Quilaquila, Huaillas, and Yotala, Indian communities were virtually wiped out. This was true also of Huata, Paccha, and Arabate. In Tarabuco, although there were 242 sales, the second-largest number for any single canton, the ayllus survived in a weakened state. In contrast, the Oruro ethnic groups controlling lands in Pocpo and Sapse were hardly affected; there were also no land sales of Tinguipaya land in Poroma.

This unequal distribution of land sales can be explained partly by the ayllus' proximity to Sucre and the consequent commercial value of the land. Here, the community's ability to stay out of debt determined which ethnic groups survived. The Yampara ayllus and those in Huata and Arabate were located very close to Sucre, making them prime targets for acquisition by the Sucre elite looking for investments outside the mining sector. Whether a community was able to remain intact depended in the end on its access to different ecological levels (and therefore to the agricultural resources of the region). As has been shown in contemporary northern Potosí, those households in the communities that maintained control over both puna and valley lands tended to be better off than those that controlled fields on only one level.[54] An examination of the revisita records makes it clear that the Huata, Paccha, and Arabate ayllus, in addition to being numerically weak, had lost control over their plots in lower altitudes and were restricted primarily to the uplands. Lack of direct access to corn and other products that could only be grown on valley lands made them extremely vulnerable to subsistence crises and assuredly helps explain their demise.

To a lesser extent, this was also true of the Yampara communities. The valley lands they had once controlled lay close to Sucre, along the Cachimayo and Pilcomayo valleys. The Indians had gradually lost these areas, which were so prized as vacation spots by the Sucre elite, in a process that began during the colonial period and was virtually complete by the mid-nineteenth century. What little land they retained was still coveted by the Sucre oligarchs and the local townspeople, and once their lands ceased to be protected by the state, they had little choice but to sell. Although they still had puna lands, without valley lands they were not self-sufficient, let alone prosperous. Their indebtedness grew, especially when the revisita officials charged them for titles, and eventually they fell prey to moneylenders.

The plight of the Yampara Indians is better understood by contrasting their case with that of the Tarabuco, Oruro, and Potosí ayllus. During the period under discussion, the Indian lands in Tarabuco had as great a potential commercial value as those closer to Sucre because of the town's need for fodder. Nevertheless, since the Tarabuco Indians maintained control over a larger variety of lands than the Yamparas to the west, they were more prosperous and therefore less vulnerable to those seeking to acquire their holdings. An indication of their greater wealth was that only 35 percent of Indian plots in the canton were sold because of debts, compared with 61 percent for the rest of the province. In Andean terms, the Oruro and Potosí ayllus were even wealthier than the Tarabuco communities, for in addition to owning agricultural lands in both puna and the valleys, they possessed large herds of llamas and alpacas on the altiplano.[55] This important additional resource, combined with the ayllus' location in a relatively inaccessible part of the province, accounts for their survival during this period.

Eventually, however, market forces in the form of the barley boomlet at the turn of the century made themselves felt in the Tarabuco communities. Indians began to participate to a greater extent in the market economy by either selling barley directly in the Tarabuco market or renting out barley fields to townspeople who had gone into the business of providing fodder for the trains of cattle, hogs, and pack animals that passed through. In other cases, Indians received cash advances to pay for tribute obligations and other expenses in return for a portion of their crops. This was a risky business, for the highland climate was always unpredictable, and a poor harvest could lose them their lands.[56]

In fact, the richest ayllu members were the ones who profited the most from the demand for barley. Such was the case with a kuraka of the Tunas Chillca ayllu, Venancio Puchu, and his wife, María Yampara. Not only was Puchu a tribute collector, a financially rewarding position, but he had married well, his wife having brought into the household a number of properties that greatly extended Puchu's resources. Puchu sold a few plots for good prices (unusual for the sale of Indian lands), and expanded his holdings between 1911 and 1928 at the expense of both Indian and mestizo landholders, using force on occasion or, when this proved impractical, applying to the local courts.[57]

Inevitably, the increased market participation of the Tarabuco ayllus in response to pressures on their land sharpened the social and economic distinctions within the communities. A new category of ayllu member, that of arrendero or colono, emerged. These were Indians who, having seemingly lost all their own land, joined the households of wealthier Indians and, as the names imply, probably paid a rent to their bosses, just as on the haciendas. Although there had been landless community Indians, often called *kanturuna*, before 1900, landlessness undoubtedly became more pervasive in the Tarabuco area, and tenancy was now an important component of the communities' commercial structure. A similar process probably occurred among the Oruro-based Indians in Pocpo. Land reform records compiled in the 1950's show that one "hacienda" controlled by the Urmiri of Quillacas had a number of plots assigned to arrenderos as well.[58]

Twentieth-Century Haciendas

In 1922, the departmental treasurer, José David Ichaso, argued in his annual report that the tribute should be abolished in Chuquisaca because "the *terrenos de origen* that pay this tax are not owned by Indians any more, but have been transferred to the *latifundistas* who have converted those lands into extensive and productive rural properties. I could cite twenty extremely distinguished capitalist gentlemen who reside in this capital [Sucre] who own one or many of those *orígenes*."[59] Although Ichaso's statement confirms the predominance of the Sucre elite in the acquisition of ayllu lands, he is clearly wrong in his unqualified assertion that the Indians no longer owned any land. Moreover, in the rest of his report, he ignored the important question of what happened to the community Indians once their lands were absorbed into the haciendas. The little evidence there is (no new tribute lists were compiled after 1877) suggests that most ended up as laborers on the new estates. One contract specified that the new owner had to keep the three sellers, their son-in-law, and their grandchild as arrenderos for as long as they lived.[60] In some instances, Indians tried to keep some of their land and, to make ends meet, work as colonos elsewhere, although this was usually not successful. Vicente Fabian, for example, was at one time a *tasero*, or tribute payer. But he first sold some of his land to Pastor Sainz and then, in 1904, sold the rest to another Indian, and thereafter presumably became Sainz's peon.[61]

Unfortunately, later catastros for Yamparaez give far fewer details than does the 1881 list and thus cannot be used to compare changes over time in the region's land-tenure structure and rural labor force.[62] Only by examining hacienda records and other sources is it possible to glean some notion of the conditions in the Yamparaez countryside after the silver crash. In the 1880's, most hacienda production had been geared to the mining market and the thriving urban markets of Sucre and Potosí. Twenty years or so later, we find Rodolfo Solares Arroyo, a prominent Sucre journalist, noting that the market for agricultural goods in Sucre was very small, and that because of the lack of easy communications with the rest of the country, it was impossible to transport them cheaply elsewhere. Solares Arroyo went on to say that simply acquiring new machinery, often mentioned in other works as the salvation of Chuquisaca's countryside, would not improve matters since this would not increase the demand for agricultural products.[63]

In fact, early in the century many new machines of various sorts were installed in the province's haciendas. This coincided roughly with the third phase of the Sucre elite's reactions to the silver crisis. Once the silver magnates realized that land had become their financial mainstay, they poured a considerable amount of capital into their estates to improve their profitability. Rodríguez Hermanos, a firm founded by the sons of the silver miner Candelaria, for example, installed a complete steam-driven chocolate factory in Hacienda Aranjuez, a short distance outside Sucre. In 1907, the hacienda produced 300 pounds of chocolate, which was packaged in a style similar to a popular French brand. The family not only made improvements on Aranjuez to increase earnings, but, as the elites were doing in the city as well, renovated the *casa de hacienda*. They refurnished the interior of the main house and had one whole side of the three-story building painted in colorful floral patterns.[64]

Another ambitious attempt to mechanize was Pastor Sainz's installation of a modern sugar mill at Hacienda El Chaco, in the Mojotoro valley. This mill produced cane alcohol as well as excellent sugar, and both products began to displace foreign imports; but after Sainz died in 1907, the expensive machinery fell into disrepair, and the mill was abandoned.[65] It was a familiar story. Comparing two surveys of the machinery on the haciendas over the ten-year period 1918–28 reveals a picture of stagnation. The 1918 list looks impressive enough, but by 1928 there was only one new item on the list: some engines for a new company that provided Sucre with electricity. Worse still, some of the distilling and milling machines had broken down and might appropriately be subtracted from the list.[66]

But even though the Sucre elites' enthusiasm for improving production through mechanization apparently waned after 1918, probably many more hacendados lived on their estates or took an active part in administering them than during the height of the silver boom. No comparable figures are available for the 1880's, but in 1908 only one-third of all properties in Yamparaez that employed a permanent labor force had absentee owners.[67] Nevertheless, even with close supervision, the haciendas seldom showed a profit simply because of the lack of demand in a stagnating southern Bolivia. With so few possibilities of selling the produce of their estates, the hacendados relied more and more heavily on exactions from the labor force to make a profit, either by increasing the peons' traditional obligations or, more often, by changing from in-kind rents to cash rents. Thus, for example, whereas even in the late nineteenth century, arrenderos still paid their proportion of the catastro in produce, which the hacendados in turn sold to the mining centers,[68] most of the landowners in Yamparaez were collecting the catastro in cash by 1908.

The exceptions, Tarabuco and Quilaquila, in both of which the majority of haciendas maintained the payment of the catastro obligation in agricultural goods, are significant. In Quilaquila, the absorption of a large ayllu Indian component into the hacienda labor force prohibited an abrupt change from produce to specie, as the long-standing struggle between government tax collectors and the Indians to change diezmo and primicia payments to cash attested. This was also true to some extent in Tarabuco, but the more important difference was the trade boom in the area, and the profits to be made on grain in the Tarabuco market.[69] The money value of the grain exacted as catastros in fact far exceeded the taxes the hacendados owed the government. For example, in 1930 the 75 colonos of Hacienda Cororo paid the owner 1,295.40 Bs worth of grain, primarily barley, but the estate paid only 427.50 Bs to the departmental treasury in taxes.[70]

What was occurring in Chuquisaca was similar to what had occurred a century and a half earlier in Cochabamba during the colonial mining downturn. Landowners were turning over a larger part of their land to colonos or increasing the number of colonos—in other words, hacendados were managing to augment their earnings while leaving most of the actual production to the colonos. And since only demesne land was counted in the tabulations, annual production figures listed in the catastros plummeted. Because of the incompleteness and unreliability of the catastros after 1881, a statistical analysis of production figures is not possible, but there is little question that the hacendados' share of output fell despite the at least theoretical increase in the haciendas' production capacity owing to the absorption of Indian lands into the great estates.[71] A couple of examples will illustrate this point. In 1881, demesne land on Hacienda Chaunaca in Quilaquila produced 50 fanegas of wheat, 220 cargas of corn, and 100 cargas of potatoes; by 1907, the figures had dropped to 20, 25, and 15, respectively. In the same period, Hacienda Tasapampa in Tuero canton registered a drop from 200 fanegas of wheat and 370 cargas of corn to 40 fanegas and 70 cargas.[72]

Giving more land over to the arrendero population meant that the modes of production changed very little. This is clear from the surviving hacienda records, which listed in great detail the peon's multifarious labor obligations. The peons of Hacienda El Recreo near Sucre, for example, worked out their obligations at thirty-three different tasks, from the spinning of a certain quantity of rough wool yarn to the threshing of grains for one day a year. These detailed obligations, put into written form at the turn of the century, were faithfully followed in the 1930's and apparently continued as the basis of the haciendas' labor regime until the 1950's.[73]

Likewise, most hacendados continued to govern their estates by traditional Andean methods, which emphasized reciprocity and redistribution. This was especially necessary once the ayllu Indians, who needed to be incorporated into the hacienda labor forces as smoothly as possible, swelled the ranks of the hacienda workers. Nevertheless, some hacendados refused to abide by the unwritten rules, adding to the Indians' growing discontent. Tensions, never far from the surface since the late-nineteenth-century drive to parcel out community lands, rose in the 1920's, to reach their peak in 1927, when both former ayllu members and those who had been able to resist the advance of the haciendas joined forces to rise up and reclaim their lost land.

Resistance and Rebellion in the Countryside

The revisita process, in which the plots of each community Indian household were measured and parceled up, brought about the first extensive resistance by the ayllus in Yamparaez—which used the court system to slow down the process, or failed to appear before the commission, or sometimes resorted to outright threats and violence. Why did the Indians oppose the revisitas? Beyond the threat that the parceling out of land would lead to the extinction of the ayllus as ethnic groups, the specific decisions of the *revisitadores* were often in direct conflict with traditional practices that the ayllus had followed to ensure their economic survival. For example, when an originario died without heirs, his land had customarily reverted to the community, which then redistributed it among other members. The revisitadores ignored this custom and simply declared the land vacant, then sold or rented it to the highest bidder. The Indians saw the removal of vacant lands from the community as an immediate threat to the survival of the ayllu and feared that their offspring would have no chance in the future to claim a holding large enough for subsistence. Their fears were justified: the depletion of redistributable land and the fixing of ownership to only certain fields gave rise to fragmentation into ever-smaller holdings as successive generations divided and redivided their ancestral plots.

The Indians also became extremely concerned about the practice of collecting fees for the services of measuring and drawing up titles during the revisita. Indeed, this practice more than any other sparked the resistance that finally brought about the suspension of the revisitadores' activities. Tristan Platt has shown for northern Potosí that by charging fees for the titles, the revisitadores broke the implicit pact that in the Indians' eyes existed between the ayllus and the state. As the Indians understood this pact, the state protected their right to their lands in return for tribute and such duties as carrying the mail and working for local officials. When the revisita officials broke this pact by charging Indians for their land beyond the tribute payments, the Indians refused to cooperate, hoping in that way to force the state to reinstitute the former arrangement.[74] There is evidence that the same reasoning was at work in Yamparaez. For example, in 1888 the prefect noted that, although it was still prescribed by law, the Indians had refused to transport the mail since the passage of the *ley de exvinculación*. The problems became so bad that the subprefect of Yamparaez finally suggested that the prefecture pay the Indians for this service, a suggestion that was apparently rejected.[75]

The numerous revisitas from the late nineteenth century onward periodically increased tensions in the Yamparaez countryside as it became apparent to the communities that the ever-larger extents of land awarded to individual ayllu members quickly passed to the hacendados or townspeople. The revisita of 1916–18 brought about the most resistance. In an effort to increase departmental income, the prefect ordered the revisitador to implement the law of 1911, which ordered that all originarios pay not the tribute but the regular catastro tax on the total income of their property. As a result, the commission collected amounts that might be double or even triple the old tribute assessments. At the same time, the revisitador, Manuel F. Mendoza, imposed stiffer requirements for proving the possession of ayllu lands. If an Indian could not prove ownership, the commission declared his plot vacant and rented it out to a non-Indian.[76]

These actions clearly broke the implicit pact between the Indians and the state. The switch from the collection of tribute to catastro meant that community lands were now in the same category as all other properties, and that the ayllus no longer had special state protection. The enormous increases in taxes simply added insult to injury. Moreover, the appropriation of "vacant" Indian lands reduced the already strained community resources even further. The actions of the revisita were unacceptable to the ayllus. As the commission moved eastward, toward Yamparaez and Tarabuco, resistance mounted to this new assault on community lands.

When the commission reached Tarabuco, Mendoza requisitioned the harvest from the lands he declared vacant, and violence erupted. The Tarabuco Indian authorities organized a crowd of ayllu members to protest the action and retrieve the crops. The commission members mounted their horses and whipped the kurakas leading the demonstration in order to disperse the crowd.

Apparently this was effective, although the Indians, among them Venancio Puchu and his wife, filed suit against the revisitador. The commission members filed a countersuit, charging that the Indians had conspired to murder them or, as the crowd threatened, make them "walk on their knees." Both parties sent delegations to Sucre to resolve the matter. From the comments printed in the annual prefectural report, the Indians appear to have won their case: the prefect publicly chastised the commission members for their conduct toward the Indians and accused them of outright mismanagement in renting out vacant lands.[77]

What is significant about this action is that for the first time since at least the nineteenth century the Tarabuco ayllu members put aside their differences long enough to join in a unified action. The kurakas, including Puchu and a young Indian by the name of Esteban Fernández, asserted their leadership by organizing the protest movement, and by collecting *ramas*, or payments to help defray the costs of litigation and sending delegations to Sucre. The prefect's decision emboldened the new ayllu leaders. Although he did not meet all of the Indians' demands, the leaders were able to hold the decision up as proof that the Indians could stand up to a seemingly all-powerful government commission and win. In a sense, this decision was a serious setback for the hacendados, who, thanks to the acquisition of Indian lands and more personal attention to their estates, had been exerting an ever-increasing influence on the countryside. The 1918 protest engendered an increasingly radical movement that lasted more than a decade and eventually threatened the legitimacy of the region's entire hacienda system.

The challenge to hacienda predominance manifested itself again in 1922, but by now the goals of the protest movement were much more far-reaching than before. This time the Indians' aim was not simply to arrest the expansion of the haciendas, but to recoup the lands they had lost in the previous decades. The first indications of this new direction came from a strike on Hacienda El Carmen, also in the Tarabuco area. As described in Chapter 2, El Carmen was formed out of ayllu lands in the late 1890's by one of the members of the Sucre mining oligarchy. Now, according to the hacienda's current owner, Lucas Vidal, some of his arrenderos refused to obey his orders, pay their rent, or perform their work obligations. The situation had become so bad that Vidal asked the local Tarabuco court to issue eviction orders for two of his peons. When the Indians were dragged to court, they challenged the validity of land sales that had occurred twenty-five years earlier, insisting that they were still *indios originarios*, or Indian community members, and so could not be expelled from their plots.[78]

Another attack on the validity of Indian land sales was launched in the same year by five Indians from the Oroncota ayllu in the hamlet of Sipoco, who repossessed lands that a town mestizo had bought from another group of Indians. One of the leaders in this action was Esteban Fernández, who had helped organize the antirevisita movement in 1918. The next year, Fernández again involved himself in a land dispute, claiming that the administrator of Hacienda Sotomayor, owned by the descendants of Candelaria Rodríguez, had dispossessed him of some of his fields.[79]

By 1924, the seeds of rebellion had spread far beyond the Tarabuco area. That year the prefect, José Pastor Sainz (son of the tin miner), decided to send *mesas revisitadoras* to measure and distribute all remaining ayllu lands in Yamparaez and Zudáñez provinces and to update the catastro rolls for the haciendas. As could be expected, the presence of the odious revisita in this explosive atmosphere sparked an uprising. Esteban Fernández began to plan a full-scale revolt with Indian leaders in Presto and individual Indians in Mojocoya, Rodeo (all in neighboring Zundáñez province, formed out of the three westernmost cantons of Tomina in 1917), and Tarabuco. Provincial authorities discovered the conspiracy, scheduled for Carnival, and arrested the leaders. According to the authorities, the Indians demanded the return of all community lands. Swift repression apparently put down the revolt without casualties. However, a few months later, when the revisita for Zudáñez entered Presto, the Indians refused to cooperate, saying that an armed detachment from La Paz would arrive to protect them from the commission. The revisitador managed to calm the Indians, but was unable to finish his job; his counterpart in Yamparaez had no better luck.[80]

Thereafter, as successive prefectural reports attest, the whole province remained on the verge of rebellion; at any word of possible conspiracies during the years 1925–26, the authorities took quick action to keep the movement from spreading. Informants reported that the Indians from Quilaquila as well as Tarabuco were in contact with others "from Potosí and other centers of the Republic."[81] Only twice in these two years were there serious threats of violence. On Hacienda Vilavila in Tarabuco canton a number of Indians insulted the landowner, Isidora de Solís, and refused to work. The colonos began to rally the rest of the field workers, and

Señora Solís was forced to flee to the town of Tarabuco. In another incident, Indians began to mass on the hills overlooking the town of Tarabuco. Pleas from the town priest and the quick arrival of a police unit from Sucre averted any bloodshed.[82]

Again, the most serious incidents took place during Carnival season, or *pujllay*, as it was called in Tarabuco. This was an ideal time for action, from the movement leaders' point of view, days in which large groups of celebrating Indians trekked from place to place, so that the conspirators could easily get together and move about unnoticed. And because the hacienda houses by custom kept their doors open to welcome all celebrants, it was easy to make surprise attacks. The heavy drinking that was usual at this time—by both Indians and landowners—was part of the whole conspiratorial, potentially violent atmosphere. Drink gave the Indians courage to fight and made it less likely that the hacendados could mount an effective resistance.

The symbolic significance of the season may have lent additional impetus to the movement. In 1816, during the wars for independence, the Tarabuco Indians and some Creole guerrillas had massacred a large contingent of Spanish soldiers in an engagement fought in early March, close to Carnival. Also, during Carnival the colonos and hacendados, like godparents and godchildren, traditionally reaffirmed their mutual ties to each other in ritualized displays. Since Carnival was the season of the *supay*, or devil, in which the world was topsy-turvy, the ideas espoused by the conspirators were appropriate. In essence, the Indians' revolutionary ideology called for a reversal of roles in the countryside: the powerful hacendados would lose their lands, and the seemingly powerless Indians would finally rule supreme. Thus, the significance-laden Carnival season provided the appropriate atmosphere for revolutionary ideas to grow.[83]

The Indians were not alone in their revolutionary ideas. According to the subprefect of Yamparaez, the local *tinterillos*, or town mestizos who represented the Indians before the courts, along with some of the Indian leaders, had "made [the Indians] consent to a supposed reconquest, in the malevolent and absurd belief that the rural properties should be restored in the not far-off future, with a new redistribution of all lands as the secular patrimony of the Indians."[84] In Yamparaez, at least, the alliance against the hacendados was probably more for economic reasons than anything else. In Tarabuco, the townspeople maintained an active trade with the Indian communities, purchasing their barley and reselling it to itinerant merchants and cattle traders. In some cases, they even drew up written contracts binding the Indians to sell their coming crop in exchange for a small advance.[85] It was therefore in the town mestizos' interest to support the Indians' cause against the hacendados. For them, Indian lands sold to the large estates meant the loss of suppliers in the lucrative grain trade.

In the end, the government could not stave off disaster. The rebellion that swept the southern Bolivian countryside in 1927 began in Chayanta province in northern Potosí, where the Indians murdered a local hacendado and then offered his body as a sacrifice to a mountain god. Soon after, the Indians in much of Oruro, Potosí, and western Chuquisaca rose up in arms. In Sucre, the large landowners organized a civil defense force and sent it to Chayanta to put down the insurrection. In Chuquisaca, the Indians in the northern part of Cinti joined the revolt, as did the arrenderos on a number of estates in Mojocoya (Zudáñez province). The areas of major activity in Yamparaez were Poroma, overrun by "Indians from the puna," Quilaquila, and, especially, Tarabuco canton.[86]

In Tarabuco, the most serious outbreak involved the Indians of Saira and Caguana, who attacked Hacienda Quichani. The Indians ransacked the *casa de hacienda*, destroyed the adjoining orchard, and butchered the domestic animals. The rebels declared that Quichani had belonged to their community and should be returned to them. They were led by Julio Ceres, a mestizo who claimed to be general delegate of the Pro-Indian League in La Paz. Ceres asserted that the political authorities did not have to be obeyed, and that he had talked to the president of Bolivia, who had given him a document authorizing him to govern all originarios and collect tribute payments.

Ceres, originally from Sucre, may have been part of a larger movement, in which Socialists from various cities conspired with the Indians in the hope of promoting a social revolution within the country. If that was the case, the conspiracy was unsuccessful. The rebellion soon degenerated into a vendetta against the Indians who had aided the hacendados. Ceres had rented a plot from Mauricio Condori, an originario from Saira. As soon as the rebellion began, Ceres's followers attacked the house of Condori's estranged wife, María Quespi, who had collaborated with various local hacendados to usurp land from other ayllu members by claiming that the land belonged to her. The rebels repaid her by beating her and taking custody of her land titles. She managed to escape from her attackers, but they caught up with her in the hills. There, after beating her again, they discussed killing her and drinking her blood in a ritual act of purification. Fortunately for her, the subprefect, aided by armed hacendados and loyal peons from the surrounding estates, attacked her persecutors and was able to capture all the leaders of the rebellion except Ceres. In the interrogations that followed, the Indians justified their intent to kill Señora Quespi on the grounds that she was a witch and had buried human excrement to put a spell on her enemies.[87]

Where the Indians acted without their urban allies, they did so with the specific aim of getting back the lands they had once owned. For example, at the eastern border of Hacienda Sotomayor, also in the canton of Tarabuco, a group of Indians led by Esteban Fernández attempted to reoccupy lands sold ten years earlier to the hacienda owners. A few days later, Fernández showed up in a different part of the canton and, in an act of defiance against judicial authorities, he and his brother and sister sowed the land that he had attempted to claim five years earlier on Hacienda El Carmen. In both cases, Fernández claimed to be the "principal cacique of ayllu Oroncota."[88] The quick mobilization of the hacendados with their rifles and their armies of loyal arrenderos put an end to Fernández's actions. He and his co-conspirators were arrested and taken off to jail. Even in northern Potosí, the site of the most violent actions, the rebellion petered out. After overrunning a number of haciendas, the Indians were stopped, their only brief triumph, significant for revealing the aims of the rebellion, having been the capture of several local officials, who were forced to go through a ritual of giving the victorious Indians formal possession of the haciendas they had taken. Any further action was thwarted by the hastily sent troops.[89] A few months later, President Hernando Siles decreed an amnesty for all those involved in the revolt.

Despite the uprising's apparent failure, tensions did not abate in western Chuquisaca. The Indians still refused to recognize the authority of constituted officials; indicative of this was an incident in 1928 involving Marcos Barron, a prominent Tarabuco merchant and tribute collector. Barron and two of his peons, accompanied by another local official, were herding some Indian-owned cattle that they had retrieved from a *rodeo*, where animals not belonging to the hacendado were rounded up and their owners made to pay a grazing fee. Suddenly five Indians armed with knives, stones, and slingshots appeared and refused to let them pass. Since there were more Indians waiting on the hillsides and in a nearby house, Barron and his party prudently took to their heels, leaving the cattle behind. The animals were then returned to their owners amid much celebration.[90] With this act, the Indians not only refused to recognize Barron's authority, but also denied the legitimacy of the haciendas' land rights, which included grazing fees.

Most attempts at repossessing Indian lands after 1927 focused on Hacienda El Carmen, with Esteban Fernández leading the assault. In 1929, he first backed a minor ayllu official, José Herrera, in his efforts to regain some of what Herrera claimed was his land. Fernández took the case to court, basing his right to petition for Herrera on a document from 1617, a *composición de tierras*, or royal grant of title, which he claimed mentioned his own paternal grandfather as kuraka of the area.[91] When Fernández's case was rejected and he began to collect a rama; or money from other members of the ayllu, to finance the defense of its claims, the owner of the hacienda, Rosa Vidal, brought suit against him to stop the mobilization of Indians. As one of her witnesses she produced Venancio Puchu, leader of the resistance movement against the 1918 revisita. He testified:

The accused Chinos, Fernández, and Herrera are accustomed to ask for subscriptions by the name of *ramas* to rouse the Indians of the district to rebellion against the *patrones*. A few days ago, they went around [the area] with this objective and also last year and the year before that said accused went around with this motive, under the pretext that those funds were [to be used] to demand the recovery of lands, and that private properties had to become *orígenes* again, and that they would not have to pay the *tasa* [tribute]. Because of this propaganda, my subordinates have refused to give their quotas of the *tasa*.[92]

Puchu apparently belonged to a more conciliatory faction in the ayllu that believed that refusing to pay tribute broke the last tenuous links in the Indians' centuries-old pact with the state in protection of their land. Puchu may also have been against the refusal to pay tribute because he had been lining his own pockets by skimming off a portion of the payments, as most collectors did. By now, the majority of Indians had left Puchu's stand, within the mainstream in 1918, far behind and had become more radical in their demands. His defense of one of the most flagrant offenders against Indian land rights lost him the sympathy of most of his remaining followers. Fernández took over the lead in the community, which clearly favored maintaining a hard line in demanding the restitution of El Carmen and other lands.[93]

As the ayllu Indians pressed their case, relations between hacendados and their Indian workers also deteriorated. Long before the 1927 rebellion, a number of colonos had taken up the communities' battle cry and refused to recognize the authority of their hacendado. In 1918, for example, the peons of Hacienda Quiscoli (Tarabuco) and neighboring community Indians, armed with clubs and stones, met the pistol-wielding hacendados in battle. Later, a Quiscoli arrendero died under mysterious circumstances after apparently having been severely beaten. One of the owners of Quiscoli was put on trial for murder but was acquitted.[94]

In the aftermath of the 1927 rebellion, a host of arrenderos from haciendas throughout the province came forth to complain about the abuses of their masters.[95] Abuses were common in a system where the hacendado had overwhelming power, but not all the problems in the relationships between worker and landowner can be blamed on maltreatment. The hacendados' attempts to streamline production and increase profits inevitably provoked problems with the labor force. Landowners often impinged on some of the arrenderos' traditional privileges in the process. For example, as haciendas became virtually the Sucre oligarchs' sole source of income, they started to crack down on the debts some colonos had accumulated. In return, the colonos refused to recognize the hacendados' authority and refused to pay or leave the property. At Hacienda Cororo, for instance, the heirs of Candelaria Rodríguez instituted at least three different trials in 1929 alone to recoup outstanding debts from the hacienda workers.[96]

The success of the Rodríguez clan's efforts shows up in Cororo's hacienda records. In 1934, though 57 of 100 hacienda peons were in debt, the average amount owed was a paltry 7.44 Bs. Moreover, the records make clear that unless a colono had special duties, such as *mayordomo* (administrator) or gardener, he was expected to pay his debts once the sum exceeded 25 Bs, if necessary by selling one of his animals.[97] Cororo's owners were not above using strong-arm tactics, especially if the debt-ridden workers participated in the resistance movement. When Miguel Yarhui left the hacienda owing money rent and work obligations, he was abducted in Tarabuco by the Cororo *alcalde* (a minor hacienda official), tied up, and kept in a room for five days until he signed a document stating that he owed the hacienda 120 Bs. A close reading of the trial record shows that the real reason for his harsh treatment was probably the fact that after leaving the hacienda, "he returned afterward and occupied himself in urging the other colonos to disobey the orders of the hacienda."[98] It is significant that many of the area's colonos like Yarhui apparently joined in the meetings of the rebel community Indians and began to use the ayllus' arguments as justification for their actions. They took the position that even lands that had not been part of communities for centuries, such as the ones the Rodríguez clan controlled, should be taken from the hacendados and given to the colonos.[99]

Although claims of this sort were absurd from the point of view of the landowners, many of whose families had owned the estates for generations, they had in a sense brought the problem on themselves when they abandoned some of the traditional labor relationships. In the minds of the peons, the ayllus' claims that the hacendados were essentially illegitimate usurpers now seemed powerful arguments. The issue of the hacendados' legitimacy became especially important in the early 1920's when a series of locust plagues and droughts made life desperate for many hacienda workers.[100] The bonds of reciprocity between landowners and peons had always been the workers' safety net; the loss of this security could mean illness and starvation. Thus, the Sucre elite's drive for agricultural efficiency came at precisely the wrong time and in all probability precipitated the labor strikes on the haciendas.

Many hacendados realized the nature of the problems they faced and tried to make their reforms more palatable. This was especially important since the workers, through such mechanisms as the diezmo and catastro, provided a large share of the estate owners' income. As a result, some hacendados retreated into traditional patterns just as, at least in Tarabuco, the communities were becoming more commercialized. The Rodríguez family, after concluding their vigorous campaign to reduce their workers' debts, generally maintained their reciprocal relations in the 1930's by, for example, giving seed on credit at sowing time after *polvillo*, a fungus disease, had ruined much of the arrenderos' wheat crop.[101] After a brief period of unrest paralleling the problems in the rest of the province, Cororo did not experience the endemic labor problems of other properties, such as La Candelaria in nearby Tomina.

The unrest among both ayllu Indians and hacienda laborers stopped abruptly during the short reign of the provisional military government that held national power in 1930–31, when soldiers rounded up suspected cattle rustlers and other perceived subversives and summarily executed them. Without written records of these extralegal executions, it is hard to put numbers to the loss of life. From eyewitness accounts, it appears that in the Tarabuco

area between twenty and thirty men met their death in this manner. But the peace was an uneasy one—and all too brief. During
the Chaco War (1932–35), widespread military recruitment struck
hard at the haciendas' work forces, precipitating a labor crisis in
the countryside. The result was renewed conflict between Indian
communities and the large estates, which attempted to make
up their losses by incorporating ayllu members into their work
forces.[102]

Despite the repression of the 1930's and the revival of antag-
onisms between communities and haciendas during the Chaco
War, the 1927 revolt effectively stopped any further assault on Indian lands. For many communities, especially those in the Quilaquila area, this came too late, for by then the Sucre elite had consolidated its hold on the Yamparaez countryside. But the switch
from mining to land had done nothing to bring Sucre back into the
national economic life. Not only had the markets of the silver-
mining period shrunk; they were often supplied more cheaply
with agricultural goods from abroad. Despite the Sucre oligarchy's
efforts to make the hacienda pay, by the late 1920's it found itself
with little income. Sucre, with its agricultural hinterland, had entered a period of stagnation from which it has yet to emerge.

CHAPTER FIVE

Cinti Province

In many respects, Cinti province in southwestern Chuquisaca, the major wine-growing region in Bolivia, was similar to Yamparaez. It depended heavily on commercial agriculture and its primary market was Potosí. Labor relations, based heavily on Andean modes of reciprocity and redistribution, also resembled those in Yamparaez. Sucre residents controlled many of the largest properties. In addition, the province suffered an economic decline in the twentieth century similar to that of Yamparaez. From the sixteenth century on, Cinti provided the Potosí mines with wine, cattle, and grains. After a post-independence period of stagnation, the silver boom revitalized Cinti and brought renewed prosperity.

Cinti was very unlike Yamparaez, however, in its response to the collapse of the silver boom. There, in the process of attempting to modernize production methods, hacendados altered labor relations to a much greater extent than in Yamparaez. The ensuing labor unrest and its consequences provide further evidence of the persistence and strength of Andean traditions, even in a highly market-oriented regional economy such as Cinti.

There are five major ecological zones in Cinti (see Map 5). The puna, at an altitude of 4,000 meters and above, extends from the department of Potosí into the northwestern corner of the province. In the high altitude, only tubers and cold-weather grains are cultivated, and some llamas, alpacas, and European livestock are bred. To the south, the puna gives way to broad, high valleys, Suquistaca, Muyuquiri, and Tacaquira, each slightly lower than the other. Cool and well watered by many mountain streams, these valleys

Potosí

Collpa

Río Pilcomayo

San Lucas

NORTHERN
CINTI

Acchilla

Suquistaca Valley

Río Chico

Muyuquiri Valley
Tacaquira Valley

CAMARGO
⊙ Camargo

Santa Elena

SOUTHEASTERN
CINTI

Río
Tumusla

Río Grande

Río Pilcomayo

Villa Abecia
(Camataquí)

La Loma

Camataquí

Tárcana Valley
Jailía Valley

Río Pilaya

SOUTHERN CINTI
San Juan de
la Torre

San Juan

Tarija

Impora

0 _____ 20 km

Map 5. Cinti province and its regions

between 3,000 and 3,600 meters are ideal for cultivating alfalfa. Similar valleys, Tárcana and Jailía, also mark the southern portion of Cinti. There wheat and corn are grown extensively, making it the granary of the province. Just before Camargo, the capital city, the Río Chico emerges from a narrow gorge into the slightly broader Cinti Valley, which stretches past the juncture of the Tumusla River southward to the provincial boundary. The primary activity of this valley (2,300–2,600 meters) is the cultivation of grapes, introduced by the Jesuits in the second half of the sixteenth century.

A view from the air reveals a narrow band of green irrigated valley bottom surrounded by a vast mountainous area of red and brown. This arid region, between 2,600 and 4,000 meters high, called *liquinas*,[1] is characterized by low brush interspersed with hardy trees, such as *chulquis* and *palquis*. In the western part of the liquinas, small streams wind through steep ravines during certain parts of the year, making irrigated corn culture possible. Farther east, the liquinas turn into a series of broad plains interrupted by mountain ranges, where level land and several small lakes allow barley, wheat, and potato farming. Except in the ravines and broad plains, the major activity is stock raising. On the eastern and southern borders, the liquinas descend abruptly into the narrow, subtropical Pilcomayo and Pilaya river valleys. Though grapes were grown in the Pilaya Valley during the seventeenth century, sugarcane subsequently became the principal crop. From there cane rapidly expanded into the Pilcomayo Valley.[2]

As in Yamparaez, the population is ethnically diverse. Most of Cinti's aboriginal population, presumably the Chichas, died or fled soon after the Spanish Conquest. Parts of three ayllus from the Oruro area, the Quillacas, Asanaques, and Yucayguaris (or Yucasa, as they are called today), were resettled in northern Cinti after the *visita* of Viceroy Toledo in the late sixteenth century. They served as warriors to defend the area against the incursions of the unconquered Chiriguano tribes to the east. Many members of the Oruro ayllus came only during certain parts of the year to work crops and then returned north, just as in northwestern Yamparaez, where the Quillacas had their "haciendas." Tribute records indicate that this seasonal migration had ceased by the end of the nineteenth century. Today the Indians in Cinti, although they preserve the ayllu names of the Oruro area, no longer remember their connections to the original groups.[3]

In addition to the Oruro-area ethnic groups, the Bisi Indians from Chaqui in Potosí (the present-day Yuras) maintained a cattle ranch in Pututaca, located in the high country midway between Cinti's western border with Potosí and the Pilcomayo River. In the late sixteenth century, this "ecological island" was attacked by the Chiriguanos. Perhaps these incessant attacks led to the abandonment of Pututaca, for by the eighteenth century the Yuras no longer controlled the area. In the valleys to the south, the population was chiefly mestizos and Spaniards, especially in the Cinti Valley, where many mine owners retreated from the harsh climate of the mining areas. Much of the mestizo blood came from the Chiriguanos, some of whom had sued for peace or had been captured and then settled as workers on the Cinti estates. Blacks brought as slaves to work on the large haciendas during the colonial period further contributed to the racial mixture. Their numbers must have been considerable, for even in the early twentieth century writers referred to the workers in the valleys as mulattos.[4]

During the colonial period, the province provided the mines with a great variety of agricultural goods, including wine, wheat, corn, sugar, and cattle. For example, from 1672 to 1698 Antonio López de Quiroga, a prominent miner who owned various large properties in Cinti, annually brought to Potosí tallow, jerked beef, and sole-leather from the cattle he had imported to his liquinas holdings from Tucumán and Buenos Aires. During the late seventeenth century, he also imported 2,228 *botijas* (goatskins) of wine and twelve botijas of sugarcane alcohol (*aguardiente*) annually, as well as other produce. This trade was worth well over 34,000 pesos a year; of this amount, wine contributed slightly more than half the total value.[5]

The independence period saw incessant warfare in the region, wreaking havoc on the province's agricultural production. The Pilcomayo and Pilaya valleys and the liquinas were particularly affected. During the 1780's, the Chiriguano Indians took advantage of the turmoil created by the Túpac Amaru revolt and sacked the town of Paspaya in northeastern Cinti, capital of the *partido* that later became the province of Cinti.[6] Fierce fighting between patriot guerrilla bands and royalist troops further destroyed the previously thriving cattle industry and the sugarcane fields. In 1825, a property assessor for the haciendas of Ingahuasi, Pilaya, and Caraparí, three of the largest and most prosperous estates in southeastern Cinti, reported that the grazing areas were bereft of cattle, and that many fields had ceased to be cultivated because the resident laborers had disappeared. The grain mills and machines to process sugarcane were beyond repair, and the hacienda houses were on the verge of collapsing owing "to the destruction by the armies of both sides that have entered and established their head-quarters in areas belonging to the estates."[7] Although the liquinas remained in a decayed state, the economy of the subtropical valleys revived in the 1840's as sugarcane expanded into the Pilco-mayo Valley, where landowners distilled rum and aguardiente to export to the mines.[8]

The wine-growing Cinti Valley was in a similarly ravaged state immediately after independence; even so, in the late 1820's, according to the British traveler Edmond Temple, Cinti's wines and brandies were still "in very great demand and [were] sent to all parts of Upper Peru."[9] By the 1850's, the wine-growing properties were as prosperous as ever, and the valley's landowners were gradually able to improve their properties as the volume of the wine and liquor trade increased during the silver boom years. Nicolas Dorado, owner of Hacienda El Pópulo along the Río Grande south of Camargo, boasted in 1865, "I have had to make great expenditures to put [the hacienda] on its feet; today [it] is one of the best of the Cinti Valley, as is evident and well known."[10]

But even though economic conditions had improved greatly in the valleys by the last half of the nineteenth century, the effects of the independence struggles lingered on the estates of the high puna in northern Cinti. Landowners were unable to exploit their holdings properly for a lack of laborers. In 1869, for example, the owners of some of the most important haciendas in the region required their colonos to pay only *yerbaje,* a grazing fee, and did not collect the customary money rent for agricultural lands. Only a few fields were being cultivated, and the owners presumably wanted to encourage workers to settle on their holdings.[11]

Land-Tenure Patterns

The ecological diversity of Cinti province was reflected in a large variety of land-tenure patterns, due to historical circumstances, such as royal policies and the level of destruction during the independence wars, as well as to differences in climate and crops. With the exception of the self-contained northern sector, each ecological zone produced products vital to the economy of the province. Land-tenure patterns in part also reflected each crop's different labor and capital requirements.

A distinct lack of economic dynamism in northern Cinti proba-

TABLE 10

Distribution of Landholdings in Cinti by Value, 1902

Region	Small	Medium	Large
North: cantons Collpa, Achilla, San Lucas	373	177	19
Southeast: cantons Santa Elena, La Loma	405	164	24
Canton Camargo	322	181	57
South: cantons San Juan de la Torre, Impora, San Juan, Camataquí	1,800	197	2
TOTAL	2,900	719	102

SOURCE: Centro Bibliográfico Documental Histórico, Universidad Mayor, Real y Pontificia de San Francisco Xavier de Chuquisaca (Sucre), Tesoro Departamental, "Registro de la rectificación del catastro de la Provincia de Cinti (1902)," 2 vols.

NOTE: "Small" = under 1,000 Bs in value; "medium" = 1,001–9,999 Bs; "large" = 10,000 Bs or more.

bly accounts for the little interest shown in the purchase of Indian lands, which were concentrated in this part of the province. Only one community land sale is listed in the Sucre notarial archives; only a few more are recorded in Potosí.[12] The three ayllus, with 600 originarios in 1871 during the last tribute count, predominated in the cantons of San Lucas, Acchilla, and Collpa—an area that stretched from the high puna lands around San Lucas to the hot, subtropical Pilcomayo Valley. Because the Indians had access to every ecological level, they were able to meet their subsistence needs either by direct control over fields in different microclimates or by the complex system of exchange between ayllu members from the uplands and lowlands.[13] No revisita was sent out to parcel out Indian lands. Moreover, these communities had a long history of resistance to encroaching hacendados, either by legal means or by mobilizing their numerous members for a show of force on the disputed land.[14] Having such a wealth of resources at their disposal, ayllu members were seldom forced into debt, and outsiders who attempted to acquire land were generally frustrated.

For the rest of Cinti also, land-tenure patterns (as reflected in real estate sales) changed little between 1888 and 1902; the earliest extant catastro, from 1902, probably indicates quite accurately the distribution of properties in the 1880's, at the height of the silver boom.[15] The figures for small, medium, and large landholdings, as shown in Table 10, are misleading, however. Small properties, defined as worth less than 1,000 Bs, appear to have predominated in the province, but the data mask the diversity of land-tenure patterns between different areas of Cinti and do not take into account the enormous size of some of the most valuable properties. Also, many proprietors, especially smallholders, often owned more than one plot and therefore can appear two or more times in the land-tax records.

Looking at the province as divided into four regions—northern Cinti, southeastern Cinti, Camargo, and the Southwest—makes the landholding pattern clearer. In northern Cinti, the ayllus controlled the core area, which was surrounded by vast latifundios interspersed with small and medium-sized properties. Here, although the Indians clearly owned the greatest amount of land, large haciendas controlled much of the rest. The hacienda complex Tambillos, possibly the largest of them, contained thirty-six square leagues, or 90,000 hectares, and virtually encompassed the whole northwest corner of the province.[16] Moreover, the latifundios had the best land. Whereas most small and medium-sized properties are listed in the 1902 catastro as containing fields or pastures without irrigation, the large properties contained prized irrigated valley lands and vineyards.[17] In fact, the 1902 and 1910 catastros indicate that over three-quarters of the land on Hacienda Tambillos was cultivable, an amazingly high proportion considering the province's generally very tough terrain.[18]

In southeastern Cinti, encompassing the hot and humid sugarcane valleys and the liquinas, there were no Indian communities at all. Most of the surface area was held in twenty-four enormous latifundios, a land-tenure pattern inherited from colonial times, when the Crown had granted vast tracts of land in eastern Cinti to various conquistadores for driving the formidable Chiriguanos from the region.[19] Hacienda Culpina, for example, valued at 140,000 Bs in 1902, controlled twenty-five square leagues, or 62,500 hectares, much of it scarce level land, ideal for growing grains and tuber crops. Most of the other latifundios averaged around twenty square leagues, such as Caraparí, on the Pilaya River, and San Jerónimo, on the Pilcomayo.[20] What smaller properties there were contained only a few hectares. As in northern Cinti, the latifundios controlled most of the good land; most other landholdings had few flat areas and no irrigation.[21]

In Camargo canton, the wine-growing center of the province, small and medium-sized properties were of greater importance. Most of the valuable haciendas, although they had vineyards, also contained considerable amounts of nonproductive linquina, whereas most of the smaller properties were all in vineyards, located in the prime bottom land of the fertile Cinti Valley. Perhaps only slightly more than half of the wine-growing lands belonged to large haciendas; the rest was in the hands of smallholders.[22]

In the cantons of the southwestern boot of the province, small properties clearly predominated—not only in total area but also in economic importance. Only two estates were valued at over 10,000 Bs, compared with 1,800 properties worth less than 1,000 Bs. To some extent, however, these numbers exaggerate the prevalence of smallholdings. Many proprietors, like Francisco Anachuri, owned more than one plot. In 1902, Anachuri had eight different plots of irrigated fields, vineyards, and orchards in San Juan de la Torre, with a combined worth of 1,844 Bs.[23] This dispersed pattern of landownership prevented the total destruction of crops by the severe but localized hailstorms that were common during the harvest season. Why there were so few big estates is not clear; perhaps the lower grape yields (because of the Río Grande's high acidity), the endemic malaria in the area, and the distance to Potosí made this zone unattractive to large landowners.

The Nineteenth-Century Hacienda Labor Regime

The nature of the labor systems on Cinti properties varied according to the crops that were grown. On both the uplands haciendas and the sugarcane plantations, labor requirements were very similar to those on haciendas in Yamparaez. Because of the low profitability of these estates, administration was relatively lax. The highly commercialized wine-producing haciendas in the valleys, on the other hand, relied heavily on a form of wage labor. But on both types of properties, though for different reasons, traditional Andean relations based on reciprocity and redistribution were extremely important.

Most of the haciendas on the liquinas and the puna in eastern and northern Cinti, which had suffered particularly during the independence period, were owned later in the nineteenth century by Potosí miners who, like the owners of the haciendas in Yamparaez, concentrated most of their energies on the more lucrative mining rather than on agricultural pursuits. For example, Simón Dorado, who owned Hacienda Tambillos in San Lucas, was a partner in Dorado Hermanos, an important mining and trading company with headquarters in Potosí. In the late 1870's, Dorado's main income from the hacienda came from his four grain mills and the yerbaje fee he charged his arrenderos, both incomes that required a minimum of supervision to collect.[24]

More is known of the obligations and labor arrangements of the arrenderos on the liquinas haciendas in southeastern Cinti. Though the amount and kind of obligations varied from estate to estate, Hacienda Ingahuasi will serve as an example of what in theory was required. The arrenderos had to work for the hacienda fifteen days a month. In addition, they were obliged to haul hacienda products down to the Cinti Valley, a task for which they used their own donkeys and for which they were remunerated. During the sowing season, the arrenderos provided a yoke of oxen for a set number of days, depending on the size of the parcels to which they had usufruct rights. Each year, they had to make a plow beam and cut a certain amount of wood for construction and for use as firewood. Besides the money rent on their parcels, arrenderos paid yerbaje and the diezmo and primicia taxes. Each year, the *patrón* had the right to a sheep for use in his household.[25] Many of these obligations were paid by *arrimantes*, or subrenters, who in return for a part of the arrenderos' land, substituted for them in the hacienda's work obligations and helped them farm the land they kept for their own use.

As in Yamparaez during the silver-boom period, many haciendas in the liquinas had absentee owners. Since most of their proprietors also possessed lands in the valleys, where a much higher profit could be made from grapes and sugarcane, they preferred to reside in the more hospitable climate of the valleys. This was the case with Mariano Linares who, in addition to Haciendas Ingahuasi and Culpina in the liquinas, owned San Pedro Mártir in the Cinti Valley and Caraparí along the Pilaya. The small quantities of produce Linares brought to market from his huge upland estates suggests a relative neglect of these properties. During the period 1889–95, he took only 777 liquinas sheep to the Cinti Valley and sold them for the relatively small sum of 1,514 Bs. He marketed even less in the way of grains and tubers during this period—only 12.4 fanegas of barley and 18 cargas of potatoes, for an approximate value of 180 Bs.[26]

Although the liquinas haciendas contributed little to the commercial revival of the province during the late nineteenth century and were largely ignored by their owners, the hacendados still kept Andean-type reciprocal relations with their laborers. Rents traditionally fell due the week after Carnival, during *Tentación*. The hacendado sponsored a fiesta that week, which allowed him to bring the workers together so he could collect the rent, and at the same time to redistribute some of the money back to his workers in the form of food and drink. Rent was the most important source of income from these properties, and landowners were careful to maintain the reciprocal arrangement.

The picture was quite different on the sugarcane estates in the Pilcomayo and Pilaya valleys, which produced a cash crop to be sold in the mining areas and depended on the resident work force mainly for their labor, and only secondarily for the income from rent payments. Although most of these properties also contained liquinas above the valley floor, the demesne lands were concentrated in the irrigated valley bottom lands, and liquinas were for the most part distributed among the arrenderos. Hacienda Caraparí, located on the Pilaya River, showed this pattern. Four of the five sections into which Caraparí was divided were cultivated exclusively by arrenderos. The fifth section, where all demesne lands were located, contained the valley area as well as the hacienda house and distillery.[27] The nature of sugarcane cultivation made this distribution of land a necessity. The crop requires little care during most of the year, but demands large amounts of labor during harvest. The liquinas enabled the hacienda to maintain a sufficient number of workers who were obligated to come down to the valley to cut cane during the harvest but could work on their own crops during the slack season. The hacienda maintained direct control over the valley, where sugarcane cultivation brought the highest profits, but it gave the greater part of the less lucrative areas, in this case the liquinas, to the arrenderos for their subsistence needs.[28]

A third system prevailed in the wine-growing areas, where the bulk of the labor force resided in the valley itself. On small properties, especially in southern Cinti, the owners themselves cultivated their plots. Larger vineyards employed between one and six peons, called *viñateros*. These laborers worked six days a week from seven o'clock in the morning to sundown and received a daily wage that was paid after the Sunday-morning *faena*, or unremunerated work period. Each viñatero had the right of usufruct to a small parcel of irrigated land, where he built his thatched hut and cultivated grapes, vegetables, and fruit trees. He paid no money rent on his parcel and had the right to distill the fruits from his own patch in the hacienda's distillery. What he did not keep, he sold to the vineyard owner. In addition, if the hacendado considered the viñatero a "good peon," he received the privilege of taking care of various fruit trees growing in the vineyards, in return for which he was entitled to their produce.[29] The peons' care of the trees benefited the *patrón*, who needed the tree branches to support the grapevines. This also gave him a greater measure of social control over his viñateros, whom he rewarded in this fashion with small, though tangible, benefits for their "good" behavior.

The large Cinti Valley estates that also contained liquinas above the vineyards usually had a number of arrenderos, who paid money rent (*arriendos*) for the small irrigated parcels of land that hugged the sides of the ravines in the uplands and nonirrigated fields on the more level mountain slopes. Crops could be grown only in a few areas, owing to the ruggedness of the terrain and scarcity of water, but the land was decent rangeland and the arrenderos' main occupation was livestock raising.

Although diverging somewhat from the general pattern, Hacienda El Patronato, located three kilometers south of Camargo, was a good example of the division between valley and liquinas labor forces.[30] This hacienda had twenty-four hectares of vineyards and 50,000 hectares of liquinas. Twenty-two workers, watched over by a mayordomo, resided in the valley. The hacendado chose the hardest-working viñatero as *capitán*, in charge of supervising work during the day. Another four workers were designated as *regadores*, in charge of the schedule for irrigating hacienda lands. Both regadores and capitán were exempt from paying a cash rent on the parcels of irrigated land they controlled. The other seventeen peons were called arrenderos and lived in the Patronato ravine behind the *casa de hacienda*. The valley arrenderos, in contrast to other Cinti Valley properties, paid a small cash rent, although they also worked regularly in the vineyards.

Only twenty-five arrendero families and some arrimantes lived in the 50,000-hectare liquinas area. A supervisor, called *capataz*, supervised the arrenderos' work; he was paid wages and also had the use of some of the most productive liquinas lands. The arrenderos were obligated to work for the hacienda at maintaining the roads in the area and weeding hacienda lands in the liquinas. Since only a few narrow ravines on the hacienda were suited for agriculture, the major activity in the high country was stock raising. In 1916, the hacienda owned 1,200 goats and sheep and forty head of cattle. The arrenderos paid diezmo on their goats and sheep. The hacendado rented teams of oxen from the arrenderos for agricultural work on hacienda lands in both valley and liquinas. The arrenderos were obligated to sell part of their barley and potato crops to the hacendado for use in the big house. Also, they had to cut firewood for use in the distillery and transport it free of charge to the hacienda house.

Haciendas with liquinas exercised an importance far beyond what their numbers would indicate. The vineyards of these properties were, with few exceptions, the largest and most prosperous in the Cinti Valley. The liquinas provided extra labor during the harvest and during the rainy season, when it was necessary to clean the ditches. The liquinas livestock provided manure for the vineyards. Crops from higher ecological levels of the liquinas, such as potatoes, barley, and wheat, made the property virtually self-sufficient in its food requirements. The firewood obligation provided the distillery with a free source of fuel. Since this lowered production and consumption costs, the Cinti Valley properties with liquinas were so profitable that their owners were able to venture into other enterprises and thus dominate the commercial circuits within Cinti.[31]

The traditional Andean ideal of reciprocity was probably best preserved in the properties that controlled different ecological levels. At El Patronato, after the harvest, the owner had to fulfill the *tincka*, a Quechua word meaning "a gift to ask a favor," used to describe reciprocal relations. During this ritual, the hacendado gave all his workers presents of wine and food. This was in addition to the daily wage each peon received. Another of the hacienda's customs had deep roots in Andean tradition: in August, when the hacienda books were balanced, all the tenants who had favorable balances received tokens that were redeemable for clothes in Camargo stores. Although reciprocal arrangements are not confined to the Andean area, the redistribution of textiles and clothes as a means of creating reciprocal bonds and confirming dependency status can be traced back at least to the Inca state.[32]

The reciprocal ideal was maintained in relations between hacendado and peon throughout the Cinti Valley. In other vineyards, in a *manteada* festival after the harvest, workers made a chair with olive branches and flowers, and to the tune of native flutes (*quenas*) and drums entered the hacienda house. They seated the hacendado on the chair, took him to the door of the wine vault, and obligated him, his wife, and the supervisors to give them wine.[33] The hacendado expressed his relationship with his viñateros by stating that they were his *socios*, or members in a common enterprise. Socios did not mean that the peon had equal status or that he benefited equally from the arrangement, to be sure, but it did express a common bond embodied in the ideal of frictionless relations between *patrón* and peon based on the recognition of mutual, though not necessarily equal, obligations.[34]

Thus, labor relations in Cinti followed traditional highland patterns, even though the area depended on cash cropping for much of its prosperity. In fact, the heavily commercialized valley regions, with their specialized wage laborers (though they also had rights to small plots), were intimately tied to the subsistence-oriented liquinas. The landowner benefited from maintaining a ready labor reserve in the uplands that could be employed at crucial points in the agricultural cycle. The sugar-producing haciendas used a similar arrangement. Self-sufficiency in labor and other liquinas resources explains why these areas, although they did not represent much hacienda income in themselves, were essential to the prosperity of the large vineyards and sugarcane-growing estates. Traditional Andean relationships helped tie the upland workers to their often distant masters and provided the moral justification for the periodic use of their labor in the valleys. Of course, hacendados also emphasized their redistributive functions and reciprocity with the valley specialists, since this created personal patron-client ties with the viñateros and helped provide stability among the valuable skilled labor force.

Commercial Circuits: Wine, Sugar, and Mules

The advantages enjoyed by the large Cinti Valley grape growers helped them to dominate provincial trade to the mining centers during the nineteenth century. The owners of the largest vineyards maintained stores in Potosí, where they sold their products directly to the consumer. In 1893, José María Linares, who owned and administered various estates in the province, such as Papachacra and San Pedro Mártir in the Cinti Valley, and Carapari on the Pilaya River, had a stock of 60,762.5 pounds of aguardiente, 3,308.5 pounds of *singani* (grape brandy), and 79 botijas of wine, worth in all 22,270.42 Bs, in his Potosí store.[35] In 1895, Linares and his partner, Napoleon G. Romero, also sold liquors directly in the silver-mining town of Huanchaca.[36]

Camargo merchants were the only ones who were able to maintain some kind of competitive edge against the Cinti landowners' commercial predominance. Those landowners who did not own stores in Potosí either sold their produce to Camargo merchants or hired mule trains to take wines and liquors to the mining centers. The merchants usually bought the finished product, since virtually all vineyard owners, even the smallest, maintained some sort of distillery. Most commonly, this wine or liquor was then marketed wholesale to Potosí merchants waiting at three *tambos* (roadway inns) outside the city. The traders from Potosí then retailed the wine or liquor in the city or the surrounding mines.[37] Very rarely did Camargo merchants keep a store in Potosí as well. Although Potosí remained the principal market for Cinti alcoholic beverages, Cinti grape growers also hired mule trains to haul their goods all over southern Bolivia, including Uyuni, Colquechaca, Tarija, Cotagaita, and Sucre.[38] Moreover, Indians from the highlands to the west periodically came down to the valley to buy wine and liquors.

Cinti Valley hacendados also controlled the aguardiente trade. Except for Linares's Caraparí, sugar estates sold most of their produce in the form of cane juice or brown sugar (*chancaca*) to these middlemen, who converted the unfinished product into aguardiente. For example, Pedro Urquizu in 1882 sold 1,500 arrobas of cane juice of the following year's crop from his property on the Pilcomayo to a Camargo merchant, Nicanor Amésaga, for an advance payment of 2,550 pesos.[39] The merchants and landowners of the Cinti Valley were able to control the aguardiente trade because the owners of the sugar estates in the out-of-the-way Pilcomayo and Pilaya river valleys had no access to pack animals for transporting the product to market. The Cinti Valley people had no such problem, for Argentine mule traders, who had attended the fairs in Sucre and Ayoma in the department of Potosí since colonial days, often traveled through the valley.[40]

Even so, pack animals were in great demand, and there was a lively trade in them. Although some merchants owned grazing lands in the high valleys north and south of the Cinti Valley, most resold the animals on credit to muleteers (*arrieros*) who lived in these fodder-rich areas. The arriero then hauled goods for the seller until he had worked off the value of the animal. A case in point, Máximo Zoto, one of the richest Camargo merchants, sold a *recua*, or mule team, to David Auza for 1,300 Bs. Auza contracted to make a trip for Zoto to Potosí every twenty days, or to Sucre, Colquechaca, or Uyuni every thirty days, and also to travel at least twice a year to either the Pilcomayo or the Pilaya River to pick up loads of cane juice or chancaca; Zoto paid Auza the going transport rate, with a 4 percent discount. Auza owned various plots in Tacaquira, which he put up as security for the deal and from which he furnished his animals with fodder.[41]

Considering the difficulties that even the traders from the centrally located Cinti Valley experienced in acquiring pack animals, it is no wonder that the proprietors of the sugar estates, isolated in the subtropical valleys far from the main trade routes, were rarely able to bring their products to market themselves. Moreover, the mule trade slowed considerably after independence; also, many mule traders began passing through the Tumusla River Valley in Potosí, bypassing Cinti. Cinti hacendados often had to provide extra incentives to attract sufficient muleteers. In 1881, Carlos Vacaflor Romero, a prominent Cinti landowner and Liberal politician, rented a medium-sized property in Muyuquiri to the owner of twenty donkeys for two years, in return for the use of the donkeys for trips to the Pilaya River to pick up the cane juice for which he had contracted.[42]

The trading network that emerged during the nineteenth century put most of the profits of Cinti province into the pockets of the large Cinti Valley landowners and Camargo merchants. Since high transport costs and lack of pack animals made it difficult for other producers to compete, the large landowners were able to use their high profits on expensive inprovements that marginally increased their production. Until the early twentieth century, for example, they succeeded in steadily increasing the always scarce acreage for grape growing by building walls to confine the rivers of the Cinti Valley to narrow channels, eliminating the problem of flash flooding. The considerable wealth that certain hacendados and merchants accumulated during the silver-boom era also led to the construction of sumptuous hacienda houses along the Río Chico and a certain kind of aristocratic lifestyle in and around Camargo that was matched only in much larger cities like Potosí and Sucre. The half-dozen newspapers published in Camargo during the late nineteenth century and the large sums of money spent on the political battles between wealthy Liberal and Conservative *cinteños* attest to the wealth and vitality of the town and its surrounding countryside.

Twentieth-Century Decline

Although the collapse of the silver boom after 1895 brought about few changes in the land-tenure patterns of Cinti province, the shrinking of mining markets, especially the market of Potosí proper, and the attendant changes in the Bolivian economic structure, plunged the province into a long decline from which it has still not recovered. The decline was evident first among the small grape growers and then even among the big valley landowners who had prospered especially during the mining boom. In time, it also destroyed the wealth of the well-connected Camargo merchants. Only a small handful of landowners were able to thrive, primarily by commercializing new crops and capitalizing their operations extensively by means of outside financial backing.

Unlike the landowners of Yamparaez, most of whom had heavy investments in mining, the vast majority of Cinti hacendados had few if any direct interests in the mining companies. Only the owners of the large puna estates in northern Cinti were heavily involved in mining; they were able to hang on to their properties. After the turn of the century, the miner-hacendado Simón Dorado began exploiting the lead and antimony deposits found on his Hacienda Tambillos. This venture was apparently successful largely because Dorado used his resident laborers to work the mines, thereby saving a large part of his labor costs, traditionally the greatest expense in the Bolivian mining industry.[43] Despite these savings, Dorado's enterprise remained decidedly small-scale and never represented serious competition to the new large international companies.

For the rest of the province, the decline of Potosí as the marketing center of the country, though not so rapid as the silver crash, nevertheless made it increasingly difficult for the cinteños to sell their crops. Although sales to the new tin-mining complexes partly offset the drying up of the Potosí market, Cinti producers faced a situation of chronic oversupply in the twentieth century. The departmental treasurer in 1911 lamented that the vineyard owner had only done half the work once the crop was harvested; the other half was finding a buyer. Consequently, many cinteños were forced to convert their wines into brandy to sell their produce, thereby, according to the treasurer, losing up to 60 percent of the crop's potential value.[44] Increasing competition from other parts of Bolivia exacerbated the problem. Peruvian alcoholic beverages, which after 1888 were allowed to enter the country duty-free, had been of such inferior quality that the Cinti beverages had easily maintained their market share; but after 1895, when cheap sugar from northern Argentina drove prices down, many sugarcane growers in La Paz and Santa Cruz started making liquor instead of transporting the sugar to market. This liquor was much less expensive than singani or wine, and better in quality than the Peruvian product, and it found a ready market among workers, miners, and Indians.[45]

The intense competition among Bolivian distilleries kept the price of alcoholic beverages stagnant from the 1890's until the second decade of the twentieth century, and this despite a general increase in the prices of wheat, corn, and other staple goods after 1906, when Bolivia moved from silver to the gold standard. In 1917, the subprefect of Cinti estimated that liquor, by maintaining the same price over the past twenty-five years, was actually selling for half its former value on account of inflation.[46] The squeeze between stagnant liquor prices and the rising cost of staple goods sharply decreased the Cinti producers' profit margins. The small grape growers who did not possess liquinas suffered first, since they were dependent on the market to buy the increasingly expensive basic goods.

Natural disasters worsened this already bad situation. In 1917, flash floods destroyed many vineyards; the subsequent rebuilding of river walls and recovery of land exhausted many property owners' limited resources. Then, in the 1920's, *Oidium*, a fungus disease that had been present in the Cinti area since 1906, took on epidemic proportions in the valley's vineyards; by that time, many proprietors, especially the small growers, were so financially drained that they could not bear the costs involved in trying to save their vines.[47]

Cinti merchants, primarily based in Camargo, suffered least during the first decades of the region's economic decline. They were not immediately affected by the natural disasters that struck the growers, and since they often had connections with foreign commercial houses, they were able to borrow from the plentiful resources of these companies to support their own endeavors. Antonio Ayo, a Spanish immigrant and one of the principal Camargo merchants, maintained a close relationship with the important German firm of Moerch, Bauer, and Company, which lent him 25,000 Bs in 1910 to purchase its merchandise. Also, merchants often had their own pack animals and so were able to avoid the complicated arrangements that Cinti hacendados had to make to obtain transport for their produce. Ayo, for example, owned pack animals that he kept on his own land in Tacaquira.[48] The merchants in fact profited from the misfortunes of the grape growers.

After the turn of the century, Cinti Valley hacendados were increasingly less able to invest the large amounts of capital that viticulture required, and although many turned to borrowing money, high interest rates (between 12 percent and 24 percent a year) made this an unattractive option, particularly in view of the stagnant price of alcoholic beverages. A much less risky alternative was to rent the property to people who had financial resources and, in return for lower rents, have them renew the vineyard. This practice was widespread in the grape-growing valleys. In 1906, for example, the owner of Hacienda Santa Barbara in the Río Chico Valley rented his property for five years at 1,600 Bs annually, during which time the renter had to convert a certain area of unworked lands into vineyards. He was also obligated to construct a storage building for wine by 1907.[49]

From the beginning, the most important renters were the Cinti merchants or their surrogates. In 1900, Rosa Romero de Achá rented the haciendas of San Francisco and Cañari to the wealthy Camargo merchant Máximo Zoto for five years at 5,500 Bs a year; 1,500 Bs was to be paid in cash and the other 4,000 Bs in singani and aguardiente placed in Sucre.[50] In 1906, Señora Achá again rented her properties, this time, at only 4,000 Bs, to a different person, who had the merchant Antonio Ayo's financial backing.[51]

Production eventually suffered as more and more owners leased their estates. The renter of course tried to make as big a profit as possible during his limited stay on the property, and his attempts to produce as much as possible over the short term inevitably led to drops in long-term productive capacity. Inevitably, also, despite the many clauses in the rent agreements that were intended to prevent the properties' deterioration, vineyards declined. Rental, meant to forestall the decay of the Cinti Valley vineyards, actually accelerated it.[52]

Many haciendas, especially those in the Río Chico Valley, eventually ended up in merchant hands. An instructive case is that of Abel Vacaflores, a muleteer-merchant who with his brothers inherited a few small vineyards in the valley. By the 1890's, he had become wealthy enough to rent two vineyards and a sugar estate. In 1902, Vacaflores not only owned one of the vineyards he had previously rented, but also bought one of the most productive vineyards in Cinti, El Papagayo, for 96,820 Bs. A merchant at heart, Vacaflores at first rented El Papagayo to an experienced viticulturist who owned various other vineyards in the area. In an extremely detailed contract, Vacaflores specified that the rent would be paid in wine, singani, and aguardiente, which he would then transport to market. Also, the renter was obligated to distill all the chancaca and cane juice that Vacaflores brought from his sugar estate. After the rental period expired, Vacaflores himself took over the administration of El Papagayo; he continued to administer the property until his death in 1933.[53]

After the turn of the century, merchants were not as interested in acquiring or renting sugar estates in the subtropical valleys. Other than Hacienda Caraparí, an exceptional case that will be discussed below, the properties along the Pilaya and Pilcomayo valleys were hit the hardest by increased competition from La Paz and Santa Cruz and the slow disintegration of the Cinti commercial circuits. The complex relationship between the owners of the sugar haciendas and the Cinti Valley landowners and merchants broke down as the latters' resources dwindled. A dramatic decrease in the number of contracts listed in the Camargo notarial archive indicates that by the second decade of the twentieth century, few Cinti Valley residents were willing to finance the arduous trip to the subtropical valleys to obtain chancaca. In the 1920's, no contracts were made at all. Many of the sugar-estate owners reverted to a subsistence economy or converted the *tablas*, or sugarcane fields, to the cultivation of the *ají* pepper as a cash crop. With pack-animal traffic slowed to a trickle, the government did not bother to maintain the already bad roads, and when the low valley proprietors petitioned for new ones, the subprefect in Camargo, faced with deteriorating conditions closer to home, did not respond. By the 1930's, after the onset of the Great Depression, the once-prosperous low valleys were, according to one knowledgable Cinti landowner, "in [a state of] complete abandonment and destruction."[54]

In 1911, the railroad finally reached Potosí, reviving hopes that the province's economic decline could be reversed by cheap access to markets beyond the city. This was not to be. The arduous, expensive, and none too reliable trip by mule and donkey from Cinti to Potosí kept costs up, while foreign and national competitors could now easily reach Potosí, previously a virtually closed market to all but Cinti producers. For the large Cinti Valley landowners especially, the coming of the railroad showed how impossible it was for the complex system of contracts between muleteers, sugar growers, and viticulturalists to compete with producers who had easy access to rail lines.

To be sure, there was at first a great outburst of new, innovative activity. The El Caserón enterprise was indicative of the problems of Cinti Valley producers as well as a harbinger of the move to different crops. In anticipation of the increased commercial possibilities, Abel Vacaflores joined two other Cinti merchants, two grape growers, an Austrian agronomist, and Fernando Mercy, a Belgian-born former inspector for the Ministry of Agriculture, in a venture to make grain alcohol from barley. With an initial capital of 55,000 Bs, the new firm, Lalanne, Vacaflores and Company, built a large distillery at El Caserón, a grape-growing hacienda along the Río Grande, with Mercy in charge of production. In 1917, El Caserón produced some 800 quintales of alcohol from 3,000 quintales of barley. However, problems soon developed; in 1918, the prefect of the department calculated that alcohol distilleries in Cinti were running at half capacity because of a lack of fuel and raw materials. El Caserón was in particularly bad shape for it had neither barley lands nor large stands of trees or shrubs for fuel. In 1921, the Austrian sold his share of the troubled company to Alcira Linares v. de Romero, owner of Hacienda Ingahuasi in the liquinas, for 7,500 Bs cash and another 7,500 Bs worth of barley, payable to the company in two harvests. This stopgap measure to obtain barley failed to revive the company. Two years later, the administrator of the alcohol tax agency in Camargo removed the alcohol-measuring device from El Caserón, pronouncing it in a state of "complete disorganization purely because of the business losses, especially last year, due to the scarcity and high price of grains."[55]

The large Cinti Valley landowners were clearly on the defensive by the 1920's and remained so until the 1960's. Instead of trying to expand their markets, they tried without success to get the government to lighten the tax burden placed on wine and singani producers while at the same time fighting a rearguard action against manufacturers of the cheaper sugarcane alcohol. In 1924, some of the most prominent Cinti Valley producers formed the Landowners' League of Cinti Province to stem the tide of cheaper products. Abel Vacaflores, who headed these efforts and became president of the league, cynically remarked, after the failure of his own attempts at producing grain alcohol: "A vineyard is a garden in which one works much but gains little; but a distillery is a source of poison put up by big capitalists to make a quick fortune poisoning the public, without leaving anything permanent and useful for later generations."[56]

The permanent removal of the seat of government from Sucre to La Paz severely weakened the once considerable power of the large Cinti landowners, but the tax reduction they sought would not have been a great help in any case. The economic decline of much of Cinti province was the result not of taxes, but of the introduction of the railroad and the decline of the once-strong Potosí market. As the silver mines, and with them the last remnants of the "Peruvian economic space," faded, so did much of Cinti's prosperity.

The Rise of Agroindustry

The process of economic decline in Cinti was a long, drawn-out affair. Most properties, except for those in the southeastern corner of the province, continued to grow and market their various crops as before in the face of ever-declining profitability. In general, labor relations remained remarkably stable. Indeed, in many cases the traditional patterns of reciprocity grew stronger as landowners attempted to make up in nonmonetary rewards what they could not pay their workers in cash. Only in two areas, the northern and southern corners of the province, did wholesale changes in the labor system result in widespread resistance.

In northern Cinti, as in Yamparaez, the silver-mining elites shifted their emphasis to their landed estates and attempted to extract a larger surplus from the resident labor force to make up for lost hacienda income in the shrinking Potosí market. This apparently led to the abuse of hacienda peons and provoked large-scale resistance. Unfortunately, so little detailed information is available for this area that it is difficult to determine the extent and the exact causes of the unrest.

From summary reports, it is clear that resistance to the new labor regime was widespread, and that it often involved violence. In 1926, the peons of three haciendas—Otavi, La Lava, and Payacota del Carmen—rose up in revolt; soon thereafter, the whole northern sector, including the cantons of San Lucas, Acchilla, Collpa, and Pirhuani, joined the uprising. The insurrection was contained after some effort, and a new subprefect was put in charge to prevent further problems. According to the new official, the principal cause of the revolt was the landowners' maltreatment of their colonos. He came down hard on the landowners who, in his words, "more than once made the Indians the object of their wrath . . . and subjected them to the most cruel treatment."[57]

Much more information is available on peasant resistance in southern Cinti. There, in contrast to the northern sector, an economic revival of certain haciendas through the infusion of large amounts of capital brought a measure of prosperity back to the area. It was not so great a prosperity as some contemporary accounts of the province described when they emphasized the commercial strength of these large but unusual estates, giving the false impression that the whole province was in economic ascendancy.[58] The vast majority of the province's inhabitants were not so well off. Nonetheless, the efforts of certain southern Cinti landowners, despite the exceptional nature of their endeavors, are important for a number of reasons. For one, they showed the possibilities of commercial agriculture in a drastically changed economic environment. Second, the resistance of the hacienda labor forces to changes in labor relations points to the continuing importance of the traditional Andean concepts of reciprocity and redistribution even in the relatively capital-intensive agriculture that the innovative proprietors practiced.

One of these successful haciendas was José María Linares's Caraparí, with lands in the hot subtropical Pilaya Valley. This hacienda was administered after 1923 by the Belgian agronomist Fernando Mercy, who left El Caserón after marrying into the Linares family. Unlike other landowners of the subtropical valleys along Cinti's southern borders, the Linares family in conjunction with Mercy decided to stake its fortunes on sugarcane. As Mercy had argued in his reports on Cinti as technical consultant to the Ministry of Agriculture in 1906, what the province needed to regain its prosperity was to streamline management, install modern machinery, improve growing techniques, and build better roads.[59] The Belgian agronomist followed his own recommendations on Hacienda Caraparí. He replaced Caraparí's outdated machinery with modern equipment and installed a large alcohol distillery and a sugarcane refinery next to the hacienda house in the Pilaya Valley. He also expanded the sugarcane fields, wresting more land from the river by constructing a new system of flood walls.[60] The heavy investment greatly increased the output of alcohol, and the labor needs of the hacienda changed accordingly.

For the sake of efficiency and higher profits, Mercy ignored the concept of mutual obligations when he changed the labor system to fit the requirements of the new machinery. As a European raised in a wholly different tradition, Mercy failed to understand the importance of acting like a "good hacendado." Presumably he saw little difference between the European worker and the Andean peon beyond the fact that it was more trouble getting the Andeans to work. His blunders led to a worsening of conditions for the arrenderos and constant friction as the peons attempted to reassert what they felt to be their rights.

In the 1920's, Caraparí had about 825 arrenderos grouped into five different sections.[61] In addition, many arrenderos had arrimantes subrenting some of their fields. The labor obligations of 150 days work a year in the sugarcane fields and the distillery remained about the same as always, but Mercy increased the peons' firewood obligation to avoid the fuel scarcity that had plagued the operation at El Caserón. Each arrendero had to bring to the distillery ten *tareas* of wood, each tarea being equal to what twelve mules could carry. He also increased the obligation to haul the hacienda's products, for an enormously enlarged amount of alcohol now had to be transported to market. Arrenderos were remunerated according to whether they transported the cans of alcohol to Tarija or to Totora, a town located between Ingahuasi and Caraparí. Arrimantes were traditionally exempt from hacienda obligations, since their rental arrangements usually involved taking on the arrenderos' obligations to the landowner. But at Caraparí, arrimantes had to transport six cans of alcohol (half as much as the arrenderos), in addition to the duties they performed in the arrenderos' stead.[62] The additional burden considerably worsened the precarious state of the arrimantes, who, with far fewer resources than the arrenderos, already performed as much if not more work.

Worse still, perhaps, Mercy refused to recognize his social obligations as *patrón* to provide certain services in return for the arrenderos' labor. According to the arrenderos' complaints, he ceased to give free quinine to those who contracted malaria, for example. More serious, he did not pay for an arrendero's funeral, as was customary, and dispossessed the widow and her family if they were unable to replace the dead man with another laborer. Quickly recognizing this threat to their families' very survival on the hacienda, the arrenderos refused to work. Mercy hired bodyguards and enforcers to keep them in line; the laborers returned to work; alcohol production continued at a high volume; and the hacienda became a showcase for those who pointed to Cinti's potential to prosper once again. However, Mercy's disregard of, or lack of understanding of, the moral system on which his rule was based robbed him of his legitimacy as *patrón* in the peons' eyes—and eventually of his life. In 1948, a time of great rural unrest, the arrenderos attacked Mercy as he was giving out the morning orders and beat him to death.

A more detailed understanding of worker resistance emerges from the other large enterprise in southern Cinti, the giant Agricultural, Ranching, and Industrial Society of Cinti (Sociedad Agrícola, Ganadera e Industrial de Cinti, or SAGIC), which combined the estates of San Pedro Martír, Culpina, and Ingahuasi. Resistance there was not shown in violence, as in northern Cinti and at Carapari, but instead manifested itself primarily in a series of relatively peaceful labor strikes. This is not to imply that there was no peaceful resistance elsewhere—indeed, it is likely that the labor strike was the principal form of resistance throughout rural Bolivia—but the documentation on SAGIC is by far the richest source for a study of that phenomenon.

SAGIC's problems are in some ways reminiscent of the early stages of industrialization in the United States. As Herbert Gutman has shown, the first-generation U.S. factory worker was likely to be a migrant from a rural area who brought a different conception of work and time to the job from that required of a disciplined labor force. In a sense, what Gutman has called a "working-class subculture" based on Andean concepts developed on the SAGIC estates, and that subculture, as in the United States, mounted an often-successful resistance to the ideas and values the new industrially oriented management attempted to impose. Gutman's concept is especially relevant and apparent in this case, for the SAGIC haciendas were by far the most heavily mechanized agricultural properties in the province and perhaps even in the country.

The SAGIC haciendas were unusual not only in their level of mechanization, but also in their market orientation, their sources of investment, their crops, and their labor organization. The company stands as the clearest illustration of the transformation of the Bolivian economy from one that was centered in the silver-mining regions of the south to one that was dominated by the tin interests of the north. From the very start, SAGIC's major market was La Paz rather than the economically moribund Potosí. Jorge Ortiz Linares, part-owner of the liquinas hacienda of Culpina, was married to the daughter of Simón Patiño, the tin king of Bolivia. Ortiz, the several owners of the two other haciendas, and Patiño founded the company in 1925, with an authorized capital of 600,000 pounds sterling. Of 235,824 shares, 100,000 belonged to Patiño, his children, and the Mercantile Bank, which he controlled. The other founders, including Alcira v. de Romero, part-owner of the ill-fated Caserón enterprise, received a combination of cash and stocks in the new company in return for their properties. Some remained active as officers of SAGIC, including José Ortiz, who was the general manager, and Jorge Calvo, who stayed on as the administrator of his former estate, San Pedro.[63] Like many members of the Sucre elite, these estate owners had become heavily indebted to the banks, and the well-financed new enterprise probably saved them from bankruptcy.[64]

After SAGIC took over the properties, the commercial emphasis shifted dramatically to the liquinas. Viticulture, once the focus of the local economy, became marginal to the overall enterprise. San Pedro, the only estate with vineyards, served primarily as an outlet to the main highway between Tarija and Potosí and as the connecting link to Camargo, only eleven kilometers away. Behind San Pedro lay Culpina and Ingahuasi, both liquinas haciendas, which became the economic mainstay of the company. The Culpina hacienda house was made the administrative headquarters, and a large distilling complex was installed a short distance away. By 1926, SAGIC had spent almost 500,000 Bs (about U.S. $180,000 at that date) on its distillery alone, half on the large factory building that housed it, and the rest on machinery imported from France. A mill imported from Belgium, with millstones from France, was assembled next to the distillery; their combined worth was 10,000 Bs. Sheds housing new agricultural machinery and trucks from the United States, worth around 170,000 Bs ($51,000), clustered on the side of the distillery. The salaried mill and distillery workers lived at the edge of the vast and desolate pampa of Culpina in a small town resembling the mining camps of the Bolivian altiplano, which sprang up in late 1925. Arrenderos from Ingahuasi and Culpina made up the bulk of the labor force. They lived in windowless thatched-roof adobe houses scattered throughout the estates, from which the distillery drew virtually all its grain.

Despite SAGIC's massive capital investments in machinery and buildings, and the owners' ambitious plans for marketing grain alcohol, its success—in the first years at least—depended fundamentally on the arrendero population's traditional obligations. In addition to almost a hundred salaried employees and San Pedro's thirty-three viñateros, the company had something over 1,400 arrenderos at its disposal.[65] Directly and indirectly, the arrendero population's arriendos, yerbaje, obligatory labor, and purchases from the company store provided by far the larger share of SAGIC's total income—the percentage never fell below 71 percent during the first six years.[66]

This was not at all what SAGIC's owners had expected. They had counted on heavy profits from alcohol production—as much as 300,000 Bs from the distillery in 1926, an amount that would have allowed them to amortize their investment in a little over two years by the sale of alcohol alone. In fact, even in 1927 the distillery was still running at a loss (3,085 Bs). When it did begin to turn a profit, the earnings were negligible: alcohol sales reached their highest level of the first decade of operation in 1930, for a total of only 41,055 Bs, a meager 14 percent of projected earnings.[67] To be sure, economic conditions in Bolivia had much to do with this lack of success. In 1928, overproduction placed the alcohol industry in crisis; soon thereafter, the Great Depression brought sharply reduced sales, especially in the mining areas, where many layoffs occurred. As a result, the company once again had to fall back on the arrenderos for its income.[68]

SAGIC also depended on the arrenderos for raw materials; during the first years, much of the grain used in the distillery came from colonos who sold their crops to the company. In 1930, for example, hacienda lands produced 48,559.69 Bs worth of the 77,637.22 Bs of grain the distillery consumed. The rest was purchased from arrenderos at market prices.[69]

The changes in the labor system were a direct result of the company's desire to earn its money from the distillery. In 1926, in the hope of instituting a more efficient and businesslike system, the administration in Culpina ordered all labor obligations standardized.[70] All arrenderos were to fulfill a work obligation of twenty-five Bs a year at the going wage rate, and all in-kind obligations were suppressed. The colonos still had to pay a rental fee on their plots, however, and it may be that at this point the company had the fields of Ingahuasi's and Culpina's arrenderos measured, and reassessed the rents accordingly.[71]

Only the vineyard area of Hacienda San Pedro was partially exempted from these reforms. The account books show that the administration adopted a modified version of the new program in 1928, but exempted the viñateros from the new regulations because they did not pay for an arriendo (plot) and, unlike the arrenderos in the uplands, were required to work daily, except for holidays. For the labor-intensive viticulture of the Cinti Valley, the old system was probably the most effective for the hacendado; but much had changed for the arrenderos of the three *capitanías*, or sections, of the estate's liquinas above the vineyards. Their firewood obligation was abolished. From 1928 on, they had to work off the twenty-five Bs they automatically owed the company in labor at thirty centavos a day (1927 rate); this amounted to about 84 days a year. New workers were invariably given cash advances as an incentive to settle on the property. In San Pedro, arrenderos who had large debts were required to work on the Ingahuasi–San Pedro road construction project; for this work, they received half of their wages in cash, and half in credit toward their debts. In general, SAGIC tried to keep debts down so as not to have too much money tied up in labor costs.[72]

The effects of the changes in labor policy are best discerned on Hacienda Ingahuasi, where the administrator, Rosendo Vargas, corresponded daily with headquarters in Culpina and kept meticulous records for inspection by the management. In 1928, rents ranged from four to 270 Bs; most arrenderos paid between twenty and 100 Bs.[73] At a daily wage of around thirty centavos, it must have taken these peons between 150 and 416 days to work off their annual rent. By demanding such high rents, which many arrenderos could not possible pay with labor on the hacienda alone, the company was actually forcing the arrenderos to provide barley and transport services that went far beyond their traditional obligations.[74] Because the installation of the distillery lagged behind schedule and was not complete until late 1926, the new regulations posed a hardship for those arrenderos who had no income other than labor. As the first six-month accounting period ended, Vargas complained that "the arrenderos' remaining considerable surplus [i.e. money not paid to the hacienda] makes it difficult to charge rents; every Monday they come by the hundreds to ask for work."[75]

The result was a new problem of absenteeism on the SAGIC haciendas, for—as the *caporales*, or supervisors, of Ingahuasi complained—many peons left the hacienda to work elsewhere to get the money to pay for their plots. By 1928, the administrator of Ingahuasi had to threaten the hacienda workers with taking a *prenda*, or security deposit, so that they would come and pay their rent.[76]

Old work habits persisted despite the company's efforts to transform arrenderos into disciplined workers. Much as it had caused concern among nineteenth-century industrialists in the United States, the workers' use of spirits disturbed the SAGIC administration. In 1926, the general manager in Culpina stopped all liquor sales during weekdays and even holidays and imposed fines of up to ten Bs on people found selling alcoholic beverages during working hours. But this policy was hardly successful. The administrator of San Pedro reported only a month later, "Easter has been much celebrated by the peons in the Quebrada section; until today [five days after Easter Sunday], I have not been able to get them to come to work although I sent the supervisor to bring them." There

are other examples of indiscipline. In one case a peon from Ingahuasi, while drunk, beat a messenger boy from Culpina. In another incident, the manager gave Culpina's blacksmith a five-day
vacation, but the employee did not return for two weeks. Apparently he had been celebrating All Saints' Day the whole time.[77]

Although most arrenderos had a few donkeys and perhaps a
mule that they used occasionally to haul goods for the company, a
few families specialized in muleteering and paid off their obligations by transporting goods for SAGIC. The Llanos family is an example. Laureano Llanos owned two parcels on Ingahuasi valued at
twenty Bs and eight Bs, which were probably grazing lands, as well
as an arriendo in the Culpina town *caporalato*, or hacienda sub-
division, valued at 170 Bs, containing a corral and his house. Llanos,
also one of the principal arrieros of Culpina, transported singani to
Potosí and Tupiza.[78]

Most muleteers lived in Culpina and Ingahuasi. Two of the three
arrieros still recorded as living in the liquinas of San Pedro until
1927 disappeared from the hacienda after receiving an advance
from SAGIC to haul alcohol.[79] Although a vehicle road from San
Pedro to Ingahuasi was completed in 1926, the one-way hauling of
grain was still more cheaply done by donkeys than by truck. In
1928, to encourage this form of transportation, the company bought
donkeys from Argentina to distribute among reliable arrenderos.[80]

Transport problems continued to plague the company, however.
Despite the intensive commercialization of the uplands estates,
the peons remained subsistence-oriented peasants who refused to
cooperate when the necessities of the agricultural cycle conflicted
with the company's duties. During the first year of operation, even
after Vargas threatened the use of force to get arrenderos to present
themselves for transport duties to San Pedro, they refused to do so,
for they were in the midst of sowing their own fields. Also imped-
ing the smooth running of the estates was the hacienda worker's
preference for performing only duties that brought the greatest
personal benefits. In 1928, the Ingahuasi administrator ordered his
arrenderos to transport goods to the city of Potosí, but they complained that their donkeys were too thin to go, because the barley
harvest, the main fodder for pack animals, had been poor. Yet ten
days later, when Vargas requested 50 donkeys for a trip to Tupiza,
a crowd of arrenderos with 74 donkeys in tow appeared the next
day, clamoring for the job. Apparently the Tupiza run was much
more lucrative than the Potosí run, since it carried the possibility
of bringing back trade goods from Argentina.[81]

The problems with the muledrivers only ended when SAGIC built a vehicle road from San Pedro to Potosí. This road, which was completed in 1929, was paid for with a special loan from Simón Patiño, in return for which the company was reimbursed by the state out of the province's alcohol tax revenues.[82] Soon thereafter, with the threat of war with Paraguay looming, the road was hastily extended to Tarija, diminishing the arrenderos' possibilities for earning cash by muledriving.

Another way to obtain rent money was to work as a petty merchant, selling goods such as coca on hacienda grounds. This was prohibited by the SAGIC administration, but judging by the popularity of the Tupiza run, it was a common practice. When the company caught anyone selling, it confiscated the merchandise, paying the culprit a price inferior to the cost. Even so, the two company stores, or *pulperías*, at Ingahuasi and Culpina, faced stiff competition, not only from enterprising peons but also from itinerant merchants—often *turcos*, petty traders of Syrian origin—who would come and set up shop on the haciendas. The Culpina administration did its best to discourage these traders by forcing them to pay exorbitant prices, twenty-five Bs daily, for the houses they used for their temporary shops.[83] Stores set up just outside the haciendas' boundaries, especially in the town of Totora, situated on the Ingahuasi-Caraparí line, also competed successfully for the pulperías' clients. As a result, the Ingahuasi company store was sometimes forced to lower its prices, as in 1927, when it discounted sugar, rough cloth (*tocuyo*), coffee, and sardines because company employees were buying those items in Totora instead, and again in 1929, when it lowered the price of coca.[84]

Despite the major changes in the labor system, SAGIC deliberately maintained many traditional customs on its haciendas and, in fact, expanded its obligations to the labor force. However, it did not pursue this policy because the administrators realized that the legitimacy of their rule over the peons was thereby maintained, but simply because it was to the company's benefit to act as a paternalistic, though modern and enlightened, employer. Simón Patiño used the same tactic in his tin-mining operations and successfully forestalled many labor problems in the mines. Although there is no evidence to suggest that Patiño intervened in the daily operations of SAGIC, he or his assistants undoubtedly had a good deal of influence on the overall management of the enterprise.[85]

Under SAGIC management, for the first time a doctor was available full-time on the haciendas; a small fee was charged for his services, but medicine was free. The distribution of Argentine donkeys to deserving peons was another important symbolic gesture. Although the firm benefited by having more pack animals available for the transport of its goods, the arrenderos undoubtedly interpreted this gesture in traditional Andean terms. For them, it confirmed the *patrones'* role as redistributive agents. Further reinforcing this view, SAGIC provided seed on credit to its colonos when they ran short because of a poor harvest.[86] This was good policy from the company's point of view, for without the peons' supply of grain, the expensive distillery machinery could not be kept working at full capacity.

At the same time, SAGIC had little patience with any traditional reciprocal arrangements that lessened the smooth working of the organization and undermined profits, and its attempts to abolish these arrangements were a direct cause of the serious labor agitation that, in turn, made it impossible to impose new standards on the workers. The most notable example of this attempt to change tradition was the company's decision to do away with fiestas that did not coincide with national holidays. Many of these fiestas held profound religious significance for the arrenderos and defined relationships among them. Through the office of *alférez*, or fiesta sponsor, the peons maintained their own cargo system independent of the owners. Moreover, fiestas, as we have seen, reconfirmed the peons' dependency on the hacendado by the latter's show of generosity during the various ceremonies. In the beginning, the company seemed unaware of this aspect of the fiestas; it only saw that they led to week-long drunkenness, an unprofitable and inefficient exercise.

Fiestas and Resistance

Changes in work patterns deeply disturbed the resident laborers on the SAGIC latifundio. The drive to mechanize agricultural production, raise rents, and change labor obligations produced stresses between the rationalizing management and a labor force securely entrenched in a subsistence-oriented, peasant way of life. Although the company tried to maintain (and in some instances even enlarge) some traditional forms of reciprocity, the enormous changes that resulted from SAGIC's unusually heavy capitalization were simply too great a threat to the colonos' household economy. It is not surprising, therefore, that the company experienced widespread resistance in the first years of its existence.

Trouble broke out as early as 1926, when Culpina prohibited the fiesta of Tentación, which the arrenderos celebrated the Sunday after Carnival with much drinking and throwing of dynamite sticks into the air. The explosions among the drunken peons often caused severe injuries—reducing the number of healthy workers and increasing the company's medical costs. Because Tentación was not a legal holiday, the administration thought the hacienda peons should work that day and the following week, which many workers inevitably missed as the drinking continued. In Ingahuasi, the reaction to the news was immediate. In the words of Rosendo Vargas, "The whole town—men, women, and children—assembled, giving *vivas* to Tentación and *mueras* [death to] the new order; there were other manifestations of protest and much loud shouting from the crowd."[87] Despite stern warnings from Culpina, the *ingahuaseños* ignored the company's orders and went ahead with the fiesta. Subsequently, the company tried to blacklist the arrenderos who were involved and refused to renew their arriendos for the next year, but too many had participated to make this practicable. Despite his marked distaste for the arrenderos' public displays of drunkenness, a panicked Vargas had to plead with Culpina to reinstate those punished, for, as the Ingahuasi administrator argued, the hacienda stood to lose many of its most experienced workers.[88]

The Tentación affair was only the first symptom of worse problems to come at Ingahuasi. In August 1926, the estate's arrenderos went on strike. Although Vargas ordered the section chiefs (caporales) to muster some peons to work on the demesne lands, they came back empty-handed, saying that the men had left the hacienda to look for work elsewhere. A few weeks later, only nine Ingahuasi peons out of fifty showed up for a work project in Culpina. The SAGIC administrator threatened to expel the missing laborers from their rental plots. Vargas blamed the obstinacy of the peons on the former owners' lack of discipline: "Before, they [the peons] had been accustomed to do what they wanted; [the former owners] did not know how to manage them and conduct them down the path of goodness and the fulfillment of duty, and today they feel put upon because their mischief is prevented."[89]

Despite Vargas's threats, the strike continued, and by December, the harried Ingahuasi administrator was at his wit's end: "The peons' resistance to work is unbearable." Finally, Vargas imposed a fine of five Bs on any section chief and two Bs on any peon who did not report to work.[90] That things came to this pass is not surprising. Vargas's emphasis on labor discipline and disregard for traditional work rhythms alienated many arrenderos. Moreover, he and the company he represented failed to understand some of the implicit rules that governed hacienda relations. For example, Vargas violated the tradition of giving all the peons cash advances to help defray the costs of transporting company goods. To him, it made good business sense to provide advances to only the most reliable arrenderos. What he did not appreciate was that by refusing to act as *patrón* for all his workers—at least in the view of those laborers who were denied this benefit—he lost his right to their labor.[91]

In 1927, learning nothing, apparently, from the near-riot of 1926, the company ordered the hacienda chapel closed except for Christmas because of "the continuous fiestas [celebrated] almost daily and the damage that these occasioned to the company as well as the arrenderos themselves." The next year, the Ingahuasi peons presented the company manager at Culpina with a petition to reopen the chapel for Tentación. In this remarkable document, they stated that "as is known in this unhappy town, we customarily celebrate or at least hear Mass on the days of Tentación. . . . In the whole town it is customary to give free the days to celebrate the God Momo." Assuring the manager that "with this petition we are not remiss in obedience and respect that we owe your person," the hacienda workers agreed to preserve order "if someone or various persons were to be negligent in their good habits during these days." The request was followed by forty-six signatures, including those of nearly all the minor hacienda officials. The document illustrates many aspects of the arrenderos' resistance. The peons grounded their request on custom, on traditional social norms and obligations. They swore obedience to the manager, so they were clearly not questioning the social hierarchy that gave the landowner the right to order them about. Nevertheless, the impressive number of signatures and the workers' confidence in their ability to police themselves suggest a high level of solidarity in the hacienda labor force.[92]

Apparently the request was denied, for that year the arrenderos clandestinely built their own chapel in an out-of-the-way section of the property and had the priest from the neighboring town of Santa Elena perform weddings and the necessary religious rituals for the Tentación celebration. Vargas discovered the building after trying to locate the caporales, who had not answered a request to bring a number of peons for work. Vargas found a completely outfitted, though as yet roofless, chapel. He also found the "*caporales* and a large part of the *arrenderos*" drinking and celebrating.[93]

Although Vargas had the chapel torn down, SAGIC began to have second thoughts and sent the harried administrator on vacation during the Carnival season, implicitly allowing the fiesta to proceed. In 1929, the priest from Santa Elena opened the hacienda chapel without authorization from the company. When the general manager from Culpina personally attempted to close it again, the Ingahuasi peons rioted. The company learned its lesson; it quickly defused the situation by hiring its own priest and keeping the chapel open. SAGIC, which by this time was in the grips of the alcohol crash, remained conciliatory. In the middle of 1929, Rosendo Vargas quit his post as Ingahuasi administrator, permitting the company to come to a compromise with the hacienda's workers without losing face. During the Depression, when the company had to fall back more and more on the arrenderos in order to make a profit, the administrators were more or less obliged to keep the old fiestas to avoid any organized resistance that would further prejudice the company's income.[94]

Conclusion

All of Cinti was severely affected by the Great Depression, but the province had started on the road to economic decline well before that. The number of business contracts recorded in the Camargo notarial office had already fallen to only a few dozen a year by the late 1920's—in stark contrast to the 1880's and 1890's, when the town engaged the services of two notaries with hundreds of documents drawn up annually by each. Even merchants like Antonio Ayo, who because of their multiple business interests had been best able to weather the region's economic woes, were brought down. At his death in 1924, Ayo, who had been one of Camargo's wealthiest merchants at the turn of the century, only owned two houses in the town and some grazing lands in the high valleys, the whole worth only 11,600 Bs. The rest of his possessions, including his merchandise and a large vineyard in the Cinti Valley, had all been sold to cover his debts.[95] As the province became more impoverished, increasing numbers of smallholders and hacienda peons, especially from the south, were induced by *enganchadores*, labor contractors in the employ of the Argentine sugar estates, to leave their plots and emigrate. This trend alarmed local authorities and landowners alike, who feared that without an abundant supply of workers, the labor-intensive viticulture of the region would decay even more.[96]

Cinti province's economic woes arose not only in the decline of silver mining in the Potosí region, but also in the resultant changes in transport patterns, which effectively destroyed an elaborate subsystem of the commercial network that had survived, with some modifications, from the colonial period. The economic decline did not lead to noticeable changes in land-tenure patterns, but it did seriously affect the profitability of the large Cinti Valley landowners and caused most sugarcane producers in the hot subtropical valleys to switch to more marginal crops. Despite the increase in commercialization, labor arrangements based largely on traditional Andean modes prevailed throughout much of the province because landowners could not afford to risk worker resistance.

Only in the far northern and southern sectors of Cinti did landowners attempt to change labor relations significantly, and even there, they achieved limited success at best. In northern Cinti, landowner-miners tried to wrest more profits by demanding more work of their peons. As in Yamparaez, the peons resisted through violent revolts. In the south, where landowners tried to create large agroindustrial enterprises, the attempt to mechanize the processing phase of agricultural production inevitably altered labor relations. Even though SAGIC attempted to keep some reciprocal and redistributive aspects of traditional hacienda rule, the drastic change in work rhythms and the emphasis on labor discipline eventually undermined the foundation of traditional landlord-peon relations. The peons were very much aware of this problem and tried to reimpose traditional relations through labor strikes. This worked in the case of SAGIC, which was much more sensitive to labor relations than Fernando Mercy at Caraparí, whose lack of understanding of traditional Andean norms was so complete that he eventually paid for it with his life.

CHAPTER SIX

Azero Province

◼︎

Azero province had a quite different history from that of the other parts of Chuquisaca. It was a frontier area in which tribal Indians fought settlers from the highlands until well past the turn of the twentieth century. As the frontier advanced into Indian territory, colonists created huge estates that slowly but surely incorporated the newly conquered Indian tribes, especially the Chiriguanos, into the labor force. The only counterweight to this process of hacienda expansion were the Franciscan missions, which also flourished during this period. Moreover, unlike the rest of rural Chuquisaca, Azero was little affected by the collapse of the southern Bolivia mining economy. Its closest ties, by the last years of the nineteenth century, were with the rapidly growing Argentine economy. The province imported most of the goods it needed from Argentina, which in turn received Azero's cattle. The province was also a source of Indian labor for the northern Argentine sugarcane fields.

Azero's geographical and ecological conditions, too, are very different from those of the highland regions of Chuquisaca. The western part of the province consists of a series of steep mountain ranges, covered in jungle and cut by a number of deep north–south valleys. To the east, these Andean foothills taper off toward the Santa Cruz plains to give way to slightly more rounded but heavily forested hills. Because of its humidity and generally warm climate, this area is excellent for the cultivation of corn and other lowland crops. In the southeast, where the province extends in a boot shape, a series of rolling hills bifurcated by deep canyons running from east to west gradually give way to vast open spaces covered by thorny scrub forest. This region in turn yields to the dry and barren Chaco, barely adequate for small bands of hunters and gatherers, which extends into Paraguay.[1]

The indigenous culture and society in Azero were very unlike those of the Andean highlands. Although the Chiriguanos, the largest ethnic group in the province, had absorbed some of the ways of the highland Indians, they belonged to a different linguistic and cultural group and had no tradition either of a unified state or of sedentary farming. They were slash-and-burn corn cultivators who, as the fertility gave out in one area, periodically moved their villages elsewhere, leaving their old wattle-and-daub huts behind and building new ones. Villages remained relatively small and were ruled by a *tubicha*, a chief who headed a number of often related families. One of the chief's primary functions was to lead his men into war; this gave him prestige and maintained his right to rule over the village. Chieftainships were not strictly hereditary, since skill and leadership qualities determined which of the chief's descendants became the new tubicha.[2]

The Tobas and Tapietés who inhabited the hostile Chaco plains were primarily hunters and gatherers, though they also practiced some agriculture. Unlike the Chiriguanos, who moved on foot, the nomadic Tobas and Tapietés became adept horsemen and frequently raided other, more sedentary tribes. Political organization among these groups were even more fragmented than among the Chiriguanos. Each band moved from place to place within the territory and only infrequently made alliances that encompassed a significant proportion of the tribe. These groups had little, if any, of the earmarks of highland Andean civilization.[3]

Conquest and Colonization of the Chiriguanos

The conquest of Azero province took over three hundred years, and the subsequent colonization of the region went through various phases, determined by the tenacity of Indian resistance, changing economic opportunities, and government policies. The land-tenure system along the frontier evolved directly from the increasingly liberal land policies that various governments promoted to populate the area. Early legislators envisioned a region densely inhabited by yeoman farmers, but the result of the laws as they were put into effect was a province divided between a small number of landowners, who controlled vast tracts of land, and several Franciscan missions, which incorporated much of the Indian population in their relatively smaller holdings.

One reason for the creation of large estates during the late nineteenth and early twentieth centuries was the Indians' ability to prevent the effective Spanish conquest of this region during the colonial period. The Chiriguanos, of Tupí-Guaraní stock, from the Paraguay region, settled in the fertile Andean foothills only a short time before the Spaniards discovered and conquered the Inca empire. Coming in waves of warrior bands across the Chaco plains, the warlike Chiriguanos enslaved the much more numerous Arawak-speaking agriculturalists, the Chanés, who largely lost their ethnic identity.[4] By the 1560's, the westward-moving Chiriguanos threated the core of the Spanish empire, Potosí, raiding within twenty leagues of the mining center. In 1574, Viceroy Toledo decided to eliminate the Chiriguano nuisance and led a punitive expedition into the Chiriguano lands, or Chiriguanía, but the Indians' guerrilla tactics and the rough, densely forested terrain were so frustrating that Toledo, ill and discouraged, retreated after only a few skirmishes.[5]

After the failure of the *entrada,* Toledo changed his strategy. He provided generous land grants to Spaniards who were willing to settle the region and deal with the Chiriguano menace, and he established a series of fortified towns—Tomina in 1575, El Villar in 1582, San Juan de Rodas (also called La Laguna, today Padilla) in 1583, and Sauces in 1596.[6] (Of these, only Sauces, now Monteagudo, was in Azero; see Map 1). Many of these settlements relied on cattle raising. Along the steep foothills of the frontier, Spaniards cleared and planted fields adjacent to small fortress-haciendas that, according to one contemporary observer, "were made with stone foundations and thick walls out of tree [trunks], roofed with strong beams and terraced with battlements and holes, with harquebuses installed as defense against the Chiriguanos who regularly attack them."[7] Similar fortresses boxed in the Chiriguanos from Santa Cruz in the north and Tarija in the south.

The failure to subdue the Chiriguanos by military means gave way to an attempt at spiritual conquest. Beginning in the 1690's, Dominican and Augustinian friars, as well as Jesuits, began establishing missions along the fringes of Chiriguano-held lands. These gentler methods were equally unsuccessful. In 1727, a revolt involving all the Chiriguanía exploded under the leadership of Chief Aruma. The missions were put to the torch, and the Indians congregated there melted back into the lush subtropical forest. Another attempt to Christianize the Indians, this time led exclusively by the Jesuits, also ended in failure after a great revolt in 1735. Only in the second half of the eighteenth century did the newly established Franciscan monastery in Tarija, the Colegio de Propaganda Fide, have some success in introducing missions. By 1810, twenty different missions dotted the Chiriguano *cordillera*, with an Indian population of 23,936. But the work of the missionaries was again destroyed when the wars for independence wracked the countryside. In 1814, the patriot governor of Santa Cruz, Ignacio Warnes, expelled all Franciscan monks in the missions for having royalist sympathies. Although secular clergy were sent to maintain the establishments, the constant warfare, with Chiriguano bands taking an active part on both sides, completely destroyed the colonial missions.[8]

During the centuries of intermittent warfare, the Chiriguano frontier underwent a series of contractions and expansions, though the overall trend was toward limiting the extent of Indian territorial control. By the beginning of the seventeenth century, the Spaniards had finally contained the Chiriguanos in the highlands of Tomina and Cinti. During the next century, they colonized the fringes of the Chiriguanía. The intermittent massive rebellions during the course of the eighteenth century that hampered the efforts of the various orders to establish permanent missions also set back colonization. A revolt in 1799, for example, resulted in the loss of Spanish lands thirty-five leagues wide and fifty leagues long along the western border of the Chiriguanía, putting the frontier only fifteen leagues east of Padilla.[9]

The Indians took full advantage of the chaos of the independence period to extend their control far into Spanish-held lands. Land grants of the late 1820's and the 1830's show the limits of white settlement in Azero. Those colonists who managed to maintain their landholdings clustered primarily in the cantons of Sauces and Sapirangui and, to a lesser extent, in San Juan del Piray and Huacareta, all in the western part of the province. Various provisions in these early republican grants were designed to ensure that neither the human population nor the number of cattle diminished as a result of the awarding of vast extents of land to private individuals. A standard contract, such as in the case of the four square leagues (5,000 hectares) granted to Juan Agustín Terán in 1833 in Sauces and Sapirangui cantons, stipulated that the owner was prohibited from expelling any small farmers or ranchers (*piqueros*) who owned less than twenty-five head of cattle. In addition, Terán was obligated to stock the tract with at least 400 cattle of his own within a year.[10] These contracts suggest that the Azero economy continued to rely heavily on cattle raising, an activity the government under the presidency of Andrés de Santa Cruz was eager to encourage.

Despite these efforts early in republican history to encourage the colonization of the province, the white and mestizo settlers—the cristianos—did not control the resources to move beyond this rather restricted area. The virtual state of civil war during the early republican period and the government's inability to aid the frontiersmen had much to do with the settlers' failure to expand into Indian territory. Land grants virtually ceased after 1838, shortly before the fall of President Santa Cruz, as the country fell into a period of political chaos and economic stagnation. Until the 1860's, the Chiriguanos maintained the upper hand over the colonists. Frequent Indian attacks devastated many of the haciendas; serious raids that often threatened even the only town of note, Sauces (renamed Monteagudo after an independence hero early during the Republic), occurred in 1848, 1849, 1854, and 1857.[11]

Even without help from the government, the settlers refused to be totally dislodged from the fringes of the Chiriguanía; though the Indians made devastating raids, their fragmented political system, in which each village only recognized a loose allegiance to a prestigious regional chieftain, did not provide enough stability or discipline for long-term conquests. The various regional chiefs and even whole villages spent much of their time making war against one another instead of fighting the men and women from the highlands. Once the Indians had burned a few houses and made off with the captured cattle, women, and other plunder, the temporary alliances disintegrated. In the long run, this lack of cohesion made the Chiriguanos increasingly vulnerable to the penetration of outsiders, who were often able to play off one village against the other for their own purposes.

This weakness became fatal when the revival of the silver-mining economy increased the demand for cattle, finally providing an economic incentive to enlarge the cattle *estancias* beyond the western fringe of the province. From the 1850's on, the cristianos took the initiative and slowly began to infiltrate the virgin pastures within the Chiriguanía. Cattle herders, called *vaqueros*, from Tarija in the south and, to a lesser extent, from the Monteagudo-Sapirangui area, entered the fertile valleys of Taperi (Ingre) and Abatire, often with the aid of local Chiriguano groups allied with the whites. In 1865, other local Indian chiefs opposed to white colonization allied themselves with the largest Chiriguano group, located in Huacaya, and attacked the interlopers, but the settlers successfully repelled the assault and, to secure their positions, in 1866 built a small fort at a strategic point called Iguembe, in the Abatire Valley.[12]

Even the colonists' Indian allies soon protested the wholesale invasion of cattle into their territory, mainly because the vaqueros let the livestock roam in Indian territory, destroying the unfenced cornfields. Corn was the basis of the Chiriguanos' subsistence economy and important not only as an edible food crop but also as an ingredient in their culture; among other things, chicha, corn beer, was an essential component in rituals and festivals and the making of alliances between various communities. The destruction of the cornfields forced the Indians to retreat to more inaccessible areas, leaving the more fertile valley bottom lands, where most of the cattle grazed, to the settlers. Some colonists intentionally drove their cattle into the cornfields, hoping to hasten the Indians' eastward withdrawal toward the refuges of Huacaya and Cuevo. In the end, the livestock did what the sparse settler population could not do—as one Franciscan missionary commented, "Instead of being colonized by men, the frontier has been colonized by cows."[13]

A similar process took place along the Chaco border during the middle of the nineteenth century. Colonists from Tarija, using the same tactics Viceroy Toledo had used some 275 years earlier, established a series of fortress-towns from which they could raid the Chiriguano settlements and also guard the hinterland. At the same time, the Franciscan monastery in Tarija renewed its missionizing. The harassed Chiriguano groups immediately to the north of the encroaching *tarijeños* were receptive to the monks' proselytization, thinking that a mission would give them some protection against the careless destruction of their crops and the raiding parties that killed their warriors and abducted their women and children. Between 1845 and 1854, missions were established in the department of Tarija at Itau, Aguairenda, and Tarairi, and by 1869, the Franciscans had penetrated into Chuquisaca, to found a mission at Machareti. The mission, established only after a series of attacks on local Chiriguanos by unconverted Chiriguano bands and their allies, the Chaco-dwelling Toba Indians, eventually became the largest and most prosperous Franciscan establishment in southeastern Bolivia. In 1872, another mission was founded at Ti-

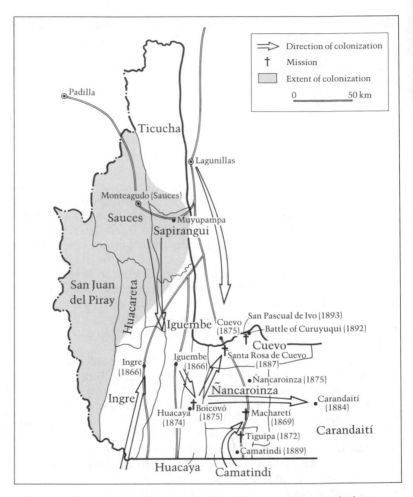

Map 6.   Colonization in Azero, 1825–1920. Dates are shown only for towns or missions founded after 1825; 1921 marks the date of the last land grant.

guipa, several miles south of Macharetí. With Tiguipa, the Franciscans—and the Tarija colonists—had finally consolidated their hold over the southern portion of the Chiriguanía (see Map 6).[14]

The progressive encirclement of the Chiriguano cordillera from the south and the west endangered the core area under the control of the Huacaya, Cuevo, and Ivo Indians. Moreover, by the early 1870's, the once-abundant grasses in the Ingre and Abatire valleys had begun to suffer from overgrazing, and, in search of virgin pasture, many of the cattle herds were driven into the area controlled by the *huacayeños*. In desperation, the Huacaya Chiriguanos secretly allied themselves with the chiefs of Cuevo and Ivo, and with some bands of Tobas, who by this time were also feeling the pressures of white colonization. Many Tobas had sought refuge in the mission of San Antonio along the Pilcomayo River. In 1874, the murder of three San Antonio Tobas at the hands of vaqueros who had caught them stealing livestock touched off a revolt. The Tobas left the mission en masse and, with the Chaco-dwelling Tapietés and the Huacaya, Ingre, and Abatire Chiriguanos, turned violently against the settlers.

After unsuccessfully laying siege to Macharetí, the hastily organized Indian raiding parties encircled the small fort at Iguembe, but were driven off by a volunteer army sent from Monteagudo. As news of the attacks spread, hacendados throughout the region called up their peons and, in some cases, their Indian allies, to put down the revolt. A few months later, government authorities launched a punitive expedition with the Monteagudo volunteers augmented by new recruits from Tarija. At Yuqui, the expeditionary members massacred 80 Chiriguano prisoners and seized their women and children for use as servants. Although a judicial hearing was held on the incident, no one was ever prosecuted.[15]

Before the last skirmishes, the national government in Sucre had authorized the Azero subprefect to grant every colonist who had helped quell the revolt one-half square league of land (1,250 hectares) in the area formerly controlled by the rebellious Indians. All qualifying colonists had to agree to live in the newly created canton of Huacaya for at least three years.[16] This was an attractive offer, and after 1874, many families from the overgrazed Abatire Valley moved with their cattle into the virgin pastures of the former Chiriguano stronghold. By 1878, Huacaya had over 200 settler families, while the population of Iguembe, whence many colonists had come, had dropped from over 1,000 inhabitants to 700. Thus, to a certain extent, a "hollow frontier" was created: the demands of the cattle frontier, with its rapid depletion of native grasses, forced the settlers to move ever-farther outward, leaving behind only a few colonists who actually settled the land.[17]

Apparently the Ingre area did not experience the same depopulation as the Abatire Valley. In 1877, the national legislature also proclaimed the Ingre area open for land grants to veterans of the 1874 war. In their haste to acquire grants, the settlers invaded the lands of Buricanambi, the *tubicha rubicha*, or regional chief, who had aided the whites in the mop-up operations in 1875. Thus, the hapless Ingre Chiriguanos, erstwhile allies of the settlers, were forced to share the fate of their Huacaya enemies.[18]

Even this new frontier proved unstable, however. Although many settlers moved to Huacaya, few actually completed the long and expensive process that was required to claim their tract. For both the Ingre and Huacaya areas, only thirty land grants were distributed for service in the 1874 war. Moreover, after the obligatory three years' residence, many grantees sold their plots to a small number of other, often absentee, landowners. The most notable among these absentee owners was Octavio Padilla, a merchant and important landowner in the neighboring province of Cordillera in Santa Cruz. Padilla himself had received one concession in Huacaya, and in the 1880's, he bought six more, or one-fifth of the total, to become the largest landowner in the canton.[19] Besides reducing the number of landowners, the sale of land grants of course negated the intent of the law, which was to settle a large number of whites in the rebellious areas.

The sale of land grants in Huacaya soon after the legal time limit may have been induced by severe overgrazing. The newly conquered territories were overrun by the ever-expanding cattle herds, but the sandy soils of that area gave out even faster than those of the Abatire Valley. In 1879, only a few years after the uprising, one observer drew a sad picture of the destruction:

It is impossible to describe the lushness of the pastures of Itau, Abatiri, and Huakaya, where gigantic grasses actually covered a horse, before the cowherds brought in their droves. And today, what remains of such richness in plant life? Nothing, . . . barren fields, clean as the courtyard of the University, sand dunes as sterile as the desert of Calama, gullies as deep as those in Quirpinchaca, where the cattle barely have enough food to live on, let alone have the necessary [nourishment] to multiply or fatten. Itao and Abatiri lasted fourteen years, Huakaya four; and now [these areas] are useless for anything but to raise goats.[20]

The land further decreased in value as many of the local Chiriguanos, after the campaign of terror waged by the settlers following the siege of Iguembe, retreated to the Cuevo-Ivo area or into the Chaco, to join their Toba allies. Thus, landowners were left with vast extents of land without sufficient manpower to work it. After 1875, when the violence subsided, many of the huacayeños attached themselves to the Macharetí mission. To attract the refugees back to the Huacaya area, the Potosí Franciscans negotiated a pardon for all Indians who had taken part in the rebellion. They settled those who returned in a new mission, Boicovo, located a few miles from Huacaya, for which the national government allotted 10,000 hectares.[21]

The colonists' vigorous campaign in the aftermath of the 1874 uprising also weakened resistance among the former allies of Huacaya. Settlers from Lagunillas, capital of Cordillera province, infiltrated from the north into the region controlled by the Chiriguanos of Cuevo and Ivo and established the tiny forts of Sucre and Bolívar close to the still independent Indian settlements. Cristianos from Azero also entered the area. The penetration of colonists from both Azero and Cordillera led to a border dispute in the Cuevo area between Chuquisaca and Santa Cruz. Finally, the government sent surveyors to delineate departmental boundaries. The surveying crew precipitated another Indian massacre in 1877. After famine-stricken Chiriguanos rebuffed the surveyors for requisitioning corn in the fertile Murucuyati area near Cuevo, Pedro Zárate, a large Ingre landowner and the delegate from Azero who had been nominated by the government to distribute conquered lands, attacked the Indians' village at night. All the men were slaughtered, and the women and children were seized; Zárate was not jailed, but the Santa Cruz press accused him of having engineered the massacre to bring the Chiriguano families into his service.[22]

This incident only served to increase the pressure on the Cuevo Indians, one of the last large groups of free Chiriguanos remaining in Azero. Although an 1880 government commission had assured the tribes in the area that their land would remain inviolable, the local vecinos sent their cattle into the Indians' cornfields to destroy their means of livelihood. Attempting to counter this strategy, the *cueveños* built fences around their holdings, but this proved unavailing. Finally, unable to continue their resistance, the cueveños asked the Franciscans of Potosí to establish a mission in their settlement. After much opposition from local colonists, most notably the merchant and landowner Octavio Padilla, the missionaries in 1887 converted the Chiriguano village into a mission. Aniceto Arce, who was to be elected president of Bolivia the following year, donated one of his own land grants in the area to the cause.[23]

Not all the factions among the remaining independent Indians were willing to give up their way of life and surrender to the *caray*, as the natives called the settlers. In 1891, a young Chiriguano, Apiaguaiqui, a survivor of the Murucuyati massacre and apprentice to one of the most respected shamans, settled near Ivo, the last center of Indian resistance. He let it be known that he was a *tumpa*, or man-god, who would drive away the whites and restore the Indians to their land. Tumpas had appeared from time to time since the eighteenth century and had sparked great revolts that often succeeded in at least temporarily freeing much of the Chiriguanía from intruders.[24]

Apiaguaiqui's revolt of 1892, like the other rebellions of the late nineteenth century, was a failure. It had a few weeks of triumph, but Chiriguano society, traditionally separated among many independent factions, was fatally divided; and in the end the mission Indians, standing with the colonists against their brethren in the last great battle at Curuyuqui, beat the rebels decisively.[25] The Franciscans founded another mission in Ivo. The nearly 2,000 Indian prisoners were parceled out among the victors. The defeat finally broke the resistance of the Chiriguanos; although they tried to revolt again in 1893, government authorities soon discovered their movement and suppressed it before it could spread.[26]

The final military defeat of the Chiriguanos confirmed the division of the Andean foothills into large properties owned by the few. By the 1890's, virtually all lands in the Chiriguanía had been given away, and the natives divided among the haciendas or the missions. In the meantime, colonists began to move into the fringes of the Chaco. The first white settlement in the Chuquisaca Chaco, Ñancaroinza, was founded in 1875 by the Castillo brothers who, in return for helping establish the Macharetí mission, had received land grants to the north of the mission. The Chiriguanos who lived there at first fled to the Cuevo-Ivo area or moved to Macharetí. Many had drifted back to their place of birth by the late 1870's, only to leave again when ethnic tensions rose after the Murucuyati massacre. In 1887, Ñancaroinza contained approximately 100 souls, of whom 70 were Indians; that number remained constant for the next several decades.[27]

The area to the southeast of Macharetí was colonized somewhat later. Settlers moved to Camatindi and Carandaití after the pastures of Huacaya gave out. The town of Camatindi was founded in 1889; by 1894, it had 700 cristiano inhabitants.[28] Carandaití, located by a pond that was a traditional meeting place for Tobas and

Chiriguanos, was settled at about the same time. In 1880, the national government gave Manuel Mariano Gómez permission to establish forts in the Chaco area, at Naguapoa and Taringuite. Each soldier-settler manning the forts was given a square league of territory in the rather desolate and arid surrounding land. Construction of the forts did not commence until 1884; a member of the government-sponsored exploratory expedition described one two years later as "truthfully not meriting the name of fort, [merely] a poorly constructed mass of branches."[29] The only fortress that could be called such was located at Naguapoa, built by the vecinos of Ñancaroinza and commanded by the Castillos.[30]

Although some colonists arrived in Carandaití in the 1880's, only after the 1892 rebellion did a large number of settlers push into the Chaco toward the town. Now the brunt of the attacks shifted from the Chiriguanos to the settlers' erstwhile allies, the Tobas and the Tapietés. Dominating these nomadic horsemen proved even more difficult than dominating the Chiriguanos had been; harnessing their labor proved virtually impossible. The colonization policy changed as the settlers confronted these hunter-gatherers who, according to local landowners, were too intractable to be drawn into the labor system. In the late 1890's, the Bolivian state gave up the policy of establishing missions to subdue the Indians and set out instead to secure the area by enticing soldiers to build and garrison a series of forts in return for grants of land. This new policy of course implied that those Chaco Indians who were unwilling to submit would either be ruthlessly exterminated or be driven farther into the desert.

In 1896, the prefect of Chuquisaca, Fernando Quiroga, boasted of the success of the new policy, summarizing succinctly the change in attitude toward the Indians along the frontier:

At present, relative tranquility can be guaranteed to new settlers, owing to the military colonies and forts founded by Gómez. [These settlers] little by little are removing to a distance the settlements of the unconquered savage hordes, making for effective and evident national sovereignty in those faraway regions, so often disputed by the neighboring republics of Paraguay and Argentina. This has been accomplished at no greater cost to the state than the small expense of rifle ammunition and the awarding of public land to the colonists and their leader. . . . The charitable and evangelical propaganda of the Reverend Fathers of Propaganda Fide, though its results are certain, is and must be slow. Their work, in which they limit themselves to the conversion of infidels and to their education by peaceful means of persuasion, cannot guarantee the life and the property of the colonizers against the attacks of the savages.[31]

The militarization of the colonization process was reflected in the behavior of both the settlers and the Chaco Indians. The same year the prefect made the above comment, news arrived in Monteagudo that a Toba had been shot and killed while stealing corn. The subprefect sent a letter to Gómez ordering him to bring in the killer, but both the leader of the colony and the local authorities refused to obey the directive. Gómez justified the shooting on the grounds that the Tobas were the "declared enemies of Christianity" and implied that killing was the correct policy.[32] In the face of this implacable hostility, many of the Chaco Indians moved farther into the uncharted areas, and when discovered by whites, burned their villages and quickly moved on to build new ones elsewhere. This happened, for example, when the Swedish adventurer and anthropologist Erland Nordenskiöld visited a Tapieté village in the early twentieth century.[33]

The change in colonization policy was also reflected in a series of new land-grant laws, elaborated in the 1880's and 1890's. Beginning in 1886, all other prefectures had to follow the regulations established in 1884 for Santa Cruz and Beni, which standardized the size of land grants and established a fee of 100 Bs for a lot of one square league, or 2,500 hectares. Also in 1886, an Office of Public Lands and Colonies was created that supervised the land-grant process.

These laws, which the legislature somewhat altered and refined in subsequent decades, fundamentally changed the rationale behind the granting of public lands. Previously, land grants had been given only as a reward for specific service to the nation, in Azero most conspicuously for combating the 1874 uprising. After the 1880's, anybody who paid a fee, had the land surveyed, and promised to settle on the tract was able to obtain public lands. But again, the lengthy as well as costly paperwork prevented most would-be settlers from gaining possession of their plots; in general, only local elites with connections in the departmental capital, where the claim had to be processed, were able to complete the process successfully.

In putting up public lands for sale, the government simply ignored the ownership rights of resident Indians, despite the pious phrases buried in the laws purporting to give them some modicum of protection. Heretofore, the grantees in their petitions had maintained a legal fiction that, ironically, described the resident Indians as the usurpers of state lands—the Sapirangui resident Diego Miranda in his 1877 request for a half-square-league tract in Cuevo asserted that he was a member of the national expeditionary force that "opened the first artery in the territorial zone [Cuevo] occupied usurpatively by the savage hordes."[34] After 1894, when claims that had been started in the late 1880's finally entered the registers of the Notaría de Hacienda y Minas in Sucre, no such justifications were included. The documents merely subsumed as part of the colonists' property any Indian villages that fell within the limits of their grants. A case in point is that of Juan Rodas, who in 1902 in his request for a tract in Ticucha described it quite matter-of-factly as containing "mountains and pasture lands, nitrous waters and *chupaderas* [water holes?] appropriate for cattle raising, and a small village of Guirapire's [a Chiriguano chief] Indians." The maps of the grants, standard after 1897, often had marked on them little houses identified as Indian villages or demarcated fields cultivated by the Chiriguanos. In one exceptional case in Camatindi, the map showed a ranchería of Tobas with at least ten huts.[35] It had been common since colonial times to take possession of lands that included Indian villages and in that way acquire the necessary labor force to work the new estates, but the blatant disregard of Indian land rights even in the official land-grant records only began in the late 1880's, when the government began to sell the "vacant lands."

The contradictions of this policy were made clear when the Indians themselves had to apply for land grants to preserve their own land. Only one case reached the Sucre Notaría de Hacienda y Minas: the Chiriguanos of the Caraparirenda Valley in Sapirangui, long-standing allies of the settlers, solicited and in 1908 received a tract of two square leagues encompassing eleven different groups in six villages. The Indians of Caraparirenda had a long history of turning to national authorities to prevent encroachment from outsiders. In 1859, just as the cristianos were regaining the initiative, Manuel Bravo, the subprefect of Tomina and Azero (which at that time were one province), ordered settlers from neighboring Vallegrande in Santa Cruz out of Caraparirenda and obtained a government decree that confirmed the Indians' property rights. Two years later the *tubicha rubicha* lodged a complaint against various colonists in the Monteagudo courts, accusing them of attempting to take over the valley. In 1894, the Indians engaged José Orias, a Monteagudo lawyer and member of an extremely influential local family, to represent them in Sucre. In 1915, José's brother, Alejandro, received a land grant, which was supposedly adjacent to the Caraparirenda Indians' property. Alejandro, however, laid claim to the six villages where the Indian allies lived, basing his claim on the rights of the previous, rejected claimant. Despite his legal maneuvering, the evidence suggests that he was unsuccessful in his attempt to assert control over the Indians.[36]

As in 1874, the regulations adopted after 1886 did not prevent the concentration of frontier land in a few hands. The 1905 law, which superseded all previous legislation, systematized the piecemeal efforts at formulating a new public-lands policy. This law gave any citizen or foreigner the right to claim up to 20,000 hectares of public lands, provided that the claimant paid ten centavos per hectare (except for rubber tree forests, for which one Bs was to be paid). It also required a density of one settler family for each 1,000 hectares of a tract. Two surveyors, one under the employ of the claimant and the other named by the government, were to locate and demarcate each lot, and any request for more than 20,000 hectares had to be approved by the legislature, a lengthy and costly process. Like the previous ordinances, the land law was modeled after the mining code, which awarded claims on a first-come, first-serve basis without considering a person's financial or technical ability to carry out the colonization as prescribed.[37]

Since wealthy and influential people easily sidestepped the regulations, the ideal—the creation of well-populated areas guarding the nation's frontiers against the ambitions of neighboring countries as well as the depredations of unconquered tribes—was not realized. Especially along the Chaco frontier, where the establishment of the privately owned military colonies had raised the government's hopes, loopholes in the law permitted the consolidation of vast tracts of land into huge cattle ranches under single ownership. Far from being settled by many colonists, the hostile Chaco environment lost most of its original military colonists; by the early twentieth century, many of the original settlers had sold their land to large cattle merchants and had either gone back west or taken jobs as cowhands. In this way a few owners brought under their control enormous expanses of land, despite the legal limit set in the 1905 law. Moisés del Castillo, a merchant from the Ñancaroinza family, accumulated eight land grants in the cantons of Ñancaroinza and Camatindi totaling 22,500 hectares. But this effort paled in comparison with the landholdings amassed by the merchant Pancrasio Sánchez, of Carandaití, and his wife, María

Balderrama, who between them owned seventeen square leagues, or 42,500 hectares, in Camatindi and Carandaití. The marriage seems to have been a strategic match: María Balderrama was the widow of the intrepid Manuel Mariano Gómez, who died in 1904, and Sánchez was the biggest cattle merchant in Azero. Together they systematically bought out many of the old settlers of the military colony and turned the land to cattle.[38]

In short, as the nineteenth century wore on, land grants and their stipulations became more and more liberal. Although the Santa Cruz government in the early republican era had permitted the alienation of large areas, provisions had been made for smaller holders as well. The growth of the cattle-ranching industry, however, encouraged an extensive rather than an intensive use of land, thereby reducing the number of possible residents. During the next phase, beginning in the 1860's, lands were given out for the grantees' exclusive use as a reward for the fight against the Chiriguanos. This coincided with the penetration of the colonists deep into the Chiriguanía, spurred by the demand for cattle in the revived silver-mining sector. Many Chiriguanos became agricultural laborers on the new haciendas. The mission system, too, flourished because of the pressures exerted by the settlers. Many Indians, at risk of losing everything to the settlers, preferred to have missions established on their ancestral grounds. In this way, they could preserve at least a degree of independence and keep some control over their lands.[39]

By the late nineteenth century, a process of land consolidation firmly established the region's current land-tenure pattern. As the frontier moved west and the settled land was exhausted, landowners bought up the old grants to create huge estates, while new legislation permitting the purchase of public lands brought equally enormous cattle ranches to the arid Chaco region. The 1905 law, intended as a reform measure, did not change the situation.

Indeed, not many years later, the government became increasingly alarmed at the reports of various ministers of colonization that the new legislation was only encouraging speculation and the formation of huge, unproductive latifundios. In 1915, the Montes regime declared a moratorium on all new grants, but by then very little productive land, at least in Azero, remained in the public domain. Since beyond the settlement of Carandaití, the Chaco turned into a vast desert unsuitable for even the hardiest cattle, the moratorium had little real effect.[40] The next phase of colonization, this time in the far reaches of the desert and under the control of the

Bolivian army, came in the late 1920's and early 1930's, and pre-cipitated the ruinous Chaco War with Paraguay.

Cattle and Commercial Circuits in Azero

The expansion of huge cattle estancias in Azero was intimately related to the decline of the highland silver-mining economy. Although the demand for beef in the mining towns provided the first stimulus for the colonization of the province, it was the Argentine market that led to the explosive growth of the cattle industry after the turn of the century. After the mining market shrank, Azero ranchers soon saw that driving their herds southward was far easier than sending them on the long trek over the eastern Andes, and what is more, that their half-wild cattle fetched much higher prices there. In short, the growth of the cattle herds on the virgin pastures of the western Chaco after the turn of the century was related more to the growth of the Argentine economy than to the decline and stagnation of the southern Bolivian highland economy.

In fact, the Azero region, like much of southeastern Bolivia, now became so closely tied to the flourishing Argentine economy that an alarmed minister of colonization could write in 1927:

At present, the provinces of Cordillera, Azero, and Chaco have no commerce except with Argentina. They export the cattle they raise, overcoming a huge number of fiscal obstacles from the Bolivian as well as the Argentine [side]. Trade between these rich and extensive provinces and Tarija, Sucre, and Potosí is virtually nil. Furthermore, the consumer demands of the Chaco . . . are met principally from Formosa, Jujuy, and Salta. The Chaco, a Bolivian region politically, is a foreign dependency in its commerce and economy.[41]

This situation, in which the largest export of the region to the country to the south was cattle, was a dramatic change in itself, for from 1890 to 1896, cattle imports to Bolivia from Argentina had still been high, reaching at their peak more than 17,000 head in 1895. The silver-mining bust all but brought an end to this trade in the first two decades of the twentieth century. These twenty-odd years correspond to the Bolivian Chaco cattle boom. Thereafter, Argentine imports increased again, but the number of animals never reached previous levels.

Unfortunately, documentation on cattle exports to Argentina is sparse and unreliable because of large-scale smuggling. On the Bolivian side, cattle merchants had to pay five to six times more in taxes on cattle bound for Argentina than on those destined for the domestic market. This gave traders great incentive to avoid customs agents and suggests why official counts were consistently low. Frontier conditions and the small number of government authorities made smuggling along the Chaco border an easy business, and the discrepancy between Argentine and Bolivian figures is indicative of the extent to which it was carried on. Estimates of actual trade, including illegal imports, by contemporary observers were much higher than the official statistics. For example, in 1918 the prefect Jorge Calvo, later to be associated with SAGIC in Cinti, said that Azero province alone had sold 22,000 head of cattle to its southern neighbor; Argentine official statistics for the same year noted the importation of only 5,811 from all of Bolivia. Another knowledgeable observer, Manuel Mendieta S., said that during the best year, 1921, the province exported 25,000 head of cattle to Argentina; for that year, Argentine trade statistics noted only 223 Bolivian cattle entering the country. Bolivian customs agents did not do much better; they found only 1,062 head crossing the border into Argentina in 1921. If these unofficial estimates by Calvo and Mendieta are closer to the true figures (which is likely), then both the Bolivian and the Argentine statistics are woefully inaccurate.[42]

Of the total number of cattle exported from Bolivia to Argentina, Chuquisaca, that is, Azero, contributed about one-quarter (assuming that official statistics can be used to determine roughly the relative proportions of cattle exports). In 1918, Azero province contributed 3,384 head, Santa Cruz (from Cordillera province adjacent to Azero) 7,163, and Tarija 3,967. The figures for Santa Cruz are probably the most accurate, since the cattle drivers had to pass many checkpoints before reaching the border. The cattle from Azero and Tarija were probably underreported because there were not many checkpoints in the prime cattle-breeding areas along the Chaco. Within Azero province itself, practically all the cantons exported cattle, though to varying degrees. According to the same statistics (see Table 11), Carandaití, at the limits of settlement in the Chaco, contributed 1,482 head. This number was probably low for a canton located in the largely uncontrolled frontier area. Even so, its dominance was unmistakable; no other canton sold more than 500 animals to Argentina.[43]

The export of cattle was part of a new and rather complicated commercial circuit that arose in the early twentieth century after the development of the railways linking Bolivia, Argentina, and

TABLE 11

Azero Cattle Exports to Argentina by Place of Production, 1918

(N = 3,384)

Place	Head of cattle	Place	Head of cattle
Carandaití	1,482	Iguembe	190
Ingre	499	Chimba[a]	111
Huacaya	474	Camatindi	86
Nancaroinza	265	Taperi, Muyu-	
Monteagudo	204	pampa, S. Miguel	39

SOURCE: Dirección General de Aduanas, Sección de Estadística Comercial, *Comercio especial de Bolivia, año 1918* (La Paz, 1919), p. 57.
[a] Location unknown.

Chile. According to the director of Bolivian customs, in 1918 the Chaco cattle exported to Argentina were not consumed there but fattened in Salta province and subsequently resold in the nitrate-mine area of northern Chile. Argentine railway spurs into the Chaco made it easier—as well as less expensive and less time consuming—to reach Chile by way of Argentina than crossing the Andes in southern Bolivia, at one of the range's widest and most inaccessible points.[44] Import-export statistics of the respective countries do not reflect this traffic, however, because Chilean officials considered the fattened Bolivian cattle to be of Argentine extraction.

For the Bolivian cattlemen, the trade was undoubtedly profitable. Although reliable internal trade figures are even more difficult to find than reliable export statistics, despite the proliferation, then as now, of internal customs checkpoints, there is little question that during the first decades of the twentieth century, the Azero region sent more cattle to Argentina than to the highlands. According to one authority, in 1926 and 1927 only 7,500 animals a year were sold in the highlands, as opposed to 12,000 driven to the Argentine border. Municipal tax records show that between 5,918 and 5,598 animals were consumed in Sucre during those two years; the rest of the 7,500 were taken mostly to Potosí.[45]

Commerce with Argentina and the highlands led to the development of new trade routes. As colonization pushed the frontier and the cattle herds eastward, the main trail between Santa Cruz and Argentina shifted in the same direction. Iguembe and to a lesser extent Ingre became the transit points for this commerce.[46] Founded only in the 1860's, both towns prospered and grew apace. By 1900, for example, Iguembe had 716 inhabitants, almost one-fifth of the total cantonal population.[47]

Merchants in these towns put up large warehouses to store their goods for later distribution, especially for the annual fairs held in Monteagudo, Iguembe, and Muyupampa, which until the early twentieth century were the principal showcases for goods from Santa Cruz, the highlands, and Argentina. The annual fair in Monteagudo, held in August, was the largest and best known of the regional markets. There, merchants from the trading houses of Tarija hawked the goods they imported from Buenos Aires. Coca traders from Tarata and Cochabamba converged on the provincial capital; so did dealers from Santa Cruz selling sugar and brandy, and Argentine mule traders from Santiago del Estero and Catamarca.[48]

As the old commercial circuits created by the silver boom disintegrated, the importance of the Azero fairs diminished. By 1928, an observer complained: "What has happened to the fairs of Monteagudo, Muyupampa, and Iguembe? They are no more than shadows [of themselves]. Today neither the Argentines nor the Cochabambinos come, and the few merchants [who do come] stay for weeks and weeks, selling the articles they have with difficulty, and mostly on credit."[49]

The growth of the cattle trade to Argentina had much to do with the decline of the Azero markets. The old fairs, located in the Andean foothills, were too far out of the way for the cattle traders who bought animals in the Chaco and then herded them directly across the border. After the fringes of the Chaco had been made reasonably safe by the advance of colonization, the new trade route from Santa Cruz to Argentina ran through the mission of Macharetí, located in the prime cattle-raising area. The shift in trade patterns can be seen in new arrangements between traders and the region's cattle barons. For example, Eliodoro Oyos, a merchant from Cuevo, put up 10,000 Bs in 1916 with which a landowner in Ñancaroinza, Juan Manuel Ordóñez, was to buy cattle in the area and, in two trips in the following three months, sell them in Argentina.[50] Such agreements completely sidestepped the former trading centers and signaled the decline of the Azero fairs.

Monteagudo, however, remained the distribution point for commerce between the highlands and lowland Bolivia. As the cattle frontier advanced, the areas behind it, such as the cantons of Monteagudo and Sapirangui, turned to corn, the Indians' traditional subsistence crop. Corn was also found to be an excellent fodder for hogs, and in the early part of the twentieth century, a small but significant hog-breeding industry developed that strengthened commercial ties between the highlands—Sucre and beyond—and Azero. In the late 1920's, some 9,500 hogs were exported to the highlands every year.[51] Livestock merchants from the highlands, especially from the town of Yamparaez, descended to "the frontier" to buy cattle and hogs, which they then sold in Tarabuco, Sucre, or Potosí.[52] Many enterprising merchants in Monteagudo also owned stores in Padilla, the capital of neighboring Tomina province. They would buy ají, potatoes, and other highland products in Padilla and market them in Monteagudo and farther east.[53]

Chiriguano Migration to Argentina

Southeastern Bolivia was also tied increasingly to Argentina as an important source of Indian labor, specifically for the sugarcane plantations of the northern Argentine province of Jujuy. Large-scale out-migration began in the late nineteenth century. What proportion of Bolivia's Indian population left is uncertain. In the absence of reliable migration statistics, one must ascribe a good share of the overall diminution of the Indian population to disease. In any event, among the Chiriguanos, the region's largest Indian ethnic group, there was a substantial decline—from about 46,000 in 1886, at the beginning of the movement, to only 26,000 in 1912. Nevertheless, the Chiriguanos still constituted over one-third of the total population of southeastern Bolivia, which of course included Azero, one of their main centers of settlement.[54]

The Chiriguanos may have begun migrating to Argentina to avoid further persecution by white settlers after the massacres of 1877 and 1892. The Franciscan missionaries encouraged the migration at first, by sending the Indians from their mission lands to Argentina during the slack season to earn money to buy clothing and other necessary goods and, as the prefect of the missions, Romualdo Dambrogi, said, to "combat idleness and extirpate [their] laziness."[55] As could be expected, the vecinos and the local authorities quickly protested sending part of the mission population to work in a foreign country when workers in the province were hard to come by.

Once the migration commenced, however, local authorities, including the missionaries, who quickly reversed their position on this matter, were unable to stop it. Many Chiriguanos living in independent villages also joined the exodus. According to observers, local climatic conditions had something to do with how many Indians left the area each year. In times of droughts, which were frequent but fairly localized, whole villages might leave—following the Chiriguanos' traditional practice of migrating to a neighboring, allied village when their crops failed. Since this was no longer possible after white settlers incorporated Indian settlements into their haciendas and forced any resident Chiriguanos to work for them, the Indians' only alternative to starving or working on frontier haciendas was to leave the country. The breakdown of the traditional system ensuring the survival of the Chiriguano tribes thus contributed to the exodus of Indians. The great drought of 1924–25, which affected most of southeastern Bolivia, probably would have strained even the old system's ability to cope. During those two years, both missionaries and local authorities lamented the virtual depopulation of the region.[56]

World economic conditions also affected migration, since the highly commercialized sugarcane plantations of Jujuy were extremely sensitive to fluctuations in the world's money and sugar markets. In 1916, as the World War intensified and a financial panic swept South America, the sugar *ingenios* suspended work and drastically cut salaries. For a time, the exodus of Indians slackened considerably, much to the relief of the Bolivian government, but the war soon stimulated Argentine sugar production, and the Indians began heading south in ever-increasing numbers.[57]

The Chiriguanos and members of other tribes in the Chaco had long since become essential to the northern Argentine sugar industry. This was especially the case in the valley of Ledezma, in Jujuy, where one observer remarked in 1904: "The Chiriguano is irreplaceable in the shovel work and in tilling, just as the Mataco [another Chaco tribe] is in the cutting and the axe [work]. The *ingenio* is his creation; do away with the Indian, and . . . this nascent civilization would die for lack of workers to keep it going."[58]

At first, migration was only seasonal; the Indians descended into Argentina during harvest time led by their chiefs. At the plantation, the captain dealt with the landowner and received a monthly bonus for each adult male worker under his control beyond whatever wages he himself might earn. Women also came with the Indian bands, though they generally did not work in the fields but did the family cooking and built the workers' huts made of sugarcane tops and leaves.[59] By the beginning of the twentieth century, many Chiriguanos remained in Argentina year round, working during the off-season on the many maintenance jobs required on the estates. For example, in 1903 the largest ingenio employing Indians, Hacienda Esperanza in the Ledezma Valley, permanently employed 800 to 1,000 local Indians and 400 Chiriguanos; during harvest time, the work force increased to between 2,000 and 2,500.[60]

Bolivians as well as Argentines worked as enganchadores, or labor contractors, enticing the Indians to leave their homes with the promise of high pay and gifts of firearms and other useful items. As could be expected, Azero landowners reviled these men, and provincial authorities threatened them with fines and jail terms. Nevertheless, the trade in Indians was lucrative, and all efforts to prohibit *enganches* went to naught. Even the *tubicha rubicha* of Macharetí, Mandeponai, and his sons were implicated by government authorities in recruiting Indians for the Argentines.[61]

The missionaries had good reason to regret their decision to send their charges to Argentina. Not only did the constant migration diminish the mission population, but those Indians who returned had often acquired, along with their new clothes and new tools, some unsavory habits. As one Franciscan complained:

[In Argentina] they live a life that is much too free; they drink liquor like water, and they get used to drunkenness. The first thing they buy is a big knife, and they learn to use it like the gauchos. They fight and are wounded or even killed, and when they return to the mission, they only have some black clothing, something or nothing for their wife, whom they give a big beating to at the first occasion for little or no reason, and afterward, with the first drink, they molest other people and disturb the public order, and always or almost always one has to lament the spilling of blood.[62]

As the labor shortage in Azero became acute in the twentieth century, local landowners protested more vigorously and pressured their allies in the national government to stem the flow of Chiriguanos across the border. In 1910, the legislature responded by passing a law making it extremely difficult for enganchadores to take laborers legally out of the country. This measure only helped for a short time. In 1912, the minister of colonization was able to report a decrease in the number of migrants, but the exodus of Chiriguanos into Argentina quickly returned to its former high level.[63]

With this legislative failure, the government sent a commission headed by a general named Villegas to the region to study the problem. Villegas was unable to come up with any new solutions; he merely suggested that the Indians be contained by force, clearly an impossible proposition in the poorly controlled frontier region. Villegas's study was included in the 1915 annual report of the minister of colonization, which gave a scathing assessment of the utility of the missions, a sentiment echoed by Villegas. In the report, the minister, Néstor Gutiérrez, an anticlerical Liberal, asserted that the missions were not fulfilling their intended function, which was "to prepare nomadic elements for the civilized life," but were merely educating certain Indian families who had been conquered many years ago. He recommended that the missions behind the frontier—which as he defined it would probably have included Azero—be secularized.[64]

The Villegas and Gutiérrez reports indicate a new turn of government policy. Now that the native populations of the region had been largely subdued, conquest was no longer important; rather, an effort should be made to prevent the indigenous peoples from leaving the country and further depleting the labor pool in the frontier regions. The Franciscans soon mounted a campaign to counter the proposed changes. Using their considerable political influence in La Paz, the missionaries were able to halt the secularization of their establishments. Three of those in Santa Cruz had already fallen to anti-mission sentiments, but after the Liberals were thrown out of power in 1920, the government no longer threatened secularization, and the missions, for their part, began to work toward the same goal of stopping the migration of laborers. Now, in addition to civilizing savages, one of the missions' fundamental duties became "to contain the emigration of the Chiriguano Indians to the Argentine Republic."[65]

There is little question that the Indians, in desperate need of employment, were easy victims of exploitation. As early as 1906, the Bolivian Congress enacted a law permitting labor contractors to recruit 5 percent of the adult male mission population for work in the rubber regions in northeastern Bolivia. The missionaries objected strenuously to the measure, pointing out that it led to an even greater depopulation of the mission. The enganchadores were supposed to leave a 500 Bs deposit for each Indian recruit to ensure his return, but the Franciscans complained that when they tried to collect the deposits, the enganchadores either tried to swindle them or took the workers by armed force. Once the Indians were in the hands of the contractors, they became slaves for life through debt peonage and never returned. The protests of the missionaries were so convincing that the law was abolished in 1910.[66] Other Chiriguanos, living in independent villages, still continued to be enticed to the rubber regions, however. Once having signed a contract, they were escorted north by armed men, never to be seen again. Myths to explain their failure to return sprang up among the Indians; according to one, there was a giant in the north who ate everyone who entered the area. Fear of the rubber regions was especially strong in the department of Santa Cruz, where recruitment was intense.[67]

By the 1920's, government officials realized that the only way to keep the Indians in Azero was to offer them well-remunerated work. When, in 1926, a poor harvest depopulated the missions controlled by the Tarija Franciscans, it was hoped that Standard Oil, which was about to start drilling in the region, would provide enough high-paying jobs to keep at least some of the Indians from leaving. The same hopes were echoed in 1927, but the oil company for reasons of its own preferred to bring in workers from Argentina. These men often presented severe disciplinary problems for local authorities. A number of times, officials accused knife-wielding Standard Oil workers of beating and killing the Indians and raping the Chiriguano women. These conditions may in fact have increased rather than prevented out-migration.[68]

The Hacienda Labor Regime

By putting their hopes in a foreign oil company to alleviate the migration problem, officials obliquely acknowledged one of the fundamental reasons why the Chiriguanos left for Argentina: poor labor conditions and extremely low wages on the Azero haciendas. One missionary frankly stated that the Indians went to the sugar-cane fields not so much to earn extra money as to escape the almost slavelike existence they were forced to lead on the Bolivian estates.[69] Manuel O. Jofre, sent by the government to report on the situation in southeastern Bolivia in the early 1890's, painted a dismal picture of the Indians who did not attach themselves to a mission. According to Jofre, many Chiriguanos wandered the countryside, contracting out their work, cheating the landowners by absconding without fulfilling their contract or being cheated out of their wages by hacendados. Like the Franciscans, he saw the poor treatment of the Indians by the colonists as the major reason for the 1892 uprising. Another observer, not particularly favorable to the missionary regime, called the labor conditions of the Chiriguanos "a type of slavery that must by all means be suppressed."[70]

The scattered population of Indians outside the jurisdiction of the Franciscans exceeded that of the mission Indians by a good deal. In 1900, at the apogee of the mission system, Azero had 17,642 Indians, of whom only 7,201, or 40 percent, lived under the control of the monks.[71] The rest lived mainly on haciendas; a lesser number resided in small and usually inaccessible villages, clinging precariously to their way of life. The Chiriguanos were especially important as laborers in Ingre, Iguembe, Cuevo, and Huacaya. According to Bernardino de Nino, "There are whites who call themselves farmers, because they have many Chiriguano peons; they order them about and direct them to work in the field for their own interest and profit. I can say that the only day laborer [*jornalero*] in the four provinces, Azero, Cordillera [Santa Cruz], O'Connor, and Gran Chaco [both Tarija], is the Chiriguano."[72]

It is extremely difficult to piece together the labor regime on Azero haciendas for any period. Settlers, many of them illiterate or close to it, rarely waited for the courts to settle disputes between themselves and the Indians. Labor contracts during the nineteenth century were generally based not on the rule of law but on coercion. Although beginning in the twentieth century, the policy was to maintain a detailed list of debt peon contracts, practically all these documents have disappeared, and the few that have survived give only a faint clue to how the labor system actually functioned on the Azero estates. Though some of the estates may have their own records, recent allegations of debt peonage and poor treatment of Chiriguano workers have made Azero landowners extremely reluctant to show even the oldest hacienda records to outsiders.

On one point, the evidence is clear: debt peonage was extremely common in the late nineteenth century and continued to be widespread until at least the 1970's.[73] The system apparently evolved during the frontier days, perhaps even during the colonial period, when landowners attempted to attract Indians, primarily Chiriguanos, to their estates during certain crucial periods of the agricultural cycle by offering certain goods, such as clothing and tools, in return for working in the fields. Often the adult males of a whole village, under the tutelage of their chief, would come to an estate to work during the harvest season. This exchange of labor for goods was probably fairly limited until late in the nineteenth century because of the modest production of the haciendas and also, it seems, because of the still very independent nature of the Indians themselves. Haciendas had hardly any commercial products other than livestock, which needed relatively few workers, and the Indians who came to run cattle left of their own accord when they thought they had worked long enough. Only those who felt that they had to remain on their ancestral lands stayed, and it was not necessary for the settlers to compel them to do so. But those who left were difficult to trace in the dangerous conditions beyond the settled frontier, so when the government authorized the establishment of Franciscan missions in newly conquered areas, the settlers welcomed them as a way of attracting Chiriguanos back to their homelands—and into the work force.[74]

Only in the last two decades of the nineteenth century, when the frontier steadily advanced to the Chaco, could landowners exert much control over the Indians. Only small pockets of independent Chiriguano villages remained, and the alternative of flight, out of the settlers' reach into the desolate reaches of the Chaco, became less attractive. Indians still frequently left the haciendas, but their goal was now northern Argentina. This out-migration and the general demographic decline, however, considerably shrank the existing labor pool.

In response to the endemic labor shortage, the region's landowners began to resort to legal mechanisms to keep the Chiriguano workers on their estates. By the turn of the century, debt peonage had become a legal system formalized by a contract signed by both employer and employee at the local police station in the presence of the *corregidor*, or highest cantonal authority. The contract specified the amount of the advance given to the peon (*conchabado*), the number of years he had to work, and the daily wages to be received. These contracts could be transferred to a different landowner, so that in effect the peon was sold. In 1929, for example, Severo Rivera transferred the contract of Manuel Rivera, who was to serve him for two years at 50 Bs annually plus two suits of clothes and daily food, to Luciano Bejarano, a landowner from Camatindi.[75] Sometimes a married couple would enter an hacendado's service together, as in the case of Jacinto N. and his wife, Inés. As recorded in the *matrícula*, the book containing the contracts, Jacinto and his wife were given an advance of 125 Bs. In return, they promised to work for the landowner, Crisólogo Florero, for five years, Jacinto as a laborer and his wife as a cook. For this work they were to receive forty and twenty centavos a day, respectively, but they were not provided with clothes.[76]

Once the Indian signed up, he was often forced to remain on the estate indefinitely in order to pay off his debts to the *patrón*, from whom he bought goods such as coca and clothes. Unscrupulous hacendados frequently juggled their account books to show debt-free peons as still owing largish sums—an easy trick because of the almost universal illiteracy among the Chiriguanos. Even if an Indian detected the wrong, he had little recourse in those desolate areas where the authorities were likely to be far away or close friends of the landowner.[77] Many wills and other legal documents attest to the perpetual indebtedness of the Indians. Some peons were apparently aware of this cheating. Witness the remarkable last testament of a Chiriguano Indian named Angel, in which, after noting that he had no earthly goods at all, he stated: "Now three years ago he [Angel] owed his *patrones*, the late Don Manuel Assencio Loaiza and his wife Cecilia Soto, the sum of 90 Bs, which they gave him in clothes for [his] service, for which he has served them three years without their having adjusted [his accounts] and without their counting the services that he gave them since a tender age for which he was not paid."[78]

The Indians tried to resist the exploitation by refusing to work without an advance payment, and they often broke their contracts by simply leaving. In a report by provincial notables in 1927 expounding on the problems the area encountered, one of their complaints was that there was no effective guarantee of keeping contracted peons: "The escape of peons to Argentina and other faraway places is frequent, defrauding [us of] the advances received (clothes and money). It must be said that it is *impossible* to obtain any peon without an advance."[79] All the same, the landowners maintained a vast advantage over the Indians. Once the police became involved in retrieving escapees, many Chiriguanos were forcibly returned to their employers. At times, the landowner settled for simply getting his money back. For example, Hachagua was inscribed in the matrícula as a servant of Guillermo T. Velasco, who had given the Indian forty Bs as an advance. Hachagua disappeared shortly after the contract was signed. Velasco was able to get hold of six of Hachagua's horses, forcing the Indian to show himself. Eventually, Velasco and Hachagua came to an agreement; the Indian would pay off his debt with the livestock he owned in exchange for having his contract annulled.[80]

In the late 1890's, as the labor shortage worsened, settlers began stealing each other's servants and peons. This led to interminable lawsuits and feuds between landowners. Such was the case with Ambrosio Hassenteufel, an Austrian immigrant and prominent Monteagudo merchant, who accused Federico Padilla, the owner of a neighboring estate, of taking away his workers by insinuating that Hassenteufel was after their women. Finally, Hassenteufel, with the help of the corregidor, retrieved "particularly said *mozos* who are indebted to me for having advanced them money, clothing, and other articles so that they pay me in work since I have contracted them through the matrícula as a better guarantee."[81]

Settlers also sometimes turned to the legal guardianship of Chiriguano children as a way of acquiring an adequate labor force. This was an increasingly popular practice once the shortage of workers became acute during the twentieth century. The number of tutelage contracts recorded by the Monteagudo notary from 1880 to 1930, although they do not by any means include all actual adoptions in Azero (most were legalized through the courts), give an indication of this trend. Over the twenty-year period 1880–1900, only seven adoptions were recorded all told. The rate started to climb in 1902, with at least one adoption a year between then and the outbreak of the First World War (the 1902–13 average was 2.9), but the truly dramatic jump came in 1914, with a figure of fourteen. Over the rest of the period, the average was almost seventeen; the lowest number, in 1917, was eight; the highest, reached in the years 1924–25 and again in 1927, was twenty-seven.

Adoption effectively gave the landowner free use of the child's labor until adulthood. Most children worked as household servants; they also did light agricultural tasks, such as goat herding and helping at harvest time. After they reached maturity, they were usually incorporated into the estate's labor force and paid the going wage. Obtaining girls was particularly desirable, since they attracted Chiriguano men, who might then become indebted and remain on the estate.[82]

Hacendados became guardians of children in three ways. One method was simply to take a child on the legal fiction of saving his soul or at least teaching him the ways of "civilization." For example, Felisindo López, the corregidor of Huacareta canton, requested permission of the Monteagudo judge to take the mestizo children of some Indian women because "immorality reigns scandalously in this region [Ñacamiri], where there are twelve married and thirty-two *amasebados*[?], the largest part with *cuñas* [Chiriguano women] with whom they have children without baptism." López hoped the judge would allow him to take these mestizos from their mothers ("these docile [*manseras*] *cuñas*") and give them to patrones so that they might be baptized and "so that the women would cease having children by Christians."[83]

Another method of obtaining Indian children was to declare

guardianship over orphans. This happened especially during the unsettled conditions after the numerous rebellions, when families were disrupted and relatives were unable to find orphaned children and take them in. After the 1892 revolt, one unscrupulous settler gathered up three children, including two orphans, and sold them to residents of Padilla and Sucre. A traveler found the buying and selling of children, presumably Chiriguanos, common practice in Sucre in the late 1890's. It continued in Sucre at least into the 1920's.[84]

Finally, there was the not-infrequent case of poverty-stricken parents giving up a child to a wealthy guardian. This at least guaranteed adequate food and shelter for their offspring until their twenty-first birthday. The documents formalizing this arrangement, quite numerous in the Monteagudo notary, usually included an admonition that the new *patrón* treat his charge well. Although it is difficult to tell the ethnic origins of the parents from the contracts, it appears that poor whites or mestizos as well as Indians were involved. Sometimes hacienda peons had their masters adopt their children. It was clearly advantageous for the hacendado to do so, for he could count on the parents staying around until their offspring reached majority.[85] Powerful or wealthy landowners might acquire quite a few children this way—as German Groc, a prominent Monteagudo lawyer, landowner, and merchant, seems to have done. In 1927, when his will was recorded, he had seven children under his guardianship.[86]

Once children were placed in the *patrón*'s hands, parents were rarely able to get them back. Most contracts specified that parents who had a change of heart had to pay a certain amount, often twenty centavos for each day the child was under the guardian's care, or a lump sum of fifty Bs. Ostensibly this money paid for the clothes and food the patrón had provided; as a practical matter, the intent was to put the child out of the parents' reach.[87] This type of clause became especially common after the turn of the century, when the labor shortage worsened.

Many requests for guardianships were made fraudulently. Applicants made no attempt to determine whether an "orphan" had living parents or to offer evidence that they were dead. A typical excuse for the lack of proof referred to the Chiriguanos' supposed nomadic lifestyle, such as the following: "It is notorious that among those of the indigenous ethnic group it is not the custom to stay long enough in any one place to make verification of deaths and births possible."[88]

The Indians, not surprisingly, resisted—sometimes to the point of violence—the abduction of their children. In 1887, Emilio Orías, an important landowner and member of one of the most powerful families in Tomina and Azero, was attacked by five or six knife-wielding Chiriguanos as he was conducting two Chiriguano children placed under his guardianship to his estate with the help of an Indian servant. The servant, also a Chiriguano, turned against Orías, and the Indians were able to make off with the children. In the trial, the *capitán grande* (or *tubicha rubicha*) of the allied villages on the Parapetí River claimed that the children were his nephew and niece, and that it was he who had engineered their return.[89] This sort of violent resistance became more and more infrequent as the Chiriguanía fell under the control of the colonists, but the Indians did not give up their children without a fight of a different kind. The Monteagudo judicial archives are full of requests by Indians to rescind landowners' guardianship rights. Most of these documents do not contain a verdict, which probably means that the Indians ran out of money to pursue the suit or simply failed to follow up on the multitude of complex legal requirements embedded in the Bolivian legal system.[90]

The Indians were fighting a losing battle in any event. Cattle breeding, especially at the primitive level practiced in Azero, where no fences or intensive breeding existed, required few cowhands. But even though cattle remained the province's mainstay until the 1930's, the settlers who stayed in the cantons behind the frontier, where many of the grazing lands had been depleted and the livestock was less productive, had to turn to farming. In addition to corn, they grew some ají, sugarcane, and tobacco (especially in Sapirangui) for export to the highlands. All these were labor-intensive crops, and therefore, as the cattle frontier moved farther east, the need for Indian laborers increased.

Although Chiriguanos were the majority of workers on Azero estates, there were also, according to one observer, a great number of Quechuas. There may not have been so great a number as he implies, but many estates, especially in the regions settled by whites early in the province's history, such as Monteagudo, Sapirangui, and San Juan del Piray, certainly employed arrenderos who were not Chiriguanos. Some of the relations of production on these landholdings, such as *yanapacu*, a form of sharecropping, were the same as in the highlands—for example, Hacienda Casapa in Sauces canton had its complement of yanapaqueros, arrenderos, and even arrimantes. As in the provinces to the west, these arrenderos paid rent for their parcels and in turn received wages for working on certain obligatory tasks, such as plowing, sowing, and fence-building. They received food and probably coca when they worked on hacienda lands. In contrast to most highland estates, however, Casapa had various vaqueros to guard the cattle. Each vaquero was given a horse and assigned a number of cattle to watch; at the end of the year, he had to account for every head. The vaquero kept some of the herd's offspring as partial payment, but was out of pocket for any cattle lost during the year.[91]

The owner of Casapa, Antonio Orías, purchased various *tierras de orígen* in Tarabuco between 1891 and 1901 without apparently ever forming them into a hacienda. Perhaps he bought the land to gain control over the labor of the originarios resident there with which to supplement his sparsely settled estates in Azero province.[92] Chiriguanos also went in the opposite direction to work in highland haciendas. In 1897, a Chiriguano tubicha named Baruca and his *soldados*, or warriors, left to work on Hacienda Pasopaya, an estate belonging to the son-in-law of former President Aniceto Arce just east of Yamparaez province.[93]

Baruca was a party in a dispute that involved his group's right to a parcel of land on an hacienda in Azero belonging to the large landowner Octavio Padilla. The case is extremely interesting for what it reveals about relations between Chiriguano laborers, arrenderos, and hacendados. Baruca and his men went to Argentina for two years. While they were gone, the hacienda administrator allowed a *subcolono* to rent part of their land. When Baruca returned, he attempted to reclaim the land. Significantly, Padilla, in a letter to his administrator, supported the Indians' cause, for he could ill afford to lose permanently the labor that Baruca controlled as tubicha.[94] It is evident Chiriguano labor was in such short supply that the Indians could sometimes wring certain concessions from their employers.

This case also illustrates some other features of hacienda rule over the Chiriguanos. When a settler absorbed an entire Chiriguano village in his hacienda, he usually kept the traditional hierarchy within the village intact; and when he wanted a job done, he gave his orders through the tubicha, who then relayed it to his men. But the tubicha—in this case Baruca—maintained a certain independence in ruling over his own group. As Yaguarenda, capitán of Hacienda Itau in Iguembe, explained in 1929, "I follow all the orders of the authorities, I direct all the works of my *soldados* and maintain the order and well-being of the district. Even the owner of Itau, Dr. Román Rivera, recognizes me in that role and makes sure that my orders are followed."[95]

Nevertheless, as hacendados increasingly controlled all aspects of the lives of their Chiriguano workers, the position of tubicha or capitán became less important. It was in the hacendado's interest to diminish the authority of the tubicha, for in this way, he could prevent the mass desertion of his prized workers. Instead, the landowners began to rely on a *repuntero*, selecting an especially hard and conscientious worker to act as liaison with the other workers and relay his orders, much as the tubicha had done but without the tubicha's control and independence. Repunteros became especially important after migration to and from the region's haciendas had greatly disturbed the old village unit. The displacement of the village chief with an official concerned only with work matters effectively destroyed whatever remained of the old authority structure. The hacendado took over many of the traditional functions of the tubicha, such as meting out justice and distributing lands. Without their traditional village structure, Chiriguanos attached to haciendas became increasingly culturally deracinated and dependent on the hacendados.

Unlike the arrenderos, hacienda Chiriguanos, by custom, did not pay rent, although they cultivated fields within the boundaries for their own subsistence. If the land-grant maps are correct, in many cases the Indians at least initially controlled much of the cultivable land within the landholdings. Some of the officials sent from Sucre to conduct the catastro, apparently uninformed about the special rules applying to Chiriguanos, unwittingly included in the Azero haciendas' incomes a certain amount for the rent "paid" by the resident labor forces. The landowners protested vehemently: they were charging, as one put it, "because of the philanthropy of the owner, not one single centavo."[96]

In one area in Azero land remained officially under the control of the Chiriguanos. This was the remarkable Caraparirenda Valley, in Sapirangui canton, where the Indians had obtained a land grant for their own lands. Life as independent allies of the whites entailed a whole host of obligations to local authorities in return for their aid in defending the Indians' interests. Accordingly, the corregidor of the canton could requisition the labor of the valley residents. Unscrupulous officials at times abused this privilege. In 1908, the capitán of the valley, Guiravaca, complained that the new corregidor, Dario Enríquez, imprisoned tubichas who were unable to fill the official's labor quota. He also took other Indians by force and refused to give them food and drink, as had been the custom. Moreover, and most seriously, Enríquez began renting out Indian land as if it were his own, thereby jeopardizing the Indians' hard-won rights to the land. After Guiravaca warned him that as a result of these practices, many of the valley residents were considering emigrating,[97] Enríquez's abuses seem to have stopped, and the community continued to maintain its independence, despite occasional interference by local officials.[98]

Conclusion

Azero's important role in the regional economy came to an abrupt end in the early 1930's. By the late 1920's, the first warnings of the impending catastrophe came when Argentina tightened up its cattle-import regulations. According to the Argentines, Bolivian cattle were infected with hoof-and-mouth disease and so could not be let into the country, but even as official exports declined, the already extensive smuggling operations took up the slack, negating the intent of the Argentine laws.[99] The days of provincial prosperity, though, were numbered. The Great Depression and then the Chaco War destroyed the province's commercial connections and threw the economy back to a subsistence level.

First, the Depression, as it swept through South America, ruined the Chilean nitrate industry, already in decline because of the invention of artificial nitrates, and so eliminated one of Azero's important cattle markets. Moreover, in 1930 the Chilean government imposed a high tariff on imports of live steers from Argentina, reducing the trade to virtually nothing.[100] As if this blow had not been enough, the Chaco War, which had started as a minor border conflict with Paraguay in the late 1920's, escalated into a major conflagration. The armies marching along the border of the Chaco, the heart of the province's cattle country, wiped out the once-numerous herds.

The Bolivian army, which had been recruited primarily from the culturally distinct highlands, viewed the Chiriguanos and other Chaco tribes with profound mistrust, partly because of their ways and partly because they spoke Guaraní, a language that was also spoken by the Paraguayans. The soldiers abused the Indians and impressed them into gangs to hack out trails for the troops and build supply lines. In 1930, an order came abolishing all missions in the Chaco. The directive was not carried out, but in 1934 the Paraguayan advance into Carandaití provided the necessary impetus; the mission at Machareti was hastily abandoned, and the converts scattered throughout the province.

The Bolivians later accused the Chiriguanos of having provided guides and information about Bolivian defenses to the Paraguayan army during the assault on Charagua in 1934. The charge may not have been true, but certainly there was some fraternization between Chiriguanos and Paraguayans, and when the war ended, various groups of Chiriguanos retreated with the Paraguayan forces and settled around some forts in the Chaco, where they are now know as Guarayos.[101]

When hostilities ceased in 1935, the provincial economy was in ruins. Many of the workers had fled, and the cattle herds had been annihilated. Without its economic base, the part of Azero still in Bolivian hands fell into a subsistence economy. It was only in the 1950's, when the Agrarian Reform cut loose the ties of the highlands' rural population, that a wave of migrants from Tomina and the department of Cochabamba swept into the province. This made possible the economic boom in hog raising and corn cultivation that has made Azero one of the few centers of growth in southern Bolivia.[102]

Sadly, however, the Chiriguanos did not share in this success. Their long struggle to maintain their independence had failed a half-century earlier, when the large frontier estates were carved out of their lands, and they became a conquered and exploited people with few or no rights. In a last-ditch effort to escape debt peonage and the exploitation of even their children, they fled to Argentina or the missions. The Franciscan mission system, which increasingly shouldered the burden of keeping the Indian population as a labor reserve, eventually failed because of the Liberal government's anticlerical policies. The Chaco War definitively destroyed the old way of life and represents a crucial turning point in southeastern Bolivia's history: not only did the missions disappear under the onslaught of the Paraguayan offensives, but ironically the Chiriguanos themselves were declared traitors in their own homeland. Perhaps this is another reason why, when the generation formed by the Chaco War took over the reins of the Bolivian government, the Indians of southeastern Bolivia were left out of the great Agrarian Reform that swept the nation after 1952.

CHAPTER SEVEN

Tomina Province

The society of Tomina province was both like and unlike the
other provinces in Chuquisaca. Its western fringe exhibited many of
the characteristics of highland society; its eastern border, with its
abundant agricultural frontier, gave it a society similar to Azero's.
Most of the province, however, was occupied not by large estates
or Indian communities, but by mestizo smallholders, who produced for the Potosí highland markets and largely based their social relations on reciprocal ties related to this trade. Once these
social relations weakened as a result of the silver-mining crash, all
but the western fringe of the province lapsed into a prolonged period of banditry and social disorder.

Tomina shares many of the geographical characteristics of the
rest of Chuquisaca. In the western part, the high plains of Tarabuco
(which in the early republican period belonged to Tomina) extend
to the town of Tacopaya. Farther south, the highest peaks of the
Cordillera de Mandinga reach an altitude of over 3,500 meters,
forming the last high barrier of the Andean range. To the west, the
extremely rugged terrain descends gradually in a series of sharp
ridges and steep valleys covered by tough scrub forests. Only in the
north, beyond Tacopaya, do the wheat-growing pampas of Mojocoya
at approximately 1,800 meters altitude provide some change of
scenery. Around the town of Tomina, the valleys become somewhat broader and the hills are progressively greener. Past the wide
basin in which Padilla is located, the jagged Andean foothills are
covered with lush subtropical jungle, a continuation of the vege-
tation prevalent in Azero province to the east, where ají and corn

are extensively cultivated. The various rivers, especially the Río Grande and the Pilcomayo, which mark the northern and southeastern boundaries of the province, form deep, humid valleys in which tropical fruits, sugarcane, and vineyards thrive.[1]

On the western fringes of Tomina, the population was and is predominantly Indian; in fact, in the northwestern canton of Presto, Viceroy Toledo established an Indian community, or *reducción de indios*, also named Presto. In 1608, it contained 194 Indian tribute payers, divided into the traditional two moieties. Baptismal records dating back to 1699 indicate that the Presto ayllu members were Guaiguas, Agoras, Charcas, Canas, and Omasuyos. The first two groups cannot be identified; the Charcas and Canas came from northern Potosí, and the Omasuyos from the Lake Titicaca area. The Tarabuco ayllus also controlled some land in the western part of Tacopaya and, as discussed in Chapter 4, an "ecological island" in canton Sopachuy, in southwestern Tomina.[2]

From the valley of Tacopaya eastward, the population was predominantly Spanish, the indigenous peoples having been wiped out or frightened away as a result of the Chiriguanos' incessant raids during the early years of the Conquest. Once Viceroy Toledo completed his policy of constructing fortress-towns farther east to contain the Chiriguano threat, the Spaniards moved in to create new estates to accommodate the burgeoning Potosí market. Antonio Vásquez de Espinosa described the area between Tarabuco and the town of Tomina during the 1620's as "populated by *estancias* and haciendas of Spaniards, with vineyards, fields of wheat, corn, and other seeds. With great herds of livestock from Spain as well as from this land, Tomina is a Spanish town [*villa de españoles*], head of the province."[3] These estates were worked primarily by *indios yanaconas*, agricultural laborers with no ties to an Indian community. Presumably many ayllu Indians entered the service of the Tomina hacendados as yanaconas to escape the mita, the notorious labor draft for the Potosí mines. Permanently separated from their highland communities, these agricultural workers lost many of their distinctive customs over the generations and eventually became classified as mestizos instead of Indians. This was especially true of those who lived in the east, in the unstable frontier area far from the influence of Andean culture.[4]

How the numerous smallholders settled in this region is not completely clear. Apparently the pacification of the area and the lush agricultural frontier led to the spontaneous colonization of much of eastern Tomina by people who did not attach themselves to any large estate but simply squatted in the less accessible areas unclaimed by large landowners. Local officials and hacendados undoubtedly welcomed the squatters as a potential labor reserve and a buffer between the Chiriguanos and the estates along the main highway. Perhaps some yanaconas simply left the haciendas and made their way into the farther recesses of the province, a movement that Spanish landowners could do little to prevent in the unsettled conditions of the frontier. There is evidence also that the land grants Melchor de Rodas, the conquistador and settler of the region, gave out in the name of the Crown were not very large. In a land title from 1569, for example, Rodas donated an area in Sopachuy of only thirty *fanegadas* (slightly less than 2,000 hectares), a relatively small grant for a frontier area. Since the Spanish customarily divided their holdings among all heirs, by the nineteenth century many of these properties had been split into relatively small parcels.[5] The distinctive land-tenure pattern of small or medium-sized properties throughout much of Tomina was due to the spontaneous settlement during the seventeenth and eighteenth centuries. During this period there was no marked growth of haciendas, as there was in Yamparaez and Cinti in the sixteenth century and in Azero in the late nineteenth century.

The land-tenure patterns established during the colonial period still characterized the province in the late nineteenth century. In the west, a few ayllu Indian lands remained. The last tribute list of 1877 shows only thirteen tributaries in the Presto community. The more vigorous Tarabuco ayllus had 70 in the cantons of Tacopaya and Sopachuy.[6] Beyond these rather restricted areas, large haciendas predominated in the west, especially in the cantons of Icla, Presto, and Rodeo, and in the prime wheat-growing area of Mojocoya (see Map 7). Sizable estates, with impressive hacienda houses, also dotted the road from Padilla to Tarabuco, as one foreign traveler remarked in 1887.[7]

Though still large compared with other estates in nineteenth-century Chuquisaca, most properties in the western half of the province had been so divided among heirs as to be only a fraction of their original size. Until 1780, virtually the whole canton of Icla had belonged to the Marquis of Otavi, and then to his widow. On her death, the estate was divided among their four daughters. By 1897, slightly over a hundred years later, these properties had been subdivided into twenty-five estates. Some were still large units, such as Hacienda Churumatas, which in 1897 produced 4,500 Bs of crops, ranging from wine grapes and ají to barley, wheat, and potatoes, and was valued at 45,000 Bs.[8] A similar process occurred in Mojocoya. In the first years of the republic, most of the canton belonged to Mariano Serrano, who received the land as payment for his services during the wars of independence. By the early twentieth century the land had been subdivided into 70 properties, of which the largest belonged to various branches of the Serranos.[9]

In the sparsely populated far eastern portion of Tomina, large estates also predominated, but these properties were large on paper only, for most haciendas cultivated only a small portion of the total territory listed in the ownership papers and at best grazed a few herds of cattle or sheep on the uncultivated land. This pattern was especially pronounced in Pescado canton. Although the southwestern corner of the canton around the town of Pescado (today called Villa Serrano) was broken up into smallholdings, the rest of the canton consisted of a handful of large haciendas that actually used only a small portion of their land.[10] A similar pattern prevailed in the southern part of Pomabamba canton, where Hacienda Rodeo Chico, valued at a mere 6,000 Bs in 1902, contained almost 10,000 hectares. Better than half this acreage remained untouched, with only 257 hectares under cultivation and slightly over 4,000 used for grazing.[11] Only one property in all Tomina, El Naranjal in Pomabamba, had been acquired through solicitation for a land grant. In 1905, the year in which the grant was awarded, the estate's 10,000 hectares were used exclusively for cattle grazing apart from a small garden, shown on one side of the hacienda house on the map accompanying the title.[12]

Large tracts like these were the exception. Most of the landholdings in this part of Tomina were of modest size. For example, according to the 1902 catastro (the most reliable surviving land census for the province), Pomabamba canton, surrounded by the Pilcomayo River on the south and west and by the high Mandinga range on the north—and thus virtually inaccessible during much of the year—contained only two large haciendas (valued at 10,000 Bs or more). Most of the other properties, 378 of 433, were worth 1,000 Bs or less, providing at best a subsistence for their owners. Significantly, both of the large haciendas were located on the Cinti border and were owned by two Cinti notables, Juan José Amésaga and Calixto Tito.[13] They represent an extension of the landholding pattern in southeastern Cinti, where the land was concentrated in huge properties. In the other cantons of eastern Tomina, what large haciendas there were mostly bordered the main east–west road, and again the hinterland was composed of smallholdings.

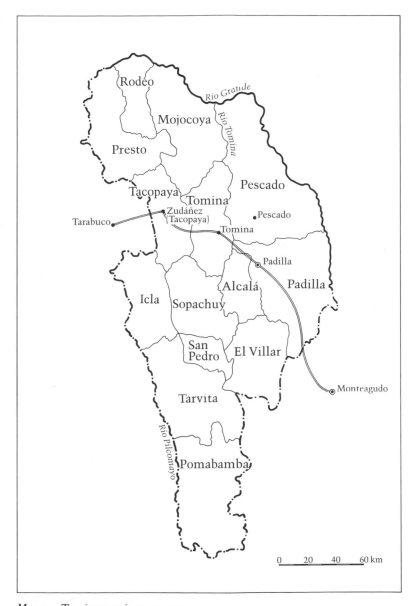

Map 7. Tomina province, ca. 1900

Commerce and Social Relations

During the nineteenth century, Tomina became one of the major domestic suppliers of cattle to the highland silver mines.[14] These cattle were not raised on vast cattle ranches, as in other parts of Latin America, but came from relatively small properties. Cattle provided the main income for many of the rural inhabitants who lived far from the main highway to Sucre; since the animals could be driven to market in herds, transportation costs were minimal, offsetting the herd's loss of weight during the drive.

A number of other products helped Tomina achieve significant prosperity during the latter half of the nineteenth century. Wines and liquors were exported from the Pilcomayo Valley in Icla, and barley from the extension of the Tarabuco highlands in the far western portion of the province. In Mojocoya, famed as the "bread-basket of Chuquisaca," hacendados sent large quantities of wheat to the bakeries of Sucre and Tarabuco. Hacienda peons of the region also participated in the wheat trade, marketing approximately 50 percent of their crops. In the valleys below the plains of Mojocoya and in Pescado, many estates cultivated sugarcane, which they processed and sold to Sucre markets in the form of molasses.[15] In addition, wool cloth from Tacopaya and Mojocoya, produced by a thriving cottage industry, was sold in Cochabamba and Potosí, as well as to provincial towns within Chuquisaca. Even in 1910, when competition from foreign textiles had severely reduced demand for the coarser locally made cloths, Tacopaya manufactured 5,000 pieces of cloth, worth 20,000 Bs, and Mojocoya 1,000 pieces, worth 3,000 Bs.[16]

The ají trade also burgeoned during the late nineteenth century. Unfortunately, the catastros' production statistics, at first glance quite detailed and exhaustive, prove unreliable on close examination because of chronic underreporting. However, it is safe to conclude that this crop was cultivated by a large number of small-holders, concentrated in eastern Tomina, and that most marketed at least part of their crop. For example, in 1910, 78 property owners cultivated ají in Alcalá alone—representing almost half the total properties (193) for which production data were collected that year. Few large landowners were interested in turning their land to so labor-intensive a crop, particularly one that consistently fetched low prices under the competition of small producers.[17]

Small producers, in fact, formed the backbone of the Tomina economy. According to a Padilla newspaper, "In general, its [Tomina's] upper class is inactive, without worries of bettering their situation; the middle class—let us use this term following established usage, among which are found farmers [*proprietarios labradores*] and all of the peasants—are those who really maintain the life of the town [Padilla], dividing their work between farm labor and the exchange of produce or the commerce of commodities."[18]

During the second half of the nineteenth century, after the region had recovered from the devastations of the struggle for independence, the province's economy was closely tied to the highland silver markets as a supplier of agricultural goods. As a result, Tomina's smallholders prospered as never before and developed a unique social system based on the production of cattle, ají, and molasses.

The provincial prosperity and the profits to be made from the cattle trade attracted a number of migrants from other parts of the country. Among them were several men from Sucre, Potosí, and Tarija who came to Tomina in the middle of the nineteenth century to settle on lands acquired through purchase or their wives' inheritance. A more numerous and important group of new arrivals were the merchants who came from Cochabamba to set up stores in Tomina's towns. Especially prominent among them were traders from Tarata. Although many of the *cochabambinos* settled in Padilla, a significant proportion went off to smaller places, like Villar, Sopachuy, Pomabamba (now called Azurduy), Pescado, and Alcalá, to populate the *calles de comercio*. Such commercial streets, found in every town and village, were the lifeblood of the settlement. One observer described Sopachuy thus: "The town has no beauty and the houses are all small; there is only one house with a second story in the little plaza, also of small dimensions. There are various narrow and short streets, and only the one that the *cochabambinos* are forming is long and straight and occupies a good position and is pleasing to the eye."[19] Some cochabambinos set up commercial networks throughout the province with their often extensive families. The Sensanos from Tarata, for example, had a family member in their hometown, another in Padilla, and three in Alcalá.[20] These traders seem to have kept their contacts with their home base, for the Padilla notarial archives contain many transactions involving Tarata real estate. Many probably returned to their native town to retire. But a number, such as the prominent merchant Pedro Pablo Uriona, married local residents and so acquired lands in Tomina province as well. Among other things, these small-scale merchants supplied hides to the important Cochabamba-based leatherworkers who exported shoes and sandals to northern Chile throughout much of the nineteenth century.[21]

The presence of a significant number of stores even in small towns indicates a widespread prosperity at almost all levels of rural society. The villages became important links in a commercial distribution system that channeled cattle, molasses, ají, and other agricultural products to the highland mining markets and brought rough cloth, coca, and other merchandise to the peasants. This marketing network was aided by the development during the nineteenth century of an interesting credit system called the *reparto*. In the reparto system, a merchant would lend a person money or provide clothes, sandals, needles, liquor, and other goods in return for ají, molasses, or peanuts after the harvest. Even cattle could be included in a reparto agreement. Sometimes, items bartered by reparto were not repaid for years.[22] This system was of advantage to both parties. The merchant could sell his goods at all times of the year, regardless of his customer's immediate financial liquidity, and received a good price on the agricultural products, which he then either resold at a higher price to other merchants or sent to his relatives for resale outside the province. In turn, the customer could buy whatever merchandise he needed on credit. The result was to increase the consumption of nonperishable goods and to raise the average *tomineño*'s standard of living.

Since the reparto system most often involved an exchange of goods, little cash circulated in the countryside, despite the overall prosperity of the region. As a result, the frequent transactions between rural inhabitants were also based on barter, and an elaborate set of reciprocal credit arrangements developed among Tomina smallholders, townspeople, and even hacienda workers. The wills registered in the Padilla notary's office are eloquent testimony to these primarily unwritten contracts. Virtually all but the very poorest people lent out agricultural goods, such as ají, molasses, potatoes, and barley, as well as money. Most monetary sums were small; they probably represented debts in produce that were converted to cash for the purposes of the testament. For example, an arrendero of Hacienda Riogrande in Mojocoya listed in his 1890 testament these assets and debts: ten people were in his debt to the tune of seven arrobas of molasses, ten pesos three reales in cash, one arroba of wheat flour, and one cattle hide; and he in turn owed twenty-five pesos payable in sugarcane, ten pesos cash, one carga of molasses and "three *arrobas* of molasses for one *cuartilla* of corn."[23] Though in some cases lender and debtor were relatives, kinship does not seem to have figured as an important consideration in these transactions; most involved people who were apparently unrelated to each other.

Cattle were a key part of this credit-barter economy. In one arrangement, called *para pelo,* a neighbor or perhaps a small-time cattle merchant butchered a sick or recently dead animal for market, and the purchaser had to replace it with a *novillo,* or one-year-old calf. This arrangement is one explanation for the frequency with which novillos are listed among the goods owed in the testaments. Healthy animals were often also "borrowed" by neighbors or small-time cattle merchants on the way to market, to be replaced usually within a year. In fact, especially among smallholders, the "lending out" of animals represented a significant form of wealth. Many smallholders had too little pasture land on the few hectares they owned to support much of a herd, and by lending their cattle to others, they were able to avoid both a grazing fee and the possible loss of their animals by theft or natural calamity. An example of the difference this could make is illustrated by the 1892 testament of Justa Espada, a resident of El Villar. She owned one of the smallest and least valuable properties in the canton, and there kept thirteen head of cattle and a mule. But she also had contracted with a neighbor to keep ten head and had given 100 pesos to another person to buy yearlings *adentro* (or in the countryside) and bring them to town for her. In addition, "many people [owed her] *novillos,* as is evident from the promissory notes." Thus, Señora Espada probably at least doubled the value of her resources by owning cattle elsewhere.[24]

In a society in which rural inhabitants had no strong communal bonds like those of the Indian ayllus or the highland haciendas, those various credit and barter arrangements provided a great measure of social cohesiveness. Economic ties among neighbors and acquaintances created mutual bonds of reciprocity. Borrowing for relatively long periods of time such valuable possessions as cattle involved an implicit trust among those concerned and undoubtedly helped solidify relationships among rural inhabitants who were scattered widely over the province's rough terrain. These arrangements were often far from idyllic—the failure to return items was common—but in most cases they worked fairly well. In fact, not having such goods as cattle returned for a long time could, as explained above, even be beneficial to the lender who could not accommodate many animals on his own small property.

Such debts continued to be counted as his estate. Almost certainly rural inhabitants included outstanding loans of goods in their estimates of a person's wealth.[25]

Well-to-do women, and to a lesser degree men, of the time also accumulated wealth in the form of silverware, jewelry, and religious objects made out of precious metals. At her death in 1885, María Nieves Cestáñez, from San Pedro, owned a small store, a plot of undeveloped land in town, 60 head of cattle, and 250 sheep, plus a jewel-encrusted golden crucifix, golden earrings, three silver plates, and thirty Fernandinos (coins from the colonial era with a high silver content).[26]

Eastern Tomina's Economic Decline

This prosperity, dependent on the revival of the highland silver-mining economy, came to an end after 1895, with disastrous consequences for the complex web of social and economic relationships in the Tomina countryside. By 1902, *El Republicano*, a newspaper from Padilla, lamented the province's sad state: "The strength of industry grows steadily weaker; commercial activity is sagging; education is being ignored; justice is ceding to the push of arbitrariness; skepticism replaces political and religious faith; the public spirit dies and civility is almost swamped by the avalanche of demagogy."[27] Although the writer's hyperbole was no doubt politically motivated, the article pinpointed a number of important components in the province's decline. For one, incentives to produce for an increasingly restricted market diminished considerably among large sectors of the population. Trade suffered as a consequence, leading to serious economic difficulties among smallholders and hacienda workers. Social relations among rural inhabitants—what the author called "public spirit" and "civility"—cemented in large part by the ultimately economic transactions of barter and borrowing trade goods, suffered accordingly.

The fate of the cattle trade, in which virtually the whole province participated as producers, most dramatically illustrates the problems Tomina suffered as a consequence of the restructuring of the southern Bolivian economy. Cattle were the province's largest export item during the nineteenth century, and most of that trade had flowed to Cochabamba and the silver-mining areas.[28] At the turn of the century, Tomina's cattle industry slid into decline. The collapse of the traditional markets was bad enough, but on top of that the colonization of the Chaco, with its enormous virgin pastures, led to ruinous competition from Azero and Cordillera cattle barons. The glut in the livestock market kept cattle prices stable while the costs of necessities escalated. Over the period 1912–30, for example, the market price of the cattle of Rodeo Chico, in Pomabamba canton, stayed constant at forty Bs a head, even during the First World War, when prices in Argentina and elsewhere shot up dramatically.[29]

In the face of an increasingly unfavorable market, many landowners, especially those with limited lands, cut production and raised only enough livestock for subsistence. As a result the herds thinned precipitously, falling from an official census of 60,088 head in 1897 to 42,364 in 1902. Even taking into account the inaccuracies of the catastros, so large a difference in the figures indicates that there must have been a huge decrease.[30] Since the bulk of smallholders lived in areas remote from the main trade routes where high transport costs made the export of most other agricultural goods unfeasible, this was the group hardest hit by the downturn.

Their economic decline was a long, drawn-out process, whose consequences were not completely evident until the 1920's. But the signs of the rural population's increasing impoverishment were there to see long before that. Growing numbers of smallholders sold their remaining cattle to large landowners and became mere hired hands watching over their former possessions.[31] In addition, the *para pelo* and other such barter-credit systems fell into disuse. As the testaments recorded in the Padilla notary's office show, the lending of cattle declined significantly by the early twentieth century. Although some people still listed livestock they were owed, the animals mentioned were in all likelihood stolen animals that the testate hoped his heirs would be able to retrieve. With the decline of mutual lending, the cattle trade among all but the owners of the largest pastures virtually disappeared.

As economic conditions worsened, some tomineños simply sold all their belongings. Sale documents do not tell us what the sellers did with their money, but it is reasonable to suppose that most used some or all of it to pay off outstanding debts. The bulk of the documents also do not say what became of the sellers. One document indicates that the seller went to Argentina, presumably to work there;[32] other sellers no doubt left the area, too. In some cases, it is impossible to determine whether a person was selling all his possessions or only his cattle. But it is clear from the notarial records that the selling trend reached new heights in the second decade of the twentieth century.

Adoptions of children also shot up, particularly after 1916,[33] a lag that suggests it took some years for conditions to deteriorate to the point where desperate parents felt compelled to give up their offspring to better-off families. What had been an extremely rare occurrence in Tomina (in contrast to Azero) became common practice as the century wore on.

In the infrequent cases of earlier times, the adoption probably redounded to the benefit of the child, as the law anticipated. Indigent parents usually gave up children to relatives or godparents. Also, many adoptees were orphans whose relatives could not or would not take them in. Now, however, children increasingly became in effect a marketable commodity. In 1902, the parents of a four-year-old girl sold her to an artisan couple in Padilla for fifteen pesos. In 1907, an arrendero couple contracted out their niece to their *patrón* for five years to meet overdue land rent catastro payments.[34] After 1913, the vast majority of guardianship documents mention a sale price. Children fetched anything from twenty Bs to, in one case, 500 Bs; most went for 60 Bs to 100 Bs.

Another sign of the impoverishment of the Tomina countryside was the departure of the petty traders from the small provincial towns; they left gradually, either moving back to Cochabamba or going on to more prosperous areas, such as Azero or Cordillera province.[35] The commercial streets of Villar, Sopachuy, Alcalá, Mojocoya, and the rest became virtually deserted, and most countryfolk found it difficult not only to find the goods they were accustomed to, but also to get credit from the increasingly strapped merchants who remained. The real estate market in these small towns, fueled by the immigration of cochabambinos and other traders during the nineteenth century, collapsed. The links between most rural inhabitants and the national economy, mediated through these villages, slowly broke down.

Large merchants, who resided almost exclusively in Padilla, fared somewhat better, but even many of them were sucked under. Beginning in the twentieth century, several important Padilla traders went bankrupt and had to sell all their belongings to make good on debts. The case of Eleazar Daza is instructive. In 1912, Daza was forced to sell his four houses (three in Padilla and one in Tomina), most of his rural properties including their livestock, and his stock of merchandise to a Padilla lawyer for 25,000 Bs to repay his outstanding debts to the German-owned Morales and Bertram merchant house in Sucre. His prompt payment apparently earned him the trust of the firm, for only two years later, he was empowered to represent it in the prosecution of two merchant-debtors. Daza remained in deep financial trouble, however; in 1915, he owed another Sucre-based German firm 2,000 Bs, and this after already having been forgiven 1,905 Bs. Eight years later, he was still in debt, and his last hacienda, Mollemolle, with its two grain mills, ended up on the auction block.[36]

Daza was perhaps more unfortunate than most Padilla merchants, but his case is particularly interesting because it demonstrates the increased importance of large merchant houses in the province. The most active were the German-owned firms Morales and Bertram and Moerch and Bauer, but merchant houses owned by the Sucre oligarchy, such as Urriolagoitia Brothers and the Tarija-based Trigo Brothers, were also important. With the rural markets shrinking, many of the large Padilla retailers were forced to rely heavily on the credit lines offered by city merchant houses. In the process, they became virtual agents of these firms and lost much of their independence and presumably much of their profit margin as well.[37] Only a few merchants, such as the Spanish-born Manuel Monterde, were able to avoid this fate.

The only members of Tomina society who continued to thrive were the small group of large hacendados, who increasingly dominated the cattle trade to the highlands. During the nineteenth century, several Tomina cattle merchants and landowners also owned ranches in Azero or had their cattle graze there, in that way benefiting from the cheap Chiriguano labor and the lusher pastures of the neighboring province. By the twentieth century, because of inheritance patterns, few hacendados, other than perhaps members of the important Orías family, owned property in both provinces. Yet the Tomina hacendados continued to prosper in the cattle trade because they could exact cattle from their laborers as diezmo or catastro obligations and use the profits to finance cattle-purchasing expeditions to the frontier. For example, Adolfo Reyes lent 1,000 Bs to a smallholder from Sopachuy, who promised to buy cattle in Azero and sell them at the Chaquí fair, located in the department of Potosí. The *sopachuyeño* was responsible for the cost of getting the cattle to the highlands; all profits from the sale were to be split in half.[38]

Adolfo Reyes's success in the face of adversity was not atypical. His family had bought Hacienda Limabamba in 1896, one of the most valuable estates in the eastern portion of the province, with a large number of arrenderos and vaqueros. Although they may not have had direct access to land or cattle in Azero, the Reyes, like other large Tomina landowners, maintained ties with their counterparts there through the *compadrazgo*, or godfather relationship, and these ties often provided them with profitable opportunities. In 1918, for example, Adolfo Reyes fetched for his *compadre* Juan Bautista Miranda some 1,700 Bs worth of merchandise from Sucre, and was paid with 422 arrobas of ají and 40 arrobas of tobacco, items that he could market at a profit in the highlands.[39]

Although large landowners undoubtedly benefited the most, several large cattle merchants based in Padilla were able to survive the breakdown of the silver-mining economy. The trade was also carried on, though in a limited way, by cattle dealers from Sucre and the town of Yamparaez who came to eastern Tomina for cattle. Since several hacendados did not participate directly in the cattle trade, most of these itinerant merchants descended on Tomina in February, after the collection of the diezmo, to take advantage of the livestock supply. During the rest of the year, this commercial activity dwindled to a bare trickle.[40]

Thus the once-prosperous Tomina became increasingly polarized between a large mass of impoverished smallholders and arrenderos and a handful of wealthy large landowners. To be sure, regions like Mojocoya and the Pilcomayo Valley were only slightly affected by the economic downturn because they produced a wide variety of agricultural goods and were relatively close to their main market, Sucre. But most of the province, and especially the more inaccessible cantons, such as Pescado and Villar, which exported primarily cattle during the brief silver boom, fell into economic disarray. The inhabitants of the remote areas, mainly small producers, were reduced to a subsistence economy. In the process, the complex social ties between smallholders began to disintegrate.

Labor Relations: Commercialization and Reciprocity

The Tomina labor picture is a complicated one, not only because of the province's diversity of climate zones, from subtropical valley to highlands, but also because of its diversity in population densities and ethnic types, from sparsely populated agricultural frontiers to areas densely inhabited by Indians steeped in Andean traditions only partly modified since the Spanish Conquest. Moreover, documentation on the ubiquitous form of land tenure, the smallholding, is even scarcer than documentation on larger properties.

There were many divisions within Tomina society, although not all are useful for the purpose of distinguishing different patterns of labor relations. There was a distinct linguistic boundary for example. Except for the extreme north of Pescado canton, most peasants who lived west of the Tomina River, especially in the more remote areas, spoke only Quechua or understood at best a smattering of Spanish. The territory east of the river, excluding the town of Padilla and its immediate vicinity, was inhabited by monolingual Spanish speakers. This linguistic boundary probably reflected the extent of colonial highland colonization, but it did not necessarily mark a cultural boundary. Many of the Quechua speakers, especially toward the east, were mestizos who shared with their Spanish-speaking neighbors an ignorance of many of the Andean traditions that were so important to hacienda peons and Indian community members in the highlands.

Still, for analytical purposes, a rough division into two sections, the western highlands and the eastern portion, can be made. Beyond the ethnic and cultural differences, there were important distinctions between these sections in the size and distribution of landholdings, geographic conditions, and crops. In fact, these distinctions had produced two very different rural societies, whose members reacted very differently to the restructuring of the southern Bolivian economy.

Western Tomina. The western highlands were an extension of the province of Yamparaez and shared many of its characteristics. This region, which included El Rodeo, Presto, and the western parts of Tacopaya and Icla, was heavily Indian and composed primarily of large haciendas. For example, in Presto canton, Indians in 1900 composed 46 percent of the population (or 1,601 in a total of 3,472).[41] Furthermore, the seven haciendas in Presto, worth over 10,000 Bs, covered the greater part of the canton; Hacienda Pasopaya, the largest, alone contained some 18,750 hectares. These estates had swallowed up much of the Presto ayllu by the nineteenth century. In 1877, there were only thirteen originarios; 194 had been recorded in the early seventeenth century.[42]

This region had remained relatively unscathed by the sixteenth-century Chiriguano invasions, so in many areas most inhabitants were probably descendants of the indigenous population. Not unexpectedly, Andean cultural ideals maintained their sway even outside the area's small Indian communities. The Andean harvest festival called the mink'a, described earlier, for example, was common in the western highlands of Tomina. This custom, with its

provision of food and other items for labor and its spirit of celebration, had deep roots dating back to pre-Conquest times. Moreover, *ayni* relationships, which entailed the reciprocal use of labor
among near-equals, were common not only among the few smallholders and ayllu Indians, but also among hacienda workers.[43]

Many landowners in the western part of Tomina were members
of the Sucre elite, a group that, as we saw in Chapter 3, began to
manage their estates more carefully after the silver bust. Some of
these hacendados, as in other parts of Chuquisaca, attempted to
change the labor system on their properties to increase revenues.
Since many of the reforms destroyed part of the traditional systems of reciprocity and redistribution, the peons resisted, and the
strategies that were relatively efficacious in Yamparaez and Cinti
did not work so well in western Tomina.

Troubles between the hacendado and peons were endemic on
Hacienda Pasopaya. When Genaro Abasto took over the estate
after the death of its owner, Aniceto Arce, he quickly attempted to
establish labor discipline and reduce the workers' debt load on the
hacienda. As a result, in the period 1909–21, at least twenty-four
arrenderos abandoned their plots and went to work on neighboring
haciendas. Abasto, who could ill afford to lose many workers in
this region of labor-intensive farming, took his former workers to
court for debts accrued from unpaid rent and unfulfilled labor obligations. If Abasto had thought by this action to force the men back
to work, his plan fell through. The arrenderos' new patrones, also
quite influential men in Sucre, had a vested interest in keeping
them. The upshot was a number of suits, which dragged on until
the 1930's without being resolved.[44]

Other haciendas in western Tomina, especially in Icla, also had
labor problems. On Hacienda El Niágara, workers staged several
protests between 1924 and 1926, raising the concern of the departmental prefect.[45] The fullest picture of labor relations in the region
is provided by a neighboring estate, the well-documented Hacienda La Candelaria, fifteen kilometers southeast of Tarabuco.
That property, owned by various Sucre miners during the nineteenth century, was called Huamampampa until 1900, when it
was purchased by Candelaria Argandoña v. de Rodríguez in a
bankruptcy proceeding.[46] A few years later, the landholding passed
into the hands of Néstor Rojas, who had married Señora Rodríguez's
daughter. Rojas's son, Nicolas, was sent to Harvard to study agron-
omy and then took over the administration of the estate in 1924.

La Candelaria produced primarily highland products: in 1925, the demesne lands yielded 272 fanegas of wheat, 370 cargas of potatoes, and 566 cargas of husked barley. The barley crop was one of the largest in the canton and perhaps in the whole province. In the nineteenth century, this crop had made the hacienda one of the most valuable landholdings in the region and constituted its main source of income.[47] After Nicolas Rojas took over the hacienda, he aggressively expanded the marketing of his crops, particularly barley and wheat. For example, seeing a perfect market for the hacienda's principal product, Rojas became a partner in a new brewery founded in Sucre and one of its major suppliers of barley.

For his wheat crop and to some extent for his barley crop, too, Rojas had to sign contracts far in advance of the harvest. To ensure a sufficient yield he changed the labor system on the hacienda. Traditionally, the 55 resident arrenderos had been divided into four different categories based on their *bajas,* or the number of times they had to transport goods to Sucre. The number of bajas also determined the amount of land each colono held and fixed all such other obligations as providing adobes, firewood, eggs, and brooms. In addition, Rojas maintained the customary services by both women and men in the *patrón*'s household and the transport obligations called *cacha,* requiring the arrendero to take hacienda produce to Tarabuco or Sucre with his own pack animals. Many of these obligations were apparently fulfilled by the increasingly numerous subrenters, or arrimantes, since there were many more households living on hacienda grounds than can be accounted for by the arrendero families. According to Rojas's 1931 census, there were 843 persons settled in La Candelaria, which probably meant at least 150 households, or more than two adult male arrimantes for each arrendero. Rojas, like the owners before him, refused to give out more demesne land for subsistence agriculture to the offspring of his peons. Only the oldest son received land once he reached majority, forcing the daughters and younger sons to become arrimantes. As a result, between 1855 and 1931, the arrimante population increased from seven to about a hundred.[48]

Rather than relying increasingly on rents and catastro payments as other landlords were doing, young Rojas held on to demesne land for commercial production. To expand production on this land, he vigorously promoted a new sharecropping arrangement called the *yanapacu,* which provided him with the bulk of his wheat and much of the barley. Traditionally, a landlord had provided a certain amount of land and the necessary seed to a sharecropper, who gave him a predetermined percentage of whatever crop he brought in. This practice was consistent with the Andean ideal of rule through reciprocity, for both the *patrón* and the peon shared the risks of farming in the always erractic highland climate. In the newly instituted yanapacu system, however, Rojas calculated how much a certain amount of seed should produce and required the arrendero to return a fixed quantity of grain no matter how dismal his crop. This new policy was convenient for Rojas, ensuring him as it did enough grain to meet his contracts, but it negated the reciprocal ideal, for the entire risk now fell on the sharecropper. True, during good years he would have the benefit of keeping a large surplus; but during a bad one, the arrendero's share (and even more so the arrimante's) might be so small that he could barely feed his own household.[49]

Rojas also required his peons to build a vehicle road between his hacienda and nearby Tarabuco, a project that lasted from 1922 to 1927 and occupied a particularly large number of workers over the years 1924–26. Although Rojas paid the peons wages, the project often pulled them away from their fields at crucial times in the agricultural cycle. It also put the hacienda's accounts in the red until 1926, so that Rojas could presumably not have been very flexible toward peons who fell behind in their debts and obligations.[50]

Other changes in the administration of La Candelaria that challenged the reciprocal relationship between the hacendado and the peons undoubtedly worsened Rojas's already strained relations with his labor force. Rojas abolished all fiestas and declined all invitations to become godfather (compadre) to any of his laborers' children. He declared that the fiestas only led to drunkenness, and rather than promote Christian practices, were based on superstitious rites. These were blatant denials of the *patrón*'s traditional ritual obligations to his peons.

From 1924 until at least 1926, the hacienda was in constant turmoil as the colonos stoutly resisted the new regime. When Rojas not only demanded extra labor from his workers, but also refused to abide by traditional rules of reciprocity and redistribution, the laborers sought a radical solution. Although La Candelaria had been an hacienda since at least the seventeenth century and Rojas had not expanded on to adjacent Indian community land, the colonos joined the movement originating from the Tarabuco ayllus and began to agitate for dividing the hacienda among the peons— an obvious solution in the arrimantes' eyes to the population crisis that condemned them to marginal status. Their support of such a radical proposal, a virtually unheard-of one so far as other long-time haciendas are concerned, points to Rojas's complete loss of legitimacy as a *patrón* in Andean terms.

Rojas's response to the turmoil was to appoint a tribunal of three hacienda members to try any cases arising from the disturbances. The panel consisted of the gardener as Rojas's representative, the *alcalde de campo*, the highest government-appointed political authority on the hacienda, and an arrendero "characterized by his seriousness and his good behavior." Rojas's tribunal succeeded in deflecting some of the antagonism from him and in giving him some measure of control over his estate. Moreover, once the road was complete, labor conditions improved because Rojas exempted the arrenderos from the cacha obligation and began to use trucks instead.[51] This was apparently sufficient to defuse the legitimacy crisis engendered by Rojas's reforms.

Protest on western Tomina haciendas was generally ineffective, partly because it was too radical. Instead of opting for reforms or even a return to the traditional ways, the workers on Hacienda La Candelaria (and probably at least on neighboring Hacienda El Niágara as well) espoused a program inspired by the struggle of neighboring ayllus to retrieve the lands lost during the last great expansion of the hacienda. Since this radical premise was unacceptable to hacendados and government alike, the movement was doomed to fail, given the balance of power in early-twentieth-century Bolivia. On Hacienda Pasopaya, though the earlier equilibrium between landlord and peon was not restored, the piecemeal resistance of a number of arrenderos—those who left to work on nearby estates—was effective to the extent that it brought them better conditions under their new masters. But in simply migrating to neighboring properties, those workers did not really challenge the *colonato* system, which, despite its emphasis on reciprocity and redistribution (at least among "good" patrones), always favored the hacendado.

Eastern Tomina. The inhabitants of eastern Tomina reacted to economic changes at the turn of the century not by mounting revolts or trading employees, but by taking up brigandage on a massive scale, attacking haciendas, merchants, and smallholders alike. Why banditry plagued this region is not immediately clear, nor can one point to a simple cause. But part of the answer may lie in the changing structure of rural society in the area.

Ethnically, eastern Tomina was predominantly mestizo and white. The 1900 census counted 21,306 mestizos, 11,668 whites, 5,020 Indians, and 20 Negroes.[52] Although much of this region had been under Chiriguano control for a time, virtually all the Indians censused were Andean Indians. A large proportion of the people owned the lands they worked. In 1902, there were 1,344 properties worth 1,000 Bs or less, compared with 453 worth between 1,001 and 9,999 Bs, and only 35 (or an average of 3.5 per canton) worth 10,000 Bs or more.[53] Although some properties in the middle category were fairly large, their assessed value, as noted earlier, was based on their low production and small number of workers and thus reflected accurately their position within the rural hierarchy.

The estates that were large enough to have peons functioned much like those in the western highlands. Here, as there, arrenderos paid in labor, in money, and in kind for the usufruct of their plots. However, labor obligations were generally less severe, and relations between hacendado and peon less imbued with Andean forms of rule than in the west. Despite the ethnic make-up of the Indian population, in fleeing their communities, the Andean Indians lost the solidarity that might have preserved their cultural heritage. Only the most basic notions of reciprocity and other Andean cultural assumptions survived in eastern Tomina, and even these varied from hacienda to hacienda, in general weakening as one moved farther east.

These distinctive conditions had evolved slowly during the colonial period, when settlers from the highlands wrested the area from Chiriguano control. To attract Indian and mestizo migrants from the west, Tomina hacendados had to offer better conditions than those found in the highlands. Even in the twentieth century, landowners offered favorable terms to new hacienda workers who were willing to colonize new land; in one case in Tacopaya, a new couple was exempted from all obligations and arriendos in return for constructing some irrigation channels and clearing new fields.[54]

The labor system on haciendas in the canton of Mojocoya illustrates the relative mildness of the obligations. Mojocoya's fertile pampas were ideal for growing wheat. As in the west, the canton's haciendas had a hierarchy of workers, consisting of full, half, and quarter arrenderos, some landless *vivientes* attached to the arrendero household, and a few subrenters, or arrimantes. Full arrenderos had to provide forty days of labor, significantly less than, for example, on Hacienda La Candelaria, where the comparable peon owed 120 days. Landowners charged a nominal money rent of less than ten Bs a year; the peons paid for their parcels in labor and in produce. The tax in produce took the form of the catastro, amounting to 20 percent of the crop and the annual gain in livestock.[55]

This method of payment was advantageous to the workers, since they shared the risk of farming with the landowner and had no fixed costs (other than in labor) that in poor crop years might prove onerous.

Mojocoya hacendados with subtropical valley lands employed socios, smallholders from the uplands, as sharecroppers to cultivate sugarcane. These men lived most of the time on plots they owned on the plains above and came down to the valleys only when the cane needed work. The proprietor and the socio shared the crop equally. This relationship was important on such valley estates as Hacienda Pasorapilla, which had thirteen socios and only four arrenderos.[56] As landowners, socios were largely independent of the hacendado: apart from a portion of the crop, they had no obligations to him, and he had none to them.

Relations between hacendados and their arrenderos were not permanent either, as they usually were in the highlands, where families remained on the same estates for generations. Many rental agreements were for a set number of years, and arrenderos could, and did, move on. Especially on the smaller properties, where the landowner had only a handful of arrenderos, the loss of even a few workers could spell disaster. The owner therefore had an important incentive to treat his labor force well. Moreover, on the smaller properties, the owner was likely to work alongside his arrenderos, inevitably closing the social distance between them.[57]

Many colonos aspired to smallholder status, and in the loosely stratified society of eastern Tomina, some achieved this. In Icla, in 1925, an arrendero and his wife and son pooled their savings and bought the plot of land they had been working on the hacienda. Relationships between servants and wealthier Tomina residents were frequently close, as evidenced by the testaments in the Padilla notarial archives. Often the testates willed significant portions of their holdings to their servants, an almost unheard-of practice in the Andean highlands or in Azero. Although most servants inherited money or livestock from their masters, a few received land. Among the lucky few were the colonos of Hacienda Lupeara (Tacopaya canton), who received their arriendo plots from the priest Manuel Martín Santa Cruz in 1856. Landless rural residents could thus aspire to getting their own plots, either by savings or by inheritance, making for considerable social mobility within the lower strata of Tomina society.[58]

The records of Hacienda Rodeo Chico in Pomabamba canton illustrate how relatively mild the working conditions sometimes were. Like many estates in Tomina, Rodeo Chico, as the name implies, ran cattle, an activity that produced half its income over the years 1912–30. Cheese, the next most important source of income, accounted for about a third of the total, and the rest came from money rents and the sale of ají, leather, jerked beef, and wooden spoons.[59]

There were twenty-four arrenderos on the hacienda, including the administrator. Their labor obligations, though not listed, must have been fairly light, considering the small contribution to income from hacienda produce. All arrenderos paid money rent and also a *ventena* tax of one Bs for each calf born during the year. The hacienda could also claim 10 percent of the resident laborers' ewes annually. Thirty-four people were listed as possessing sheep. Since Rodeo Chico did not allow nonresidents to graze on hacienda lands for a fee (yerbaje), the ten non-arrenderos were perhaps arrimantes or vivientes.

Two men listed in the records did not pay any type of rent. These were the vaqueros, who took care of the hacendado's 313 head of cattle. They, like the mayordomo, were salaried employees; one, José Gomez, was paid 8.00 Bs, and the other, Florentino Morochi, received 6.40 Bs annually. Of course, such small sums were not sufficient to live on; the vaqueros earned most of their income from the cheese they made from the milk of the hacendado's cows. At certain times of the year, landowners also provided their vaqueros with clothes, coca, and foodstuffs. As in Azero, vaqueros were a distinctive group within the hacienda labor force, and their rights over milk production and other privileges made them relatively well off compared with the other workers. On Rodeo Chico, as on most other Tomina ranches, the vaqueros also owned small plots of land and received the services of the hacendado's teams of oxen but were not required to provide labor beyond their herding duties.[60] Freedom from this obligation provided a measure of prestige over the arrendero population and allowed the vaqueros' households to work exclusively at their own enterprises, further increasing their economic advantage over the other hacienda workers. The deep divisions implied in these economic and social distinctions between arrenderos and vaqueros partly explain the absence of hacienda-wide revolts in eastern Tomina.

The workers had little sense of the Andean notions of reciprocity, though some vestiges remained. Although the hacendado of Pescado provided the usual rations and a handful of coca (deducted from the peons' accounts) at harvest, there was nothing approaching the mink'a that accompanied the work in the west. Instead, after the harvest the *patrón* threw a three-day fiesta with food and drink for all, rather like European harvest festivals that celebrate the completion of work. The Andean notion of work and celebration, which incorporated deeply felt pre-Conquest religious ideas and served to reaffirm ties within the community, was lacking.[61]

As noted earlier, it was the smallholders in Tomina province who suffered the most from the decline of the silver-mining economy. The dramatic decline in cattle raising by smallholders, the most important contributor to provincial prosperity during the nineteenth century, led to serious economic dislocations in the countryside. As a result, there were increasingly frequent complaints about the severity of the catastro tax collected by the state (in contrast to the catastro collected by hacendados from their arrenderos) and the inability of tax collectors to get what was owed. The magnitude of the shortfall suggests that the problem traced primarily to the financial woes of provincial smallholders. In 1919, a Padilla newspaper, *El Deber*, commented that in the previous year 50 percent of the land tax had not been collected. Conceding that the immediate cause was the economic crisis that swept through Bolivia at the beginning of the First World War, the newspaper nevertheless suggested that many landholdings were chronically being charged much more than the stipulated 10 percent of their earnings, and were having to use all the year's income for taxes.[62]

Although large properties clustered around the main Monteagudo–Sucre trade route continued to prosper, those in the marginal areas suffered. Again, the failure to collect the catastro tax was a symptom of the area's economic malaise. In 1926, the *informe* of the subprefect of inaccessible Azurduy (a province formed out of Pomabamba, Tarvita, and San Pedro cantons in 1917) lamented the continued inability of landowners to pay off the catastro. He stated that by this time there were some properties worth only 50 Bs that owed the state 400 Bs in back taxes. The subprefect, Aniceto Reyes Barron, himself a large landowner, recommended that, to recover the money, all interest should be forgiven: "It is a pity to see what sacrifices the landowners have to make to cover this obligation; at times they even have to sell their beds."[63]

The problems of the freeholding peasantry went far beyond the economic sphere. The decline of the cattle trade, on which so much of the fabric of provincial life depended, was in itself devastating, since smallholders (and to a lesser degree arrenderos) relied on the cattle and other goods exchanged in such barter systems as the *para pelo* to cement social ties among the widely dispersed settlements. With the economic incentive in these relationships gone, the bonds of mutual trust and friendship tended to break down, in effect isolating eastern Tomina smallholders from one another precisely when mutual support and aid were most urgent.

Within this context of social marginalization and increasing poverty, there came an alarming increase in the incidence of banditry, severely aggravating the province's economic malaise. The Padilla judicial archives, the main source for examining this phenomenon, are fragmentary, but the surviving lists of court cases indicate a steep rise in banditry during the second and third decades of the twentieth century.[64] Between 1882 and 1888, only 211 cases dealing with cattle rustling and five armed attacks were noted; in 1905 alone, 296 cattle-rustling cases and twenty-eight armed attacks came to the attention of the court.[65] Five years later, the prefect reported that bandit attacks were lessening, but this respite proved to be short-lived. A report in 1915 warned: "Farmers and livestock owners, disheartened by the assaults of which they are the object, are seeking to give up their work and look for other places and ways to earn a living. Landholdings are devalued and earnings are depressed, to the harm of the [departmental] treasury." The situation became so bad in Tarvita that the largest landowners of the canton sent desperate petitions to Sucre for troops and rifles to put down the constant attacks on their hacienda houses. By 1930, at the height of bandit activity, the Tomina subprefect complained that, on average, he received two to three cattle-rustling reports daily.[66]

Who were these bandits? As Eric Hobsbawm postulates in his classic work on bandits, this was a peasant phenomenon;[67] *labrador* (laborer) was by far the most common profession of those brought to trial in Padilla. Though the term was applied to both hacienda peons and independent smallholders, most of those taken in hand appear to have been smallholders. Only in a few cases were other professions mentioned; one bandit described himself as a carpenter, and another, according to the victim, "has no profession other than robbery."[68] In two cases proprietarios were accused of being chiefs of highwaymen, but in both cases the facts are so unclear that it seems likely these accusations were motivated by personal and political animosities.[69]

Bandits came from all cantons of eastern Tomina, although one region in eastern Tacopaya, an area of smallholdings called

Sayanchaca, was particularly notorious for its bandits and cattle rustlers. The mountainous territory was strategically located close to the main east–west trade route and served as ideal refuge for those who scourged the highway. One man was arrested in Tarabuco merely because he professed to be from Sayanchaca; once in jail, he was accused of a spate of cattle rustlings near the town.[70] Another area that was much infested by bandit gangs was Pescado canton, but no area in eastern Tomina was immune from the bandits' depredations.

The gangs might have as few as three members and as many as twenty; the usual number was about ten. What is most striking is that many gangs contained members from quite distant areas. For example, a group of bandits implicated in the robbery and murder of an Indian from Tomina and the rape of his daughter hailed from three different cantons, Alcalá, Tomina, and Padilla. It is possible that an extensive information network existed that allowed peasants from different areas to hear about potential marks and temporarily band together for the job. This hypothesis is supported by testimony given in the trial of the above-mentioned gang, where one of the defendants admitted that the attack had been instigated by a Saturnino N., an Indian from Miscamayoc in Padilla who did not join the attack. The Indian asserted that the murder victim had just received a large quantity of money and therefore was a good target.[71]

Bandits were not the only ones to profit from their criminal activity. Cattle merchants often bought stolen livestock cheaply in search of high profits. In fact, in eastern Tomina cattle traders were looked on with suspicion; many inhabitants believed they were rustlers themselves or hired others to take the animals. The mayor of Villa Serrano (formerly Pescado) asserted that a band of robbers had been "supplied by the Sucre butchers or cattle dealers who bring [supplies] clandestinely from that capital city in return for cattle, particularly to those who have the reputation of being rustlers." Unscrupulous lawyers in Padilla who defended rustlers took in fee the cattle their clients had stolen. Many bandits crossed over to Vallegrande, in Santa Cruz, and sold their loot there. There they could also dispose of stolen livestock to the cattle traders who marketed the animals in Argentina.[72]

In a limited sense, the bandit phenomenon had the potential of becoming a social movement against the wrenching economic changes that Tomina underwent in the early part of twentieth century. There is a hint of this potential in the oral tradition that inevitably makes the merchant or the hacendado the bandits' target. Most local tales elevate the bandits to heroes and emphasize their sense of honor, perhaps in contradistinction to their victims' considerable power over others in usual circumstances. For example, Pío Romero, perhaps the most famous of the Tomina bandits, sneaked into the small village of Pescado with his gang at night and roused one of the local merchants, demanding forty suits for himself and his companions. The frightened merchant complied. On his departure, Romero promised to pay the hapless trader in one month. According to local legend, Romero returned exactly a month later and paid up in full.[73]

The cases in the judicial archives hardly support the myth of the bandit-hero. In fact, the Tomina bandits attacked Indians, smallholders, and hacienda peons just as frequently as they did the more powerful and wealthy members of rural society. One arrendero on Hacienda Punilla graphically described the situation when, in 1928, a number of bandits used the estate as their base, "sowing such terror among all the inhabitants of the district that [the local residents] have not felt safe a single instant, especially at night, passing cruel moments of fear until the light of day has dissipated with the shadows the feared danger." The items stolen in some assaults clearly indicate the poverty of the victims. The bandit leader Olegario Cabrera, working with eight or nine others, at gunpoint robbed and then murdered an Indian, an arrendero of Hacienda Huancapampa in Alcalá. Cabrera's gang stripped the Indian's hut of all of his meager possessions, including some rough cloth, a new poncho, a small weight, and a sack of jerked beef.[74]

By preference, of course, bandits chose richer targets—traders, for example, who usually had cash as well as goods. In 1903, four men raided the house of two cattle traders in Villar, making off with over 7,000 pesos cash, a Winchester rifle, and other items.[75] Attacks on landowners were frequent. In Tarvita in 1929, a gang of twelve bandits armed with rifles, revolvers, knives, and sticks overran three hacienda houses in a week, taking all their contents, and also assaulted travelers and the huts of arrenderos. Two people died of severe beatings during this crime spree.[76]

Since authorities and victims alike considered all bandits mere criminals, it is unclear to what extent, if any, attacks on merchants and landowners may be seen as a form of resistance against changing social and economic conditions. There is a hint of banditry as a nascent resistance movement not only in the selective popular memory of bandit exploits, but also in the experiences of the

Reyes family, one of the most important landholders in eastern Tomina. In 1915, the prominent Liberal Aniceto Reyes, scion of an old established Padilla family and owner of the Hacienda Limabamba, was attacked on his estate and brutally murdered. Reyes had only recently begun to devote himself exclusively to farming after the ouster of his party from government cut short a long career in public service. The Padilla elite was alarmed at the murder of one of their most distinguished members, and the town's newspaper decried the growing strength of bandit gangs in the countryside.[77] Considering Reyes's inexperience as a *patrón*, he may well have instituted some changes that angered the work force. Apparently there was a considerable amount of social tension on the hacienda, for as late as 1929, Enrique Reyes Barron, Aniceto's nephew, was attacked with slings and stones by cattle owners, presumably his own arrenderos, when he attempted to collect grazing fees. The seriousness of this case is evident in the fact that it was brought to court; the Reyes family traditionally administered their own justice on their estate because the region's judiciary was dominated by the family's political rivals.[78]

The government did not make concerted efforts to repress banditry until the second decade of the twentieth century, and even then it did so only under intense pressure from the region's elites. In 1912, the prefect of Chuquisaca authorized the stationing of a contingent of mounted police to combat the bandits in Tomina, but this force existed on paper only. Two years later, in response to increasing pressure by Tomina vecinos and provincial authorities, the prefect sent several soldiers to the beleaguered province. These were meant to be temporary protection only, and they were no match for the well-armed brigands. Also in 1914, the corregidor of Pescado charged one of the bandit strongholds at Salto with a force of twenty soldiers. The robbers, many of whom were from adjacent Vallegrande in Santa Cruz, forced the small band of soldiers to retreat. Incensed by this defeat, the subprefect of Tomina sent in more soldiers, accompanied by the Padilla commissioner and five of the Padilla jail wardens, to root out the criminals. Again the brigands repulsed the attack, in part because the robbers owned modern Winchester rifles, far superior to what the authorities could muster.[79]

The defeat of national forces emboldened the bandits, and the corregidores complained the following year, "The leaders of the bandits, some of whom have been condemned to death [by the courts], strut around in the villages, with no authority daring to capture them." According to the prefect, this was in part because the few existing jails were falling apart, allowing many escapes. Consequently, local officials did not attempt to capture the bandits lest they later wreak certain revenge on those who had brought them to justice.[80]

Finally, in 1918 the mounted police corps that had been authorized six years earlier went into action. With their mobility and modern arms, they were quite successful in reducing the bandits' activities. They eliminated virtually all the gangs in the new province of Azurduy within a year. But when, in 1921, the force was halved as a cost-cutting measure, banditry again increased.[81] The mounted police were responsible for Azero province as well, and the force was spread very thinly over a huge and inaccessible territory. However, banditry was not as widespread in Azero as in Tomina. Most attacks in the eastern province were perpetrated by Tomina and Vallegrande gangs who made brief incursions into bordering areas such as Ticucha canton.[82]

The relationship between bandits, hacendados, and merchants was not so antagonistic as the pleas by the provincial elites to suppress criminal activity suggest. Besides the cattle merchants, who were in a position to buy rustled cattle at rock-bottom prices, landowners sometimes found it advantageous to reach an accommodation with the armed gangs. A number of bandits happened to be arrenderos, making relations with their patrones a delicate matter. For example, the infamous bandit Olegario Cabrera, who in 1922 had already been in jail at least three times for various misdeeds and who later entered into local folklore, was ostensibly a peon on the hacienda of the wealthy Spanish merchant Manuel Monterde. Although it is unlikely that Cabrera completed the usual obligations of an arrendero, the bandit did not molest Monterde. According to Monterde's son, Cabrera left the merchant alone because he "was a good *patrón* and all the *arrenderos* liked him."[83]

In some instances, landowners seem to have actively shielded their workers from the full force of the law. Such was the case in 1926, when Mariano Alvarado admitted to his *patrón* that he had been a part of a gang that attacked the residence of a moderately wealthy farmer in Padilla. As punishment, the hacendado had Alvarado sign a contract with his victim, obligating him to return his part of the booty and imposing a fine of forty Bs as additional restitution. This was a mild punishment in view of the size of the gang—between eleven and twenty men—and the fact that they had stolen 500 Bs in cash in addition to other items.[84] The hacendado may have used his influence to keep his arrendero out of jail because he was more interested in keeping his peon's labor than in combating banditry.

Hacendados at times even used the threat of prosecution to enlist bandits as workers in the always labor-short economy of eastern Tomina. These workers, it stands to reason, were not always very reliable. In 1902, Felipe Núñez of Tacopaya was taken in hand for stealing thirty pesos worth of goods from the hacienda of a prominent landowner, who then contracted with the robber to work off his debt in labor for one year and remain as colono for another two years. But after Núñez stole again in 1903, the landowner had him put in jail.[85]

In 1930–31, the provisional military government, as in Yamparaez, sent a commission of soldiers, apparently with an adviser from the German army, to Tomina and summarily executed all men in jail on banditry charges. Perhaps more than 60 suspected brigands lost their lives.[86] This action, drastic though it was, apparently did not eliminate the problem, for in 1932, the new civilian government sent six policemen from La Paz to Tomina as an anti-bandit force. These men were hardly on the spot before they were recalled and sent to fight the Paraguayan army in the Chaco, whereupon banditry again increased. As the Chaco War continued, deserters replenished the ranks of the gangs and made life behind the front, which included much of Tomina, as dangerous as before, if not more dangerous. In a sense, as René Arze has suggested, the Chaco War opened a second, internal front, which the Bolivian army, because of its manpower problems in its fight with the Paraguayans, found impossible to combat effectively.[87]

To add to the province's problems, the Great Depression had a devastating effect on Tomina and virtually eliminated the commercialization of its products and thus much of the surplus that the bandits appropriated. The subprefect in 1932 painted a desolate picture: despite the fertility of the area and its access to abundant water, agricultural production was barely sufficient to cover subsistence needs, and the immense grazing areas were scarcely used. Although the subprefect blamed these circumstances on the laziness of the inhabitants, a more likely explanation was that Tomina's traditional markets, especially Sucre, were so depressed that the costs of growing and taking the produce to market were higher than the sale price.[88]

Furthermore, as we have seen, the Chaco War destroyed the lucrative Azero–Sucre trade route from which the province had derived its last remnants of prosperity. As bandit activity turned from a potential social resistance movement to mere criminal activity with the addition of armed bands of army deserters, the Tomina landowners and merchants who previously had continued to do well also plunged close to the subsistence level. The resulting economic and social stagnation made it impossible for the province to improve rural conditions. Even in the 1950's and 1960's, when neighboring Azero began to prosper again, Tomina, mired in minifundism, remained poverty-stricken. Tomina residents began to leave in increasing numbers for economically more dynamic regions, such as Argentina, Monteagudo, and Santa Cruz. Although this out-migration had begun in the 1910's, by the second half of the twentieth century, the flight from the province turned to a flood.

Differing reactions to changing economic conditions in Tomina mark the region's diverse cultural background and social organization. In the western highlands, society organized primarily into large estates and based on traditional Andean cultural models produced resistance to new work patterns through labor strikes. The movement's leaders, who adopted from the Indian communities their call for the return of usurped ayllu lands, in fact had a more radical proposal in mind, since in Tomina there had been virtually no hacienda expansion at the expense of Indian communities. As the experience at Hacienda La Candelaria shows, the adoption of the ayllus' ideology called for an agrarian reform in which hacienda lands were to be distributed among the increasingly land-starved resident workers. This, of course, was totally unacceptable to the hacendados, and they were eventually able to suppress or coopt this movement.

In contrast, in eastern Tomina, where a frontier heritage and a much more diverse ethnic mix created a rural society of mostly smallholders with a decidedly commercial and much less traditional Andean orientation, reactions to economic decline were quite different. Since social relations were based to a large degree on commercial transactions, smallholders and the relatively mobile hacienda labor population became much more isolated after the turn of the century. This sense of isolation and consequent anomie resulted in a marked increase of banditry—at best an inefficient type of social movement incapable of stemming the tides of change. Banditry and cattle rustling were the last rearguard effort—even if of a minority only—to escape from the social and economic dislocations following on the structural changes in the Bolivian economy. The concluding chapter will compare and contrast the different rural resistance movements that sprang up in the various provinces of Chuquisaca and examine the effects on the Agrarian Reform of 1953 and beyond in the context of the historical legacy of this crucial period of change during the late nineteenth and early twentieth centuries.

CHAPTER EIGHT

Conclusion

As the preceding chapters have demonstrated, resistance by rural inhabitants to changes in social and economic conditions during the late nineteenth and early twentieth centuries was widespread and manifested itself in many different ways. The commercial impetus that closely integrated many of the Latin American economies into the world economy had enormous consequences for rural peoples throughout the region; indeed, the changes at this time were perhaps more profound than at any time in their history. This was even the case, as in large portions of Chuquisaca, where the restructuring of the economy on the basis of new exports led to stagnation, because there, elites attempted to compensate for their loss of income in the export-oriented economy by squeezing larger profits from the peasantry. What is significant, however, is that countryfolk, whether Indians, mestizo smallholders, or large estate owners, actively participated in the reshaping of rural society. For all the power and influence of the elites, non-elites played no small role in affecting the amount and type of change.

How do we make sense of the strategies that rural peoples adopted to cope with the massive changes around the turn of the twentieth century? For one thing, it is clear that not all rural inhabitants resisted these transformations; occasionally some were able to use new opportunities to enrich themselves or to increase their power. Perhaps the best example of this is the Tarabuco kuraka Venancio Puchu, who, with the assistance of his wife, expanded his landholdings and increased his power over the members of the community. But this kind of success was relatively rare. For most rural inhabitants at the turn of the century, standards of living deteriorated. This was apparent as much in Yamparaez, where many Indians lost their lands and were forced to hand over a larger proportion of their surplus as hacienda peons, as in Tomina, where smallholders lost much of their social cohesion as old commercial exchange networks broke down with the increase in competition from Chaco cattle and shrinking mining markets. Similar cases can be made for Cinti, which experienced a general economic decline after 1890 with only a few exceptions, and for Azero, where the dominance of white settlers meant increasingly worse conditions for Chiriguano workers and the eventual destruction of their culture. The worsening of social and economic conditions for the majority of rural inhabitants is a general trend discernible for much of the rest of Latin America during this period.[1]

Chuquisaca's rural inhabitants were well aware of the fact that most of the changes during this period meant declining conditions for themselves and their neighbors. To avoid a drastically lowered standard of living, most attempted to resist in one way or another. In fact, resistance to change, a wholly rational decision considering the circumstances, marks the history of the vasty majority of the diverse peoples living in the department throughout this period. But it is striking that the strategies and tactics countryfolk employed to arrest the decline in their social and economic positions varied so widely according to region, cultural background, and conditions of employment.

How do we account for the types of resistance that the rural inhabitants of Chuquisaca engaged in? What are the implications of the varieties of resistance for the study of peasant movements in general? The literature on peasant movements has burgeoned since the Vietnam War, when it became apparent to scholars that peasants were not simply modern-day anachronisms soon to fade away, but were, on the contrary, an integral part of the present-day world who would continue to play extremely important roles in the social and political turmoil of the twentieth century. The inspiration for much of the new research came from Arthur Stinchcombe, who in a short article published in 1961 hypothesized that types of land-tenure systems determined how rural inhabitants mobilized for political action. In Stinchcombe's model, tenants were the most likely to produce what he called "revolutionary populist movements." Other types of property systems, such as

manorial, family smallholdings, plantation, and ranching enterprises, were not so effective and tended to produce low, disorganized, or corrupt political activity among the rural masses.[2]

New scholarship on peasant movements in the main followed
Stinchcombe's framework and attempted to find correlations between type of property and peasant rebellion; this was certainly
true of the work of Jeffery M. Paige, and, to a lesser extent, Eric
Wolf and James C. Scott. Theda Skocpol, in a recent review article
on this subject, divided these scholars into two groups: those who
asserted that landless laborers were revolutionary (Paige) and those
who concluded that peasant villagers were the most likely to en-
gender a revolution (Wolf, Scott).[3] These startlingly different conclusions point to a number of problems in approach. One fallacy,
especially in the work of Stinchcombe and Paige, is the emphasis
on land-tenure systems as the decisive variable in the quest of
finding the rural group most likely to rebel. In Chuquisaca, different types of land tenure undoubtedly had a certain effect on whether
rural inhabitants rebelled or did not rebel, but they were at best a
minor factor so far as the patterns of resistance were concerned.

Both Wolf and Scott—though they hypothesize that one type of
peasant, the independent villager, was the most likely to participate in revolutionary activities—take pains to place the peasant
movements they discuss in their respective historical contexts.
Scott, however, while showing great concern for the changes in
village elite relations precipitated by the penetration of capitalist
methods in the Southeast Asian countryside, assumes that villagers over the widely diverse region subscribed to essentially the
same moral economy that existed in the precolonial period. He
largely ignores many of the diverse arrangements within the village economy between non-elites, which in fact must have changed
well before the end of the nineteenth century and probably varied
from area to area in this enormous region.[4] Thus, Scott and to
some degree Wolf fail to recognize the implications of the changes
in the internal structures of the villages they study on the non-
elite level. But these changes in the internal cohesion of peasant
society are, I believe, crucial to an understanding of the potential
for peasant rebellion and revolution. One can see this very clearly
in the case of Tomina, where the disintegration of smallholder society, people who are the logical candidates for both Wolf and Scott
as revolutionaries, failed to go beyond a destructive type of banditry in resistance to economic changes.

Another major problem with the literature is the excessive emphasis on revolution, or, at the very least, violent rebellion. This emphasis is perhaps not surprising in view of the wealth of information that such episodes have created, or of the interest in peasant violence after Vietnam and, in the Latin American case, the legacy that the Mexican and Cuban revolutions created for the study of the region; yet it has too often meant that other, perhaps more subtle, methods of resistance have not been adequately taken into consideration.[5] Rebellion is often only the ultimate response to pressures, and is preceded by other actions. A case in point is the community Indians of Tarabuco (Yamparaez), who engaged in a gamut of behaviors that can all be described as resistance to the encroachment of the haciendas—a progression from judicial challenges, a restructuring of the ayllu economy to take advantage of new commercial possibilities and creating sufficient resources to avoid encroachment, to demonstrations against the revisita, and, finally, to the takeover of hacienda lands and participation in the great Indian rebellion of 1927. Rebellions are undoubtedly significant, but I would argue that day-to-day responses, which often involve a lower level of overt conflict, are perhaps more important to understanding the dynamics of rural resistance (and, therefore, the structures of rural society) than the infrequent and sporadic violent episodes.

I do not mean to imply that authors who stress massive violent conflict altogether ignore other forms of behavior. Stinchcombe and Paige, for example, try to account for other types of political movements as well. But their models fail to hold true for Chuquisaca, and, I suspect, for many other rural areas. Paige sees no overt conflict occurring at all on commercial haciendas; yet laborers from both Yamparaez and Cinti haciendas frequently clashed with hacendados. On the other hand, smallholders in Tomina never engaged in "reformist commodity movements," since they were incapable of uniting under a common cause, nor did the Chiriguano migratory laborers ever contemplate nationalist or socialist revolution, although they had been proletarianized to a great degree in the sugarcane fields of northern Argentina.

Part of the problem in most of the models of revolution and revolt, particularly in those that are based primarily on land tenure, is the failure to note the dynamism that in fact exists in the constantly changing conditions in the countryside. In the case of Chuquisaca, it is possible to show that violence actually can decrease, even though resistance to changes in the rural society of Latin America as a whole remained high. For example, in Azero province after the 1892 rebellion, the Chiriguanos found it virtually impossible to strike back at the encroaching colonists using violent means. Earlier, violence had been fairly effective, even in getting back Indian children who had been taken away by landowners. After the failure of the 1892 rebellion, even the most recalcitrant Chiriguano village chief realized that fighting the white man would not bring back the earlier period of independence. Instead of joining the hacienda labor force, many Indians chose to leave the area altogether, and go to work in northern Argentina where, presumably, conditions were better and the pay higher. If one accepts emigration from the Chiriguanía as a type of resistance to oppressive conditions, then one can say that levels of resistance went up at the same time that violent resistance, at least as measured by actions the Indians instigated, went down. Thus the concept of resistance, which takes into account a wide range of behavior, is much more useful for understanding the reality of the rural inhabitants' reactions to unfavorable changes in economic and social conditions than the concepts of revolution or rebellion are. By examining resistance rather than just large-scale, violent reactions, one can more nearly approach the reality of life and its changes in the countryside.

Why do rural inhabitants resist in certain ways and not in others? As I have tried to show, resistance varied from case to case and over time. Three factors appear to have been particularly important: the economic forces that led to changes in living conditions, the alternatives that each group of rural inhabitants disposed of in resisting change, and the internal cohesion of the various groups that constituted each rural society. All three factors changed over time and were largely interconnected. Since in each type of rural society these factors differed, it is essential to take a regional perspective (thus approximating the actual experience of the largely localistic countryfolk) to account fully for the types of resistance.

In most areas of Latin America in the late nineteenth century, as in Chuquisaca, there were a number of economic incentives to change land-tenure patterns and labor conditions that often led to a lower living standard for the majority of rural inhabitants. Most scholars have defined these economic incentives as part of the increasing direct commercial integration of the Latin American countryside into the world economic system. These economic incentives certainly existed in Chuquisaca, particularly in Azero and on the haciendas of southeastern Cinti. The expansion of frontier estates into the Chiriguanía was a direct result of the new opportunities for profiting from cattle raising opened up by the revival of the silver-mining economy. Likewise, the formation of the enormous SAGIC latifundio linked the economically secondary Cinti uplands to national markets, particularly La Paz. In both areas, resistance to changes from rural inhabitants was evident, as most scholars examining this period would predict.

Nevertheless, most of Chuquisaca during the early twentieth century, when presumably the forces for integration into the world economy were at their strongest, became increasingly marginalized. This topic, relative stagnation and consequent changes in the rural economy, has rarely been broached in the discussion of this period. Even stagnation, however, brought about new stresses in the rural economies. This was quite clear in Tomina and Yamparaez, where the faltering of the silver-mining economy resulted, in Tomina, in the decline of the networks of barter and exchange, and in Yamparaez, in hacienda expansion. These processes, directly attributable to economic decline, also led to widespread rural resistance. Thus, the expansion of export economies during the late nineteenth and early twentieth centuries, or, as Eric Wolf would put it, "the spread of North Atlantic capitalism," though perhaps the most common phenomenon, was not the only cause of rural unrest. Conversely, the shrinking markets could, and did, also bring about resistance.

The intensity of economic change, and thus social change, also varied widely and must be taken into account. Although Cinti province experienced an overall decline, grape growers continued to produce wines and singani, although on a reduced scale. The skilled vineyard workers, the viñateros, for example, suffered little change in their labor conditions. The paternalistic measures that vineyard owners employed (echoing older, Andean customs) provided enough of a cushion for the viñateros to keep them from suffering much change in their comparatively well-off existence. In fact, the combination of market incentives, such as wage labor, and reciprocal measures appears to have been fairly effective in maintaining good relations between patrones and laborers; it also helps to explain why resistance to hacienda expansion in Yamparaez was not stronger. The downturn in the economy forced hacendados to rely more heavily on traditional, Andean methods of rule, while certain members of the Indian communities reacted to the expansion of haciendas by participating to a greater extent in the market. Economic stagnation, in this case, brought about an increasing similarity between hacienda and ayllu. Although there was concerted, and eventually effective, resistance to the loss of community lands, it is significant that the communities were unable to regain the fields they had lost. Most affected were the Chiriguano Indians, who were forced from a largely natural economy into debt peonage or wage labor in Argentina.

That the alternatives available to rural inhabitants depended on a number of factors is apparent in the Chuquisaca case. Generally speaking, highland inhabitants were more integrated into national society and often had more choices, which included a larger range of nonviolent behavior, than peoples on the lowland frontiers. These alternatives included lawsuits, refusal to appear before governmental bodies (such as the revisita), migration, and labor strikes. Only after these methods had failed did most highland rural inhabitants resort to violence. This is quite clear in the history of the Yamparaez ayllus, where a radical faction dedicated to direct action to retake former community lands developed only after two or three decades of hacienda expansion. It is also necessary to take into consideration the power wielded by the various actors on the local scene. Not surprisingly, both hacienda work stoppages and efforts to regain Indian lands became especially numerous in the early part of the twentieth century, after the Sucre elites had lost their economic and political predominance on the national scene. Weaker elites did provide greater opportunity for resistance, but since elite control over the Bolivian countryside was always tenuous at best (and remains so today), this factor is not of primary significance.

The case of the Chiriguanos and other tribal groups on the Azero frontier is far different. Unlike the highland people, the Chiriguanos had no effective juridical identity before the state. The landgrant process, which (except for one case) completely ignored aboriginal property rights, is indicative of this lack of status. Rather, a type of "conquest society" existed in which the white or mestizo conquerors arrogated to themselves all power over the Indians' lands, labor, and women.[6] Moreover, on the frontier the state wielded little independent power, permitting local elites to do as they wished. This clearly affected the ways in which the Chiriguanos could resist encroachment. While the Indians still maintained control over some territory, mutual violence marked frontier society; after the Indians' last effort to throw out the settlers failed in 1892, the colonists, unchallenged, used violence to institute a labor system characterized by poor working conditions and debt peonage.[7] From the available evidence, one cannot easily determine whether the Chiriguanos engaged in the type of resistance so common among black slaves both in the American South and in Latin America, such as work slowdowns and the deliberate breaking of tools, but even if they did, it probably had relatively little effect on their general welfare. Apart from the few Indians who still lived in the remaining handful of independent villages, the best most could hope for was to flee the country or live on a mission. Either option meant eventual deculturation. In Jujuy, Indian sugarcane workers quickly became proletarianized; and in the missions, Chiriguano children were effectively indoctrinated into alien patterns of thought. These forms of resistance, though not particularly attractive alternatives and not conducive to the long-term survival of the group, were all that were left to the powerless lowland tribes.

Although the type and strength of economic forces and alternatives available to rural inhabitants explain to a large degree what type of resistance, if any, they engaged in, these two factors by themselves fail to take into account the whole picture. A third factor, social cohesion, is necessary for understanding how rural peoples resisted. Otherwise, it would be difficult to explain the incidence of banditry in the Tomina countryside. From Wolf's point of view in particular, and also Scott's, the independent smallholders should have been most capable of revolutionary activity. Instead, numbers of inhabitants resorted in the end to criminal activity that weakened rural society even further. Tomina smallholders and even hacienda workers were perhaps even better integrated into national society than were the Indian communities, but they were unable to react effectively to their declining position in the rural economy. Of course, the economic forces battering the Tomina peasant household were much more diffuse than elsewhere, not represented by any one person or entity. In Yamparaez, Indians could organize against the usurping landlord; in Cinti, SACIC hacienda workers could blame the administrator for the lack of time to work on their own fields. In Tomina, the petty traders simply moved out of town and the cattle merchants traveled farther east, to the Chaco frontier, to buy their livestock. The absence of any type of collective action, even perhaps what Hobsbawm has termed "social banditry" (other than in later myth), shows that the social disintegration of Tomina society that attended the decline of mutual exchange and bartering systems severely limited peasant resistance. Independent peasants in Tomina were the least likely to engage in effective political action because—contrary to the hypotheses of some scholars—the internal organization of this group varied over time and according to particular economic circumstances; in this case, social cohesion became weak when new economic forces lowered the smallholders' standard of living.

The numerous instances of hacienda labor strikes also go against current theories of peasant unrest. All theorists hypothesize that manorial labor systems are the least conducive to revolutionary activity. Yet in Chuquisaca, hacienda peons came closest to a radical vision of society, namely on Hacienda La Candelaria, where the workers' stated aim was to redistribute the entire estate among its residents and eliminate the landlord completely. Why were the most radical movements to be found on haciendas? Perhaps the paternalistic system was not as strong as previously believed; the "open triangle" model in which peons depended almost exclusively on landlords for goods and favors, to the exclusion of ties between hacienda laborers, does not work for highland Chuquisaca estates. But there was a continuity between communal and hacienda structures and modes of authority. The hacendado did not rule directly over his peons; he delegated most of his day-to-day authority to trusted overseers, themselves workers deeply imbued in Andean culture. Cooperation and mutual aid, in the form of ayni and other reciprocal arrangements, were common among arrenderos. When the landlord did preside directly over the hacienda community during crucial points in the agricultural cycle, he did so in a community-reaffirming manner by sponsoring celebrations that, according to traditional mechanisms of reciprocity and redistribution, strengthened the bonds not only between *patrón* and peon but also among the peons themselves.

If the landowner refused to participate in this system of mutual obligations, he threatened the whole hacienda community. The hacendado was an essential actor in the peons' continued struggle for survival, since he usually possessed considerable resources to help prevent subsistence crises. Furthermore, changes in the hacienda regime that lessened the safety net of paternalistic measures exposed the full extent of the exploitation the peons suffered. As Joel Migdal has pointed out, the ties between urban activists and peasants are crucial to an understanding of the ideology that peasant movements adopt. In the case of La Candelaria, it appears from the scanty evidence available that these ties were probably indirect. The peons joined in meetings with the comunarios, who had some connections with the Pro-Indian League. Nevertheless, the Indian communities' program of throwing the hacendados off former ayllu lands had powerful appeal for La Candelaria's workers. The interesting question is why peons from that hacienda would adopt this ideology. It seems unlikely that there was still a strong collective memory from the time, far back in the sixteenth century, when the estate was Indian land. But it is quite possible that the hacienda community was still cohesive enough, despite the fragmentation of peons into groups such as full arrenderos, half arrenderos, and arrimantes, that if the hacendado refused to fulfill his traditional role, the peons would feel free to get rid of him and run things on their own. This revolutionary vision was a logical step once the Andean notions of reciprocity and redistribution were no longer valid in relations between peon and hacendado. In turn, however, the hacienda workers themselves were able to strike (which called for considerable organization) and to maintain their solidarity by emphasizing the strength of these same Andean notions among themselves.

The radical stance of La Candelaria's peons earned them little or nothing—the hacienda remained intact and the landowner apparently was eventually able to diffuse much of the subversive tendencies of his laborers.[8] Resistance with more limited objectives was much more effective, precisely because the social relations governing the countryside permitted much flexibility and some victories for the non-elites. Otherwise it would have been impossible for the large landowners of the highlands, for example, to maintain the hacienda regime. Conflict was endemic to the countryside, but the goal was usually accommodation rather than a radical restructuring of society. This meant that the groups that were relatively well integrated into society were more likely to achieve their objectives than those that were not. Although the strains of economic and social change of the late nineteenth and early twentieth centuries exacerbated conflict, even groups such as highland Indian communities (shorn of their legal status, but maintaining some de facto legitimacy before the courts) were able to channel some of the conflict over lands through the courts.

The integration of peons into national society was not as complete, yet they used the courts to fight what they considered abuses; and a solidarity based on Andean mores made them a formidable force to contend with. The hacendado's need to reach some kind of accommodation with his workers made strikes and other drastic actions much less frequent than otherwise would have been the case in this period of severe economic strain. In a sense, both the Indian communities and the highland hacienda peons were eventually effective in their resistance, since the 1927 rebellion and subsequent actions forced the elites to take seriously the demands of the majority of the rural population. Similarly, the economic constraints of the Great Depression forced the SAGIC administration to compromise with its workers. The always tenuous equilibrium between elites and masses was reestablished along traditional Andean and paternalistic lines.[9]

In Tomina and Azero, most rural inhabitants did not fare as well. In both provinces, at least by the turn of the century, community organization was extremely weak. Tomina smallholders and peons, like the Chiriguano Indians, were unable to unify and attempt to change their destiny. Moreover, the forms of resistance they chose were ineffective. In Tomina, banditry, as Hobsbawm has rightly asserted, was an ultimately ineffective way of resisting change because it tended to destroy community organization and did not swing the balance of power in favor of smallholders and peons. As for the Chiriguanos of Azero, migration to Argentina and acceptance of Franciscan missions, though effective in the short run (and very annoying to the settlers), ultimately meant the destruction of traditional Indian culture.

Thus, internal cohesion, the alternative actions available to each group according to their level of integration and relative power within rural society, and the kind of economic changes in the countryside determined the type of resistance that rural inhabitants engaged in to maintain their way of life in Chuquisaca. Resistance, if one includes nonviolent actions, was much more widespread and perhaps also more effective than previously thought. The excessive emphasis on revolution and rebellion by many theorists on rural conflict helps mask, rather than illuminate, other forms of significant resistance in the countryside. The type and nature of this resistance varied: it occurred in areas that became more closely integrated into the burgeoning export economies and in those that were disengaged. Resistance was also a type of adaptation, and led to mutual accommodation between elites and the rural masses. We must discard the previous image, in which the elites (or worse, foreign capitalists) determined the nature and speed of change in the Latin American countryside during the late nineteenth and early twentieth centuries. Instead, it is necessary to place close to center stage the many groups within the rural masses, who often were able to control a surprisingly large part of their own destinies.

Developments in Chuquisaca after 1930 are beyond the compass of this study. Besides, much further research remains to be done on the events of the past fifty years. Yet certain contemporary problems relate so clearly to the crucial period under study that a brief summary of the department's subsequent history is in order.

The Great Depression had a tremendous impact on much of rural Chuquisaca, showing that, despite the marginalization of the region, the department was still greatly affected by outside economic forces.[10] Tomina, already depressed, was particularly hard hit. The desperate conditions there finally became a high priority for the authorities when the bubonic plague made its first appearance in the province. In 1932, the disease left 730 dead, killing 90 percent of its victims.[11] Banditry increased again, despite the often brutal methods of suppression during the Chaco War as armed deserters, fleeing army patrols, joined remnants of the old Tomina bandit gangs.

In the highlands, the state again forbade the sale of Indian land. Once this prohibition, a major goal of the Indian ayllu leaders, went into effect, agitation in Indian communities subsided. On the haciendas, the further shrinking of markets during the 1930's forced landowners to rely even more heavily on their tenants for profits. Those hacendados who had experimented with modifications in the labor system during the 1920's had to compromise with their workers a decade later to preserve at least part of their already much diminished income. Similarly, the SAGIC management in Cinti had to accede to the demands of its laborers as the tin mines and urban employers in northern Bolivia continued to lay off workers. In the rest of Cinti province, the global economic downturn only reinforced the landowners' reliance on self-sufficiency and paternalistic measures.

The Depression also had a profound effect in Azero. Trade policies in Argentina and Chile suddenly veered toward protectionism, severing many economic ties with southeastern Bolivia. The cattle trade to Chile would probably have virtually stopped anyway, because northern Chile's mining economy, with its enclave features and dependence on foreign markets, suffered particularly during the Depression.[12] The Chaco War made seasonal Chiriguano migration to the Argentine sugar plantations impossible, and as Ian Rutledge has shown, Argentine cane growers in the 1930's turned for their seasonal workers to the resident laborers from highland estates they bought in northern Argentina.[13] With Argentine competition for Chiriguano workers much diminished, Azero landowners were finally able to attract enough Indians to meet their needs, despite low wages and generally poor labor conditions. But this respite came too late; the destruction of the Chaco War and the severing of commercial ties with Argentina forced most Azero inhabitants back to the subsistence level.

Political tensions rose after the Chaco War as large numbers of veterans, many of them Indians from the highlands, returned to their communities with vastly expanded political horizons. During the 1940's, rural movements protesting conditions in the countryside gained strength, especially in Ucureña, in the Cochabamba Valley, and around Lake Titicaca in La Paz. Katherines Barnes has documented pre-Reform agitation in parts of Potosí and in Mojocoya (Zudáñez province) as well. In Cinti, peasant revolts seemed to have been endemic during the 1940's. In 1946, the arrenderos of Hacienda Las Canchas, along the Potosí border, refused to work and threatened to plunder the hacienda house. Troops were called in, and the crowd was dispersed only after several peons had been killed. After similar troubles on Hacienda Payacota del Carmen, the landowner, in 1947, bequeathed the estate to the tenant laborers. The SAGIC haciendas also experienced another round of unrest. In 1945, the company lost 101,044.33 Bs in rental payments when the arrenderos called a rent strike. Thereafter, the SAGIC administration began keeping dossiers on various inhabitants of their haciendas, often former miners, who were suspected of organizing protests against the company. No doubt contributing to the company's concern was the incident in neighboring Hacienda Carapari, where the hapless administrator, Fernando Mercy, was killed in an uprising in 1948.[14]

In 1953, a year after the National Revolutionary Movement (Movimiento Nacionalista Revolucionario; MNR) overthrew the government in one of the few real social revolutions in Latin America, constant uprisings in the countryside forced the new administration to sign a radical Agrarian Reform law. This law gave the tenant laborers on the haciendas the land on which they worked, prohibited the use of remunerated labor by the patrones, and expropriated the large estates defined as latifundios.[15] Popular myth attributes only a minor role to Chuquisaca's inhabitants in furthering the revolution in the countryside. One observer, the anthropologist Charles Erasmus, noted of rural inhabitants of Chuquisaca and Tarija: "They are an even-tempered, passive people who are not easily provoked to violence. Had it been up to the people of this area to bring about a revolution, I believe it safe to say that it would have never taken place. Chuquisaca and Tarija have benefited from changes instigated in Cochabamba, La Paz, and Potosí; they have followed the lead of peoples elsewhere. There are very few 'angry men' in this part of Bolivia."[16]

Because we know so little about rural society in Chuquisaca in the several decades before 1953, one cannot be certain, but it appears from preliminary information that outbreaks of agrarian unrest were much more frequent than suspected. There is perhaps some truth to Erasmus's assertion, however, for as we have seen, the rebellions in the highlands during the 1920's accomplished many of the goals of the Indian insurgents, and these goals, which included the maintenance of reciprocal relations between hacendado and peon as well as the end to hacienda expansion at the expense of ayllu lands, gave the rural inhabitants a stake in the old system, making them relatively immune to the call to revolution.

Despite this supposed lethargy, the 1953 law completely changed the complexion of the countryside in Cinti and Yamparaez. The many enormous estates in these provinces were expropriated and given over to the former peons. Only in the Cinti Valley—where landowners had always paid their viñateros wages, the vineyards were fairly small, and the estates could be classified as commercial enterprises—did the old landowners keep most of their land. There, the viñateros received the plots that they had been given in usufruct by the hacendados, but little else. Anthropological research from the 1960's has shown that social relations changed relatively little in the valleys.[17] This, however, was not the case with the SAGIC haciendas. Thanks to political pressures generated by a new and strong peasant union in Ingahuasi, coupled with Patiño's prominent role as the leader of the opposition to MNR policies, SAGIC lost its liquinas haciendas and was left with only the valley bottom lands of San Pedro. Indeed, most of the large estates that contained both vineyards and liquinas forfeited their liquinas during the Agrarian Reform. The severing of the two deprived vineyard owners of a resource that had helped to insulate them from the vagaries of the market. This was offset, however, by the enormous expansion of the market in Bolivia as a result of the Agrarian Reform, which thrust the marginal hacienda population into the monetary economy.

Many Indian communities did not fare well under the Agrarian Reform, despite official pronouncements that promised a restoration of community rights. As Tristan Platt has shown, the reformers imposed a unitary land tax on both communities and privately held properties. In carrying out this law, officials attempted to divide the ayllus into individual properties, an action reminiscent of what Platt has called the "first agrarian reform" of the 1880's.[18] Moreover, the provisions regarding the distribution of lands to renters applied to the ayllus as well. Thus, on Hacienda Piosera in Pocpo canton, property of the Urmiri de Quillacas community located in the department of Oruro, the ayllu had to give up 40 hectares of arable land and 216 hectares of pasturage to arrenderos who had settled there. These "arrenderos" were in fact related to the Oruro Indians and were probably members of the community who lived permanently on the hacienda.[19] Thus the Agrarian Reform, instead of protecting and supporting communal organization, actually promoted the further fragmentation of the ayllu.

The Agrarian Reform brought changes in the hacienda system that, perhaps more than any of the economic forces of the early twentieth century, destroyed the elaborate system of reciprocity and redistribution. For one thing, the hacendado was effectively removed from the estate's life, eliminating a key player as well as a large part of the economic resources that made the system function. Moreover, from the beginning, the syndicate organization, which to a certain extent replaced the hacendado, was highly politicized. Officials of the syndicate were often appointed by Agrarian Reform or party officials rather than elected by the community. To remain in power, these officials had to satisfy the outside political authorities instead of, as formerly, achieving legitimacy by maintaining a consensus within the haciendas. Under this system, traditional mechanisms that had formerly ensured the smooth functioning of the estate were inevitably neglected.[20]

Ironically, the massive infusions of aid and the proliferation of rural development agencies also contributed to the breakdown of traditional Andean customs. Although these agencies set up agricultural cooperatives that could have exploited these traditions, they most often did not. On the one hand, many cooperatives encompassed (and those that survive, still do) regions larger than individual haciendas, throwing together peasants who often had no history of common ties. The complex internal web of relationships within the former haciendas was ignored to achieve economies of scale. On the other hand, the cooperatives and the efforts of the development agencies emphasized the production for the (largely urban) markets and the integration of the peasant into the monetary economy. As this integration progressed (and it is by no means complete today), the largely nonmonetary mechanisms of traditional Andean customs lost much of their importance. This, in turn, exposed a larger part of the peasantry to the vagaries of market prices and removed much of the subsistence insurance that the peasants enjoyed under the old system.

Despite diminishing traditional modes of organization, hacienda peons in particular gained much as a result of the Agrarian Reform. Although little land was in fact redistributed, since most of the hacienda land had already been subdivided among the labor force as arriendos, the peons did gain control over their resources, especially their labor. The reforms applied only to the arrenderos, however. The rights of the subrenters, or arrimantes, were ignored in the elaborate 1953 legislation; this important group within the hacienda population received no lands. As Daniel Heyduk has argued, this oversight has led to a perpetuation of the *patrón*-peon relations typical of the southern Bolivian hacienda system between arrenderos and arrimantes.[21]

The Sucre elite lost perhaps the most in the Agrarian Reform. With most of their money invested in land, they forfeited the last vestiges of their once enormous wealth. It is hardly surprising that many actively opposed the reform, and that many former landowners still remember with fondness "the good old days" when they controlled vast numbers of peons and huge expanses of land. Indeed, Erasmus found that it was this group, which had lost so much, that came closest to harboring the "angry men" he had expected to find among the peasants.[22]

The effects of the land reform were less drastic farther east. Although the large estates of Tomina were expropriated, smallholders received nothing. Moreover, in the more remote areas of the province, large landowners were able to maintain control over their lands by joining the MNR and bribing or otherwise hindering the implementation of reform measures. In Belisario Boeto province (the former Pescado canton), one researcher found that "in the early 1970's twelve big landowners controlled almost half of the total area of the province," a land-tenure situation not much different from the one that prevailed at the turn of the century. To this day, the province's large landowners are still able to manipulate the political system so as to keep their estates intact.[23]

This pattern is even more evident in Azero province (subdivided after 1947 into Hernando Siles and Luis Calvo provinces), where the landowners have actively and successfully resisted the reform laws. In Huacareta in 1957, landlords ambushed and killed several syndicate leaders sent to organize the peasants. Although the murderers were sent to jail in La Paz for a time, they continued to control local politics after their return; some even joined the MNR, the party responsible for the Agrarian Reform.[24]

The Monteagudo area is the only region in Chuquisaca that has registered strong economic growth. An epidemic in 1959–60 finished off the remaining livestock in the region and forced the landowners to convert pastures into cornfields and raise hogs to make ends meet. The efforts of CORDECH (Corporation for the Development of Chuquisaca) to commercialize pork production, though impeded by widespread corruption, met with considerable success. Combined with the discovery of significant new oil deposits in the old Azero province, the region experienced an economic boom during the 1960's and 1970's.[25]

The rights of the Chiriguanos are ignored today, just as they were ignored during the Agrarian Reform. Once commercial corn cultivation again became important, landowners were loath to let go of their most important labor source. Despite a strong case for receiving land, by the 1953 law the Indians continue to serve as peons at below-subsistence wages on the former land grants, actually a modified form of debt peonage. Not surprisingly, many Chiriguanos still flee the oppressive conditions and migrate to Argentina or, more recently, to the sugarcane and cotton fields of Santa Cruz. Only the small number of arrenderos, mestizos who migrated to the province during the colonial period and the nineteenth century, became owners of their plots. As Kevin Healy has shown, a handful of large landowners continue to control the best lands. These landowners refuse to let the former arrenderos cut down trees on communal property to construct fences, and so, as before, the landowners' livestock enters the small farmers' cornfields and often destroys the crops.[26] Relations between workers and hacendado today greatly resemble those of pre-Reform days. In many respects, the frontier society of 80 years ago persists in this region. The only exceptions are among the rural migrants since the Agrarian Reform, many of whom came from adjacent Tomina province with their tradition of independence and banditry; they have to a certain extent successfully challenged the absolute predominance of the old elites in the area around Monteagudo.

In sum, though the forces of change are inexorably transforming the countryside, economic stagnation continues to characterize most of Chuquisaca, unable to break free of the patterns of resistance and accommodation of the past.

Reference Material

A Note on Source Citations

Published works are cited in short form in the Notes. For full authors' names, titles, and publication data, see the Bibliography, pp. 243–59. Most of the archival material is cited as explained below. In some few cases, documents are cited by title; in those cases, the full title is given at the first occurrence in a chapter and cited in short form thereafter. Documents cited across chapters are re-cited in full.

Many of the archives used in this study had never been tapped by a researcher, and some were in a state of considerable disarray, organized by whatever system suited the person in charge at any given time. Citing the materials in the notarial and judicial archives is especially difficult because they are not always consecutively paginated. Most of these archives can be sensibly cited by year and case number, however, and that is the system I have adopted in the Notes so far as possible.

For those few notaries whose papers are not arranged by case number, I give the year and the *foja*, or sheet, number, abbreviated as "f" (or in the plural, "fs"); overleaf fojas are indentified with a "v." For simplicity, I do not include the notary's name unless there were two or more notaries keeping separate books in a town.

The lack of numbers on court cases in some of the judicial archives creates a more intractable problem. In that event (or where the top, identifying sheet is missing), I cite the year and "nn" for "no number." Imprecise as this is, there are so few cases per year in the provincial archives that future researchers should have little difficulty tracking these materials down.

The abbreviations used in citing archival documents can be found in the Archival Sources section of the Bibliography.

Notes

CHAPTER ONE

1. See, for example, Cortés Conde; Cardoso and Faletto; and Furtado. There are a number of excellent national studies for this period, such as Graham; McGreevy; and Thorp and Bertram.

2. See especially Mallon, passim.

3. The literature on rural conditions during the Porfiriato is vast. See, for example, Katz; Wasserman; and Cerutti.

4. For an excellent analysis of this oligarchical project in Latin America, see Carmagnani.

5. For the colonial period, see, among others, Chevalier, *Land*; Gibson; Martin; Keith; Davies; and S. Ramirez.

6. McCreery, "Coffee"; McCreery, "Debt Servitude."

7. Chevalier, "Témoignages"; Piel, *Capitalisme*; Condarco Morales, *Zárate*; S. Rivera C., "La expansión."

8. Grieshaber, "Hacienda."

9. On the Yaquis, see Hu-DeHart, "Pacification"; and Hu-Dehart, *Yaqui Resistance*. On the Maya of Yucatán, see Farriss; Katz; and Chacon, "John Kenneth Turner." Much of the burgeoning literature on Yucatán is usefully summarized in Joseph.

10. Most of these articles can be found in Murra.

11. Among the numerous works of Platt, see also *Espejos* (on the concept of reciprocity), "Dos visiones," and "Liberalism."

12. Bauer, "Rural Workers"; Loveman; Arnold J. Bauer, "Reply," *Hispanic American Historical Review*, 59.3 (1979), pp. 478–89; Gonzales; Langer, "Debt Peonage."

13. A pioneering study on accommodation and reciprocity in Peru is Martínez Alier.

14. U.S. historians concerned with the slave-labor regime on Southern plantations have provided the most extensive treatment of pater-

nalism up till now. The seminal work is Genovese, *Roll, Jordan, Roll*, which has given rise to too many works to mention here. For a recent critique of Genovese's argument, see Oakes.

15. Gutman. See also Montgomery.

16. Thompson, p. 79.

17. For a critique of Scott, see Popkin. Despite Popkin's claims of revisionism, his views are closer to Scott's than he would admit. Rational economic behavior by peasants and adherence to the moral economy are not really antithetical, but quite clearly mesh in many instances. Although Pearse's *Latin American Peasant* predated Scott's influential book, Pearse anticipated this solution; see pp. 39–75.

18. Handelman. For an important corollary of this approach, the "closed triangle" model, which posits that peasant mobilization is dependent on internal cohesion, see, for example, Cotler; Whyte and Alberti; and Jorge Dandler, *Sindicalismo campesino en Bolivia: Cambios estructurales en Ucureña, 1935–1952*, 2d ed. (Cochabamba, 1983). For a useful summary and critique, see Singelmann.

19. See especially Jenkins. For a useful summary of the debate, see Skocpol.

20. See, for example, Hobsbawm, *Primitive Rebels*; Tilly; and Stern, *Peru's Indian Peoples*.

21. For a similar point, see LeGrand.

22. Following the French example, Bolivia is divided into departments, provinces, and cantons. The department is more or less equivalent to the state in territorial size, though not in degree of political independence; the canton is roughly equivalent to a county. For a similar breakdown of Chuquisaca into territorial units of analysis, see Lenz B.

23. This is, of course, not to say that rural conflict was only present in this period. I quite agree with William B. Taylor that "conflict is normal rather than exceptional in societies where power and wealth are not distributed evenly or to the satisfaction of all members" (*Drinking*, p. 131). It is just that a combination of economic, political, and social conditions during the late 19th and early 20th centuries increased conflict far beyond "normal" levels.

CHAPTER TWO

1. Schoop, pp. 109–11. See also Bakewell, *Miners*, pp. 111–12. For a classic overview of Potosí's development and importance, see Hanke.

2. Cobb. For the concept of the "Peruvian economic space," see Assadourian, *El sistema*.

3. Cushner, pp. 156–84.

4. Mitre, *Los patriarcas*, p. 39.

5. On the effect of British trade on coastal areas, see, for example, Halperin Donghi. The incomplete penetration of imports into the in-

terior of the central Andes is detailed in Mitre, *El monedero*; and Langer, "Espacios."

6. Pentland, pp. 102–4. The original (English) version of 1827 was only partially reprinted in 1974. Since the Spanish translation of 1975 is more complete than the English reprint, all references are to the Spanish edition. The tanning industry in Tucumán and the links to Bolivia are discussed in Guy, pp. 11–14.

7. Sánchez Albornoz, p. 198. On the first years after independence, see Lofstrom.

8. Sánchez Albornoz, p. 205.

9. Mitre, *Los patriarcas*, pp. 46–49; Benavides M., pp. 38–39.

10. Mitre, *Los patriarcas*, p. 157; Guy, pp. 11–22; Dalence, p. 279.

11. Mitre, *Los patriarcas*, pp. 86–93. See Arce, p. 83, for a critique of Mitre's assumptions about the role of Chilean capital.

12. Mitre, *Los patriarcas*, pp. 59–60; Arce, p. 82. For a comparison with 18th-century Mexico, see Brading.

13. Arce, p. 82.

14. Dalence, pp. 251–57, 279–80. See also Wittman, pp. 177–93.

15. Mitre, *Los patriarcas*, pp. 116–21.

16. Ibid., p. 68.

17. During the first decades of the 20th century, significant land purchases were still made with the old, debased coins. See, for example, the land sale summaries in DR. For a discussion of this phenomenon and its significance in the countryside, see Platt, *Estado tributario*.

18. Grieshaber, "Survival," pp. 198–200; S. Rivera C.

19. Grieshaber, "Survival," p. 202.

20. However, some of the silver miners collaborated with Melgarejo, such as Félix Avelino Aramayo, who in 1869 attempted to negotiate a railroad concession in Europe. See, for example, Baptista, 5: 1–29.

21. The La Paz periodical *Illimani*, no. 8–9 (1976), contains a valuable sample of the large pamphlet literature that argued the merits of community land sales in the 1860's. See, especially, B. Sanjines U.; and the two articles by Santiváñez listed in the Bibliography. The authors of these pamphlets argued against the legitimacy of the 1842 law.

22. See, for example, Barragán y Eyzaguirre, pp. 5–7; and *Solicitud*, pp. 9–14. For the most comprehensive, though flawed, work on the debate over community lands, see Ovando Sanz. A useful summary of this subject, based on secondary sources, is Peñaloza Cordero, 3: 109–64.

23. For a full text of the 1874 law, see Flores Moncayo, *Legislación*, pp. 235–45. Sánchez Albornoz, pp. 211–12, argues that the increase was 25% with the change from *pesos febles* to bolivianos.

24. Vargas, p. 15. See also Platt, "Dos visiones," for an excellent treatment of the urban white elites' liberal views on the "Indian problem."

25. The literature on the War of the Pacific is exceedingly large and, as might be expected, very polemical. Some of the best recent works are Basadre et al.; Burr; Querejazu Calvo, *Guano*; Peñaloza Cordero, vol. 4; and Démelas, *Nationalisme*, chap. 1.
26. Klein, *Parties*, pp. 14–20. See also Klein, *Bolivia*, pp. 150–51. Platt, *Estado boliviano*, asserts that both Conservatives and Liberals implemented a "Liberal Project" in their Indian policies that did not differ in its aims and its effects on Bolivian society.
27. For an example of the same argument in the 1860's, see Dorado. The quote is from Cabrera, p. 18. On the importance of Social Darwinism in Bolivian Positivist thought, see Démelas, "Darwinismo."
28. Cabrera, pp. 18–19; Sánchez Albornoz, pp. 212–15.
29. For the text of these laws, consult Corvera Zenteno, pp. 115–20, 124–37, 167–72, 181–99. For a discussion of public lands legislation, see Peñaloza Cordero, 3: 173–204.
30. Averanga Mollinedo, p. 64; and Schoop, p. 116.
31. Mitre, *Los patriarcas*, pp. 146, 148; Bolivia, *Censo*, 2: 221.
32. Tristan Platt, personal communication, Dec. 1981. For information on the mita and its effects on the city of Potosí, see Bakewell, *Miners*, pp. 41, 111–12.
33. Mitre, *Los patriarcas*, p. 147.
34. Ibid., pp. 123–24.
35. See O'Brien, "Chilean Elites"; and Kirsch.
36. Fifer, *Bolivia*, pp. 56–58; O'Brien, "Antofagasta." The Chilean domination of the Littoral mines began early in the 19th century. On copper during the period 1825–42, see Cajías.
37. Mitre, *Los patriarcas*, p. 106; Arze Cuadros, p. 246.
38. Mitre, *Los patriarcas*, pp. 98–99; Arce, p. 83; Abecia, p. 32.
39. José Rivera, p. 475. The Bolivian shares were distributed in the following manner: Sucre, 600; Cobija, 525; La Paz, 178; Potosí and Tarija together, 150; Cochabamba, 140; Tupiza, 50; Oruro, 30. It is probably wrong to assume that the majority of the bank's stocks was in Bolivian hands. Because of the preponderance of Chilean residents in Cobija, its 525 shares were almost certainly not owned by Bolivians. Also consult Giménez, p. 46.
40. José Rivera, p. 476.
41. Giménez, pp. 60–64; Schurz, pp. 243–44. For the most recent summary of banking history in Bolivia, see Peñaloza Cordero, vol. 5.
42. Fifer, *Bolivia*, pp. 67–69.
43. O'Brien, "Antofagasta Company," pp. 12, 23, 27; Fifer, *Bolivia*, p. 69; Mitre, *Los patriarcas*, pp. 164–68.
44. Mitre, *Los patriarcas*, pp. 25–42.
45. Ibid., pp. 163–65, 173.
46. Kaerger, 2: 297–98.
47. Ibid., pp. 298–99; Mitre, *Los patriarcas*, pp. 175–77; Grieshaber, "Survival," pp. 222–28.

48. GP, July 1893–May 11, 1895, in Valda 1895, p. 274.
49. Luis Peñaloza, *Historia*, 1: 491.
50. GP, July 1893 . . . , Valda 1895; GP, May 18, 1895–June 20, 1896, Valda 1896 2.
51. Mitre, *Los patriarcas*, pp. 109, 191–92; Schurz, p. 130.
52. Bolivia, *Censo*, 2: 159.
53. Kaerger, 2: 290–91.
54. Condarco Morales, *Zárate*. See also Roca, pp. 115–36, 309–42; and Gade.
55. Klein, *Parties*, pp. 37, 41–42; Klein, *Bolivia*, pp. 167–68; S. Rivera, "La expansión," pp. 105–8.
56. For tin production between 1897 and 1902, see Bolivia, *Sinopsis estadística y geográfica de la República de Bolivia*, 2 (La Paz, 1903), pp. 136–38. For the percentage of total exports, see Arze Cuadros, pp. 248, 251. Also consult Hillman; and Gómez. See Gómez, pp. 218–20, for tin production in the period 1900–1970. Manuel E. Contreras is presently working on the tin-mining industry. See his "La minería estañífera boliviana."
57. See Fifer, *Bolivia*, pp. 108–40; and Fifer, "Empire Builders."
58. International Bureau of American Republics, p. 114.
59. Ibid., p. 111; Schurz, pp. 120–37.
60. Mitre, *Los patriarcas*, Appendix 11, p. 205; Klein, "Creation," p. 9.
61. A list of companies and their owners appears in Schurz, pp. 120–37. Of the 32 companies listed, Bolivians owned the majority of stock in only 5 (excluding those in the Patiño group).
62. Klein, "Creation," pp. 15–16. For extensive and largely favorable biographies of Simón Patiño, consult Carrasco; and Geddes.
63. See Marsh, p. 48; and Albarracín Millán, p. 164. See also Mitre, *Los patriarcas*, pp. 96–97, for a comparison with the silver miners.
64. Schurz, p. 122; Marsh, p. 48; Klein, *Parties*, pp. 119–20; Klein, *Bolivia*, p. 166.
65. Peñaloza, *Historia*, 2: 323–24.
66. Querejazu Calvo, *Llallagua*, pp. 18–26, 75–86.
67. Giménez, p. 75.
68. Schurz, p. 243. For a panoramic view of Chuquisaca's slow decline, see J. Querejazu, pp. 63–67.

CHAPTER THREE

1. The number of inhabitants fell from 21,800 in 1815 to 15,400 in 1880; by 1900 the population was 20,907. See Schoop, p. 154; and Bolivia, *Censo*, 2: 71.
2. Chevalier, *Land*.
3. Mendoza, p. 154. Aniceto Arce lived in the department of Potosí and in Chile for many years before he bought his first large agricul-

tural estate, La Florida, near Sucre in 1870 (Condarco Morales, *Aniceto Arce*, p. 236). Of course, not all followed suit. Perhaps the most important exception was the Aramayo family, on which see Crespo. For a biography of the family's patriarch, see Rück.

4. CR, Yamparaez, 1881. The 3% range was confined primarily to the Cachimayo Valley, where the construction of ostentatious buildings skewed the usual relationship between property values and income from agricultural production.

5. GP, July 1893–May 11, 1895, Valda 1895, pp. 256, 278, 323–24, 378.

6. See ibid., pp. 41, 54; and GP, Dec. 1880–May 1882, pp. 19, 87–88.

7. GP, Dec. 1880–May 1882, p. 242. Condarco M., *Aniceto Arce*, pp. 233–54, makes a similar point: that the haciendas Arce purchased were important money-making enterprises into which he poured much capital to improve agricultural production.

8. For the Melgarejos' mining interests, see NHM, 1886: 65. Antonio Rojas and Tristan Platt kindly furnished me with a list of all northern Potosí mining company stockholders appearing in the mining company literature at BNB; this supplied references to some of Melgarejo's stocks. On haciendas, see CR, Yamparaez, 1881, *San Lázaro*: 6, 12C, *San Sebastian*: 2, *Chuquichuqui*: 19, Quilaquila: 14A, *Siccha*: 2B; and DR, bk. 1, "1888–92, Sucre y su Cercado," 1888: 203, 1889: 1, 221. On houses and steamship stock, see DR, "Libro de propriedades de la capital y su Cercado, no. 2, 1893–1899," 1893: 19; and NHM, 1887. On Melgarejo as tax collector, see NHM, 1884: 18; 1887.

9. DR, Sucre y su Cercado, 1892: 40, 68, 83; DR, "Libro de propriedades de la capital," 1894: 12, 1895: 50; Centro Bibliográfico, Protocolos Notariales, Not. Ezequiel Cabrera, 1892: 59.

10. DR, Sucre y su Cercado, 1892: 89, 90.

11. There are many lists of commercial establishments available for early-20th-century Sucre. See, for example, *Guía de Bolivia: Comercial, industrial y administrativa* (Santiago, 1915). The Harriague firm is mentioned on p. 700.

12. See NHM, 1886: 75, 76; DR, "Libro de propriedades de la capital," 1893: 94–97. See also CR, "Libro de resúmen de títulos de propriedad, año 1907," Yamparaez: 18.

13. DR, "Libro de propriedades de la capital," 1893: 3; DR, Tomina 1889–1902, bk. 3, 1895: 5, 1898: 19.

14. These account books are in the possession of José Rodríguez, a descendant of Candelaria Rodríguez. All information in this section, unless cited otherwise, refers to these documents.

15. NHM, 1900: 4. The debt was 29,876 Bs.

16. CR, Yamparaez, 1881, *San Lázaro*: 4C, *Huaillas*: 3A, 1B, *Palca*: 1B, *Chuquichuqui*: 10; DR, Sucre y su Cercado, 1888: 62; CR, Tomina, 1889–1902, bk. 3, 1897, *Rodeo*: 6, *Presto*: 7. The earliest information I have on Arce's properties in Tomina is from the 1897 catastro, but he

must have bought them before 1889, since DR lists all land sale documents after that date.

17. IP, 1895, annex.

18. Platt, *Estado boliviano*, pp. 121–32.

19. Téllez Hermanos was a family-run business with no public shareholders, and I have not been able to find a list of participants. Considering Eulogio Téllez's business activities, it is very likely that he was a member of this firm.

20. DR, "Libro de propriedades de la capital," 1897: 144, 1898: 7; NHM, 1895: 41–48, 50, 1896: 5, 10, 12, 15, 42, 44, 50, 56, 64.

21. See DR, "Libro de propriedades de la capital," 1897: 81–84, 135–38, 146, 148, 151–53; and NHM, 1897: 8, 22, 23. The dispute is recorded in NHM, 1901.

22. Blanco, pp. 300–301. See also Mitre, *Los patriarcas*, p. 192.

23. AHH, "Hacienda La Calera"; interview, Hortensia Hernández, Sucre, Nov. 16, 1981.

24. See CR, "Libro de resúmen . . . 1907," *Mojotoro*: 10, and *Yamparaez*: 25. Unfortunately the 1907 catastro is incomplete. By 1907, Sainz had died; and at the early date of the previous catastro (1881), he did not own any rural property in Chuquisaca. From other sources, however, notably the prefectural reports and NHM, it is clear that he owned Hacienda Guzman in Huaillas and El Chaco in Mojotoro. His heirs appear in the 1923 catastro as owners of these estates. NHM, 1899: 23, 1900: 6, 1901: 7, 13, 31, 1902: 7, 10, 23, 24, 1903: 14, 21, 33, 1905: 13–16, 31, 32. Sainz also bought one Indian plot in Paccha, probably adjacent to his property in Yamparaez canton (NHM, 1903: 25).

25. Bingham, p. 145. See also Walle, p. 187.

26. *Memoria y balance del Club de la Unión correspondientes a la junta general ordinaria de 18 de febrero de 1900* (Sucre, 1900).

27. Payne and Wilson, p. 70.

28. Rossells. My sincere thanks to Ms. Rossells for giving me a copy of her important manuscript.

29. See Schoop, pp. 157–59. Schoop incorrectly asserts (p. 157) that the neoclassical remodeling was done mainly during the years of the silver boom, "around the beginning of the twentieth century." A comparison of photographs taken during the presidential inaugurations in the 1890's (in the Casa de la Libertad in Sucre) with others taken during the 1910 and 1925 centenary celebrations shows that the remodeling was not done until after the silver boom.

30. Walle, p. 187.

31. Ibid., p. 187; Bingham, p. 145.

32. For García, see CR, Oropeza, 1923, *Quilaquila*: 1; and EM, 1912: 2. His partners were Antonio, Eduardo, and Mamerto Urriolagoitia, Augusto Marión, Mamerto Querejazu, and Josefa Urriolagoitia de Bonel. Except for Bonel, all owned haciendas worth in excess of

30,000 Bs each. See CR, "Libro de resúmen . . . 1907," *Yotala*: 8, 14; and CR, Oropeza, 1923, *Huata*: 19, 20, *Yotala*: 28, *San Lázaro*: 1, 2.

33. For Rouma's non-mining activities, see Démelas, "Darwinismo," pp. 65–66; and Condarco Morales, *Historia*, pp. 286, 288–89. The mining venture is recorded in EM, 1928: 4. Antonio Cosulich, the notary in charge of the NHM, whose father was one of the original members of the Sindicato de Platino, gave me the information on the failure of the enterprise.

34. EM, 1913: 4.

35. EM, 1922: 8.

36. EM, 1927: 6.

37. See Schurz, p. 123. Tristan Platt and Antonio Rojas kindly provided me with the names of the shareholders. The sale to Patiño is recorded in NHM, 1922: 3.

38. NHM, 1913; IP, 1921, p. xxix.

39. EM, 1914: 1; 1916: 8; IP, 1917, p. 46.

40. IP, 1921, p. xxix; EM, 1914: 4, 1912: 6, poderes.

41. See Schurz, pp. 139–40. For an excellent summary of the history of petroleum in Bolivia, see Klein, "American Oil Companies." Other important studies are Almaraz Paz; Fernández Soliz; and Mariaca Bilbao.

42. IP, 1917, p. 45.

43. Klein, "American Oil Companies," p. 49.

44. EM, 1914: 4; 1920: 1; Schurz, p. 141.

45. Klein, "American Oil Companies," pp. 51–55. Standard Oil paid $2.5 million for the Richmond Levering claims and over $3.0 million for the Braden holdings.

46. For the amount of debts, see LP, "Testimonio de deudas de Ingahuasi y Canahuaico," and "Testimonio de deudas de San Pedro." The appraisals come from CR, Cinti 1910, *Santa Elena*: 25; and CR, Cinti 1902, *Camargo*: 123. San Pedro was not listed in the 1910 catastro.

47. Jáuregui Rosquellas, *Sucre*, 2: 91.

48. Mallon, pp. 125–246.

CHAPTER FOUR

1. Dalence, p. 93. For a detailed geographic description of what is now Oropeza province, the western half of Yamparaez in 1900, consult Acción Cultural Loyola, *Estudio Oropeza*, 2: 19–39.

2. D'Orbigny, *Viaje a la America meridionial*, pp. 1477–79.

3. Grieshaber, "Survival," pp. 139, 141.

4. Ibid., pp. 143, 145.

5. See Payne and Wilson, p. 89; Flores Moncayo, *Derecho*, pp. 208–9; Reyeros, p. 53.

6. See, for example, FP, Administrator of Correos to Prefect, Sucre,

Sept. 23, 1881; and on military service, FP, Corregidor of Huata to Subprefect of Cercado [Yamparaez], Huata, Sept. 1, 1899.

7. CR, Yamparaez, 1881.

8. Concolorcorvo, p. 345.

9. Mallo and Suárez, p. 419; Robinson Wright, p. 185; Jáuregui Rosquellas, "Monografía," p. 642.

10. CR, Yamparaez, 1881, *San Lázaro*: 9. La Glorieta, now part of the Sucre military academy, can be seen along the road to Potosí.

11. Ibid., *Yotala*: 2A.

12. Ibid., *Yamparaez*: 13A; Espino, p. 10.

13. GP, Dec. 1880–May 1882, p. 19.

14. This was the case with Gregorio Pacheco's properties. See ibid., pp. 230, 257.

15. NHM, 1882–87. That this was one of the motives for collecting this tax is also evident from the correspondence of Gregorio Pacheco, whose secretary authorized the purchase of the diezmo rights to "avoid the abuses that the *diezmeros* commit against the poor colonos" (GP, July 1893–May 11, 1895, in Valda 1895, p. 245).

16. Payne and Wilson, p. 90. For an analysis of festive labor, see Erasmus, "Occurrence."

17. See Alberti and Mayer, especially the chapter by Orlove, pp. 290–321. This ceremony was similar to the festival that accompanied work on the Inca's lands before the Conquest and probably had similar functions: "For this occasion, they wore their festival dress, ornamented with gold and silver, and on their heads, crowns of large bouquets of feathers. They sang praises to the Inca while working and this labor was thus transformed into a festival, by virtue of their great love for their god and king" (Vega, p. 157). See also Murra.

18. I have not found any evidence of uprisings on Yamparaez haciendas during the 19th century. But because the documentation on rural conditions in the 19th century is so poor, particularly in comparison with the rich sources for the 20th, this conclusion might have to be revised as more research is done, especially in the Sucre judicial archives. I feel, nevertheless, that my contention that rebellions were relatively scarce during the silver boom compared with later periods will hold up to further scrutiny.

19. Sánchez Albornoz, pp. 188–218.

20. Calancha, p. 519.

21. Ramírez del Aguila, p. 63. See also Gisbert and Mesa, pp. 166–68.

22. Rojas, pp. 170–71. See also Cook, p. 31; and Archivo Parroquial de Tarabuco, vol. 1.

23. They were called Yanaguaras by Calancha and Condes Arabates by Toledo (Calancha, p. 519; Cook, p. 30). On the Moyos, Churumatas, and Condes Arabates, see Gisbert and Mesa, pp. 174–77.

24. The information on ayllu size in 1877 comes from TD, "Matrícula de la Provincia de Yamparaez formada por el apoderado fiscal René Dulon (1878)."

25. Information about ownership patterns in the valley lands was gleaned from an interview with the parish priest of Tarabuco, P. Edgar Torrelio, Jan. 19, 1982; and Xavier Isko, an anthropologist under contract to Agrocentral who was working in the region, kindly confirmed the information in a personal communication, Aug. 1985. For an example of a similar pattern, see Platt, "Role." The term "ecological island" comes from Murra. The number of Tarabuco originarios comes from Erwin Grieshaber, personal communication. See also NHM, "Registro de escrituras de adjudicación del canton Tarabuco (1898)."

26. TD, "Matrícula de Yamparaez (1878)"; also TD, "Matrícula . . . de Tomina (1877)," *Tacopaya, Sopachuy.*

27. TD, "Matrícula de Yamparaez (1878)," *Huata, Paccha.* Paccha had 17 originarios, and Huata 11 originarios and 9 forasteros. A note under Huata says, "All lands that appear [in the Matrícula] canceled earlier have been owned by the doctors Mariano Navarro and Vicente Garnica since the time of Melgarejo."

28. Ibid., *Arabate.* In 1573, Toledo counted 326 tributary Indians (Cook, p. 30).

29. L. Navarro Careaga, "Litigio sobre indios residentes en canton Poroma, Departamento de Chuquisaca, que son tributarios de canton Tinguipaya, Departamento de Potosí," as reproduced in Platt, *Estado boliviano,* pp. 187–91.

30. Ibid.; IP, 1896, pp. 66–67, 1910, p. 30; FP, Prefect of Potosí to Prefect, Potosí [of Chuquisaca], Sept. 28, 1881, no. 99, Nov. 21, 1881, no. 106.

31. CR, Yamparaez, 1881, *Sapse:* 4B. Ocas and *papa lisa* are root crops common to the Andean area.

32. Ibid., *Pocpo:* 7A, 9A, 10A.

33. AJS, Juzgado de Instrucción, 1909, bk. 2: 171, f. 6.

34. See, for example, NHM, 1898: 8.

35. As Platt, "Symétries," points out, the designation ayllu refers to various levels of Indian organization and so must be used with caution. The same can be said of the term kuraka, since it also refers to leaders of various levels of ayllus. Because no ethnographic fieldwork on ayllu organization has been done in Yamparaez province, it is impossible to define these terms precisely. New research by Philip M. Keyes should help resolve this matter.

36. See Alberti and Mayer, for some of the different forms of labor obligations. For present-day examples, see Acción Cultural Loyala, *Estudio Oropeza,* 2: 438–40.

37. For a detailed discussion of stratification in Indian communities, see Alberti and Mayer; Sánchez Albornoz; Platt, "Role"; and

Carter. Much historical and anthropological research must be done before it is possible to understand what such terms as *originario*, *agregado*, and *forastero* mean in the context of Indian society.

38. McBride, pp. 19–20, 24–25. See also Grieshaber, "Survival," pp. 21–23, for a critique of the methodological problems in McBride's work.

39. IP, 1895, p. 29, 1896, p. 65.

40. See IP, 1924, annex, p. xxxviii, for a concise discussion of this type of resistance by a frustrated revisitador.

41. Revisitas were conducted in 1881–83, 1891, 1894–96, 1897, 1898, 1908, 1912, 1916–17, and 1923–24.

42. A total of 567 sale documents listed both the residences and the professions of the buyers; of that number, 289 purchases were made by the Sucre elite. I included under elite professions the designations *propietario*, lawyer, *agricultor*, priest, *militar*, accountant, medical doctor, housewife, and miner. The names, when possible, were checked against other sources to determine the correctness of these categories.

43. See NHM, 1898: 37, 1901: 1, 17, 18, 29, and 1904: 17. Whether this change in category merely reflected the notary's opinion or actually signaled a change in status in the ayllu is not clear; the latter appears the more likely because of the extreme care with which the Indians used these terms.

44. NHM, 1913: 10, 1914: 1, 3, 20, 1915: 7.

45. See CR, Yamparaez, 1881, *Quilaquila*: 10A. On the rental, see NHM, 1902: 27; and on the sales, NHM 1896: 52, 53, 1897: 3, 1900: 5, 1901: 27, 15, 1902: 15, 26, 1903: 16, 19, 26, 36, 41, 44, 1904: 22, 1905: 23, 26, 33, 42, 1906: 11, 1908: 22, 1909: 5, 12, 14, 17, 23, 1910: 14, 17, 20, 1911: 3, 7, 12; and CR, Oropeza, 1923, *Chaunaca*: 28, *Quilaquila*: 4, 52–57.

46. JIT, 1909: 29; CR, "Libro de resúmen de títulos de propriedad, año 1907," Yamparaez: 18, *Tarabuco*: 40, *Yamparaez*: 49.

47. The canton's crop could be identified in 105 of 242 sales: 53, or 50%, were barley, 27% wheat, and 17% corn; only 5% were fruit orchards and 1% potato fields.

48. NHM, 1898: 6, 30, 31, 32, 35, 38, 39, 1899: 3, 13, 1900: 17, 19, 1901: 10, 12, 1902: 14.

49. NHM, 1903: 16, 17.

50. In New Spain (Mexico), the Crown established a special court (see Borah). In Peru, Viceroy Toledo appointed protectors to represent the Indians before the Audiencias, the highest judicial bodies in the viceroyalty.

51. Wachtel.

52. See S. Rivera C., "La expansión." Erwin P. Grieshaber conducted new research on this topic as well, based on an exhaustive statistical study of the La Paz Indian land sale records. See his "Export Expansion" for a summary of some of his findings.

53. Of the total 626 land sales, 288 cases mention what proportion of the land was sold; in 55 it is clear that they sold all.
54. See Platt, "Role."
55. For a discussion of these Andean modes of adaptation, see "El 'control vertical' de un máximo de pisos ecológicos," in Murra.
56. Langer, "Comercialización."
57. NHM, 1910: 13, 1912: 31, 36; JIT, 1911: 257, 1912: 113, 266, 1913: 322.
58. ASNRA, *Pocpo*: 3745, Hacienda Piocera, fs. 1–6.
59. IP, 1922, annex, p. xxx.
60. NHM, 1903: 17.
61. NHM, 1904: 21.
62. Neither the 1907 nor the 1923 catastro lists all properties, only those whose owners paid taxes on time. Moreover, no production figures accompany the 1923 catastro.
63. Solares Arroyo, pp. 63–64.
64. Robinson Wright, pp. 184–85. These floral designs are still evident today on the walls of the former hacienda.
65. Jáuregui Rosquellas, *Sucre*, p. 84.
66. IP, 1918 and 1928 annexes: "Cuadro demonstrativo del movimiento industrial de la Provincia Oropeza."
67. TD, "Libro de convenios entre proprietarios i colonos (1907 y 1908)."
68. See, for example, GP, "A administradores 1894–95," pp. 13–14; and GP, July 1893–May 11, 1895, in Valda 1895, p. 189.
69. See IP, 1897, pp. 31–33; and TD, "Libro de convenios."
70. AR, "Cuentas 1922–1937," pp. 49–50.
71. For a discussion of the problems with the catastros, see Langer, "Promise."
72. On Hacienda Chaunaca, see CR, Yamparaez, 1881, *Quilaquila*: 15A; and TD, "Libro de declaraciones: Catastro de la Provincia de Yamparaez año 1907–1908 (riquezas)," *Quilaquila*: 10. On Hacienda Tasapampa, see CR, Yamparaez, 1881, *Tuero*: 13A; and TD, "Libro de declaraciones . . . (riquezas)," *Tuero*: 13.
73. Archivo Marcelo Zamora, Hacienda El Recreo, Libro Diario (1937). See also hacienda account books in AR and Archivo Virgilio Toledo.
74. IP, 1896, p. 65. See also Platt, *Estado boliviano*, pp. 78–80, 102–9; and Platt, "Dos visiones."
75. IP, 1888, p. 5; FP, Antonio Vellido to Prefect, Sucre, Dec. 24, 1894.
76. IP, 1916, pp. 39–40; FP, M. P. Mendoza to Prefect, Tarabuco, Nov. 23, 1916.
77. JIT, 1918: nn, Criminal; 1918: nn, Subversión; IP, 1918, p. 36. The quote comes from JIT, 1918: nn, Subversión, f. 9.
78. JIT, 1922: nn.
79. Ibid.; JIT, 1923: 88.

80. FP, Corregidor of Mojocoya to Prefect, Mojocoya, Feb. 21, 1924; Subprefect of Yamparaez to Prefect, Tarabuco, Feb. 29, 1924; S. Bacano to Prefect, Sucre, Mar. 1, 1924; Exujerancio Sardan to Prefect, Presto, May 24, 1924; Fiscal of Chuquisaca District to Prefect, Sucre, Mar. 1, 1924; Comisión Rectificadora del Catastro de la Provincia de Zudáñez to Prefect, Presto, June 4, 1924; IP, 1924, annex, pp. xxxvii–xxxviii.

81. IP, 1925, p. 2, 1926, annex, p. xxxii; FP, J. M. Oroza to Prefect, no. 198, Tarabuco, Feb. 25, 1925.

82. FP, J. Torres Goitia to Prefect, Tarabuco, Feb. 25, 1925; J. M. Oroza to Prefect, Tarabuco, Feb. 25, 1925; J. Muñoz D. to Vicario Foraneo del Beneficio de San Pedro de Tarabuco, Tarabuco, Feb. 22, 1925.

83. For information on the pujllay, consult Costas Arguedas, pp. 72–77. Historians of early modern France have best explored the opportunities for revolt and its implications during Carnival. See, for example, LeRoy Ladurie; and Davis.

84. IP, 1926, p. xxxii.

85. JIT, 1905: 166. See also JIT, 1901: 67, 1905: nn, 1907: 6, and 1912: 187.

86. See Platt, *Estado boliviano*, pp. 132–47; and IP, 1928, pp. 7–19. The most valuable document on this episode is AJS, "Criminal: Denuncias y querellas, sublevación indigenal, primer cuerpo (1927)." The first work exclusively dedicated to the 1927 rebellion is Andrade. Philip M. Keyes is currently writing a doctoral dissertation on the subject.

87. JIT, 1927: 1, 155.

88. Ibid.: 38, 90.

89. AJS, "Sublevación (1927)."

90. JIT, 1928: 48.

91. JIT, 1929: 149.

92. JIT, 1928: 55, f. 2v.

93. See JIT, 1929: 23, 262, 263, 269; and 1930: 94, 105. For Puchu's role in the resistance to the 1917–18 revisita, see JIT, 1918: nn.

94. JIT, 1927: 170; JIZ, 1918: 148, 481.

95. See especially *El País*, one of the few Sucre newspapers of the period that chronicled the 1927 rebellion in a fashion sympathetic to the Indians. The editors also received numerous reports from arrenderos about abuses from their masters.

96. JIT, 1929: 57, 12, 7.

97. AR, "Libro de caja."

98. JIT, 1929: 57, f. 8.

99. See AER, "Libro copiador de Hacienda 'Candelaria' de Junio 1924," pp. 72–79.

100. Locust plagues and drought were especially bad from 1922 to 1924 (interview, E. Arancibia, Tarabuco, Dec. 23, 1981; JIT, 1927: 1, f. 11v).

101. AR, "Libro de caja." Information about the polvillo plague is from IP, 1931, p. 48.

102. Arze, "Las implicaciones." For a development of his argument, see Arze, *Guerra.* My thanks to Lic. Arze, who kindly let me consult the book manuscript before publication.

CHAPTER FIVE

1. Bertonio defines *liqhuina* as "hot lands as *yungas.*" Harris, p. 52, defines *likina* as valley lands of 2,000 m to 3,000 m altitude. This suggests that only the perspective is different. The Aymaras, living in the high puna, would consider liquinas valley lands, whereas Cinti hacendados, in the valley, would see them as uplands.

2. Bakewell, *Antonio López*, p. 13, mentions the Pilaya Valley haciendas as cultivating only grapes in the 17th century. However, sugarcane probably replaced grapes by the late 18th century in some of the low valleys. In 1803, Hacienda Caraparí, on the Pilaya River, is described as a property with "Lands, Black Slaves, a Sugarcane Field, a House, a Mill, [and] Additions"—no mention is made of vineyards (AML, Prevendado Dn José de Lizarazu: cuentas y ajustes de sus bienes," Planilla 1a). See Dalence, p. 94, for the early 19th-century expansion of sugarcane cultivation into the subtropical valleys.

3. My efforts at delineating the ethnic makeup of Cinti have been a work of collaboration, and I am indebted to various scholars studying the colonial period for much valuable information. The reference to the Chichas is from J. Ramírez R., *Cinti*, p. 2. Information on the resettlement of the Oruro ethnic groups is from the Archivo General de Indias, Charcas 270, "Libro y relación sumaria que de orden del Exmo Senor duque de La Palata . . ." My thanks to Ann Zulawski for bringing this document to my attention.

4. On the Yuras, see Mujía. The document cited is from 1584. Inge Harman and Roger Rasnacke kindly alerted me to this reference. On the residence of mine owners in the Cinti Valley, see Arzáns de Orsúa y Vela, p. 5. That the Chiriguano population declined is evident from a letter dated 1689 in the "Representaciones y quejas" over the Duque de la Palata's *numeración general.* My thanks to Jeffrey Cole, who shared this information with me in a personal communication. On the presence of black slaves in the colonial period, see Bakewell, *Antonio López*, pp. 12–13. Even at the late date of 1919, Jaime Mendoza, a noted physician who had been sent to Cinti as part of a medical commission, stated that the Cinti workers were "a mixture of mulatto and white" (IP, 1919, "Informe del Dr. Jaime Mendoza, enviado en comisión sanitaria a Cinti," p. xxxvi).

5. The provision of the mines from Cinti (then called the Partido de Pilaya y Paspaya) has been documented in many works. See, for ex-

ample, Vásquez de Espinoza, pp. 616, 621; and P. Ramírez del Aguila, pp. 20, 36. The reference on López de Quiroga comes from Bakewell, *Antonio López*, p. 15. According to Bakewell, a botija held 100 pounds of liquid.

6. J. Ramírez R., *Cinti*, p. 9.

7. ALP, "Títulos," "Inventarios de las haciendas Ingahuasi, Caraparí y otros nombres [1825]," fs. 20–20v.

8. See Dalence, p. 94.

9. Temple, p. 346.

10. Archivo Juan José Dorado, "Año 1865, del testamento i codicilio cerrados de don Nicolas Dorado," f. 3v.

11. Ibid., "Tasación de las haciendas de Cocha, Tirahoyo, Corma y otros" (1869), f. 12.

12. Only one sale is recorded in Sucre (NHM, 1922: 34). A few sales were apparently registered by the Potosí notary. However, I briefly examined the Notaría de Haciendas y Minas in Potosí and was unable to find any sale documents; in all probability 10 or fewer sales are noted therein.

13. See Ulpana Vicente, pp. 35–37. Also, interviews with the ayllu authorities of Yucasa—Feliciano and Felipe Mollo, and Gregorio Zegarro—and of Asanaque—Damian Clemente, Cesáreo Gomez, and Basilio Colque—in San Lucas, Oct. 17, 1981, and Yapusiri, Oct. 25, 1981. Norberto Espino, son of a Quillacas (pronounced Qhuellajas in San Lucas) cacique and now agronomist for the Instituto Boliviano de Tecnología Agrícola, also provided valuable information in an interview in Tarabuco, Dec. 7, 1981.

14. See Archivo Juan José Dorado, "Deslinde de las estancias . . . (1595)," "Hijuela de don Simón Dorado 1871," fs. 46v–48v, and "Testimonio 1901," f. 3v. See also Archivo Judicial de Camargo, 1910: 95, 1938: 323.

15. DR, Sucre y su Cercado 1888–1892, and "Libro de propriedades de la provincia de Cinti, año 1889–1902," no. 4. There are up to 90 transactions recorded per year for the 1890's. This is a small number compared with Yamparaez, where, for example, over 250 sales were registered in 1889 in a province that was half the size of Cinti and had 10 times fewer properties. Furthermore, many of the Cinti documents refer to sales made before 1888. There were two earlier catastros, in 1887 and 1895–96; unfortunately I have been unable to locate copies either in the Archivo Nacional de Bolivia, in Sucre, or in the Fondo Prefectural of the Centro Bibliográfico Documental Histórico.

16. TD, "Libro de resoluciones 1911: Cinti," pp. 43–45.

17. See TD, "Catastro Cinti 1902," *Acchilla, Collpa, San Lucas*. The vast majority of less valuable properties were described as *temporal* or *pastal*, indicating that irrigation was not possible. All large haciendas contained lands with irrigation.

18. See TD, "De autos del Juzgado de Apelaciones de la rectificación del catastro de la Prova de Cinti (1902)," p. 6; and TD, "Libro de resoluciones 1911: Cinti," pp. 43–45.

19. J. Ramírez R., *Cinti*, pp. 5–7.

20. TD, "De autos . . . (1902)," pp. 7–8, 10; ASNRA, Sud Cinti, *La Loma*: 77, f. 292.

21. Unfortunately, it is impossible to determine the exact size of most properties from the catastros, since only land under cultivation by the owner was listed in the tax rolls. That few of the small properties had irrigation is shown in the land classifications. Only 92, or 16%, of the 569 landholdings worth less than 10,000 Bs had access to water for their fields.

22. My estimate of the percentage of total Cinti vineyards on large haciendas is based on the 1902 and 1911 catastros and my familiarity with the Cinti Valley. An exact figure cannot be determined from the catastros, since all cultivated land, regardless of crop, was included in their estimates. In the absence of a breakdown by crop, there is no way to calculate what proportion of land each property devoted to vineyards.

23. CR, Cinti 1902, vol. 1, *San Juan de la Torre*: 209, 211, 226, 252, 267, 268, 335, 340.

24. Archivo Juan José Dorado, "Inventario de las haciendas La Cocha, Tiraoyo, Corma y Andamarca (1878)."

25. SP, Correspondence between Culpina and Ingahuasi, 1925–26.

26. LP, "Títulos primordiales de la hacienda Ingahuasi," no. 26. See also DR, Sucre y su Cercado, 105–8, 116. For the haciendas' income, consult AML, "Mi tio Dn Napoleon."

27. ASNRA, Sud Cinti, *La Loma*: 77, f. 292.

28. See Guerrero for a similar distribution of demesne and peon-controlled land.

29. Interview, Humberto Leyton, Camargo, Aug. 9, 1981. See also López Avila, pp. 80–81.

30. The information on El Patronato is from J. Ramírez R., "Historia."

31. In this sense, Cinti haciendas with liquinas employed similar strategies to those of Andean ayllus. Compare, for example, Platt, "Role."

32. This custom is described in J. Ramirez R., "Historia," p. 3. For the redistribution of textiles in the Inca state, see Murra, pp. 145–70.

33. J. Ramírez R., "Monografía," p. 24. The reciprocal aspects of this celebration are confirmed by the words that the peons traditionally changed at the wine vault door during the Manteada festival: "Considering that the *zambos* [Negro and Indian mixture] have suffered much, considering that the barrels were filled with the sweat of their brows, considering that during the year they had nothing with

which to quench their thirst, considering that the *patrón* was stingy, he is condemned to give as a present a bottle of aged wine so that the *zambos* may drink."

34. J. Ramírez R., *Cinti*, p. 24; López Avila, p. 83. The term socios is still used by the Cinti Valley hacendados.

35. AML, "Balance de la bodega de José Ma Linares," p. 23.

36. Interviews, Humberto Leyton, a prominent hacendado and former owner of El Papagayo, Camargo, Aug. 9, 1981, and Ismael Raya, San Pedro, Aug. 11, 1981. Sr. Raya is one of the oldest employees of Hacienda San Pedro. The fact that virtually all Cinti vineyards, no matter how small, had distilleries is clear from the inventories of small and large properties. See ANC, 1881: 49, 125, 1891: 52, 76, 1893: 95, 1894: 49; Archivo Notarial de Villa Abecia, 1912.

37. AML, "Mi tío Napoleon G. Romero en cuenta con la testamentaria de mi señor padre Dn. Mariano Linares, al 1 Septiembre/95," p. 1.

38. ANC, 1904: 15; 1906: 99; Archivo Judicial de Camargo, 1894: 70, 1906: 45, 1911: 102; JIVA, 1904: 232, 235.

39. ANC, 1882: 125. For similar arrangements, see ANC, 1881: 31, 53, 1882: 33, 70, 126, 1890: 20; Archivo Judicial de Camargo, 1887: 182, 1898: 33, 1906: 4; and JIVA, 1913: 563, 1921: 882.

40. IP, 1927, p. 95; interview Dr. Juan Ramírez, El Patronato, Aug. 15, 1981. In addition, see Assadourian, *El sistema*, pp. 222–76.

41. ANC, 1904: 15.

42. ANC, 1881: 55. A short summary of Carlos Vacaflor Romero's life is given in J. Ramírez R., "Monografía." See also Lawrence Whitehead, "Vineyards," p. 13.

43. Interview, Dr. Juan José Dorado, Sucre, Dec. 12, 1981. On the cost of labor in Bolivian silver mining, see Mitre, *Los patriarcas*, p. 114.

44. IP, 1911, pp. 44–46.

45. See Monroy Cárdenas, p. 69; J. Ramírez R., *Cinti*, pp. 30–31; and Calderón, p. 51.

46. IP, 1917, p. 48. See also AML, "Balance," of José María Linares's bodega, which includes the period 1890–95; no price increases were recorded.

47. MC, 1906, annex, p. 158: Informe de F. Mercy, Camargo, June 2, 1906; J. Ramírez R., *Cinti*, p. 39; IP, 1927, p. 83.

48. CR, Cinti 1902, *Camargo*: 502; ANC, 1910: 84.

49. ANC, 1906: 69.

50. ANC, 1900: 74.

51. ANC, 1906: 67.

52. For a similar process in 18th-century Cochabamba, see Larson.

53. CR, Cinti 1902, *Camargo*: 109, 321, 324; IP, 1910, p. 29; ANC, 1906: 105; J. Ramírez R., "Monografía," p. 43.

54. J. Ramírez R., *Cinti*, p. 23. The testament of Laureano Olarte is one example of this conversion to ají. By 1916, on Hacienda Santa

Rosa, along the Pilcomayo in a heavy sugarcane-growing area, various cane fields were abandoned and ají was more heavily cultivated than sugarcane (ANC, 1916: 23). The quote is from FP, Damian León to Prefect, Palmar, Mar. 30, 1929.

55. ANC, 1910: 64; IP, 1917, pp. 47, 51, 1918, p. 48; AJS, Juzgado de Partido 3° 1927: 1980, f. 5v.

56. FP, "Copia del acta de la sesión del directorio de la Liga de Propietarios," Papagayo, Sept. 13, 1924, p. 1.

57. IP, 1927, p. 79.

58. Cevallos Tovar is prominent among those who gave this erroneous impression.

59. MC, 1906, annexes, pp. 158–60, 230–31.

60. SP, folder no. 12, Linares (1928), indicates that SAGIC transported 100 tons of machinery to Caraparí, but does not say what kind of machinery it was. The information on the containing walls is from interview, Humberto Leyton, Camargo, Aug. 9, 1981.

61. No population figures for Caraparí are available for the 1920's. To arrive at my figure, I took the arrendero population from the 1902 catastro and applied the rate of increase between 1902 and 1920 in Ingahuasi and Culpina. Since the vast majority of arrenderos on all the haciendas in those areas lived in the liquinas, they probably grew at the same rate. But the 1920 estimate is probably low because the 1902 catastro consistently underestimated the arrenderos.

62. ASNRA, Sud Cinti, *La Loma*: 77, fs. 13, 111, 113, 114. This source is tainted by the political atmosphere in which it was made and must be used with extreme caution.

63. See articles of incorporation in NHM, 1925: 13. See also SP, Price, Waterhouse, Faller and Co., "SAGIC: Balance general al 31 de diciembre de 1926," pp. 1–2, for a list of shareholders.

64. For the amounts of the debts, see LP, "Testimonio de deudas de Ingahuasi y Cañahuaico," and "Testimonio de deudas de San Pedro." The appraisals come from CR, "Cinti 1902," *Camargo*: 123, and "Cinti 1910," *Santa Elena*: 25. San Pedro was not listed in the 1910 catastro. Information on El Caserón and Jorge Ortiz's involvement is from AJS, Juzgado de Partido 3° 1927: 1980.

65. SP, "Arriendos Ingahuasi 1928," "Hacienda Culpina 1924," "Libro diario San Pedro 1927–1928."

66. For a table of profits and losses for the years 1927–28 and 1930–31, see SP, Price, Waterhouse, Faller and Co., "Informe y balance general al 31 de agosto de 1931, SAGIC," Planilla B, n.p. The information contained in this table is reproduced in Langer, "Peasant Labor," p. 20.

67. "Libro de actas de SAGIC 1925–1970," pp. 2–3. See also LP, Price, Waterhouse, "Informe y balance . . . de 1931," Planilla B.

68. For the alcohol production crisis, see CORR, Zeller, Moser y Cía to Culpina, La Paz, May 23, 1928; and SP, Price, Waterhouse,

"Cuadros y balances de enero de 1927 a marzo de 1928," p. 2. An excellent summary of the effects of the Great Depression is Whitehead, "El impacto."

69. SP, Price, Waterhouse, "Balance general al 31 de agosto de 1930," pp. 128, 136.

70. CORR, Culpina administration to Rosendo Vargas, Culpina, Jan. 29, 1926.

71. CORR, Culpina to Vargas, Culpina, Jan. 9, 1926; LP, "Libro de actas," p. 66.

72. CORR, Culpina to Vargas, Culpina, Sept. 2, 1927; LP, "Libro diario San Pedro 1927–28."

73. The mean for arriendos was 59, the standard deviation 39 (SP, "Arriendos Ingahuasi 1928").

74. This is what Witold Kula has called "forced commercialization" (*Teoría económica del sistema feudal;* Mexico, D.F., 1974, pp. 45, 77, as cited in Platt, "Acerca").

75. CORR, Vargas to Culpina, Ingahuasi, June 23, 1926.

76. Ibid., Aug. 11, 1926, May 31, 1928, Aug. 29, 1928, June 6, 1928.

77. CORR, Vargas to Culpina, Ingahuasi, Aug. 28, 1925, Culpina to Jorge Ortiz, Culpina, Mar. 9, 1926, Nov. 4, 1927, Ortiz to Culpina, San Pedro, Apr. 10, 1926, Nov. 6, 1927. See Gutman, pp. 19–21, for similar incidents in 19th-century North America.

78. SP, "Arriendos Ingahuasi 1928," p. 16; SP, "Hacienda Culpina: Arriendos 1926," p. 5; CORR, Ortiz to Culpina, San Pedro, Nov. 16, 1925.

79. CORR, Ortiz to Culpina, San Pedro, Oct. 4, 6, 7, 1927.

80. CORR, Culpina to Vargas, Culpina, June 10, 1927, Mar. 16, 1928, Vargas to Culpina, Ingahuasi, Jan. 7, 1928.

81. CORR, Vargas to Culpina, Ingahuasi, Oct. 17, 27, 1928.

82. SP, *La Villa Imperial* (Potosí), 42 (1929), 3a: 5.

83. CORR, Culpina to Vargas, Culpina, June 25, Oct. 10, 1926, Vargas to Culpina, Ingahuasi, June 26, Oct. 10, 1926.

84. CORR, Culpina to Vargas, Culpina, May 13, 1927, Mar. 11, 1929.

85. My information on Patiño's paternalism comes from Tristan Platt, who with Ramiro Molina is studying the tin-mining operations in northern Potosí. Documents from both the San Pedro and the La Paz archives make it clear that Patiño was kept apprised of SAGIC's operations. Although I did not find any personal correspondence from Patiño, his representatives in Paris often sent detailed letters to the administration in La Paz. And his representative in La Paz was able to play a dominant role in the board of directors' meetings because the tin miner and his Mercantile Bank were a major source of financing. For Patiño's management techniques in the tin mines, see Platt, "Conciencia andina."

86. SP, "Arriendos Ingahuasi 1930"; CORR, Culpina to Vargas, Culpina, Mar. 31, Dec. 28, 1928.

87. CORR, Vargas to Culpina, Ingahuasi, Feb. 2, 1926.
88. CORR, Culpina to Vargas, Culpina, Feb. 3, 1926, Vargas to Culpina, Ingahuasi, Feb. 22, Sept. 2, 1926.
89. CORR, Vargas to Culpina, Ingahuasi, Aug. 11, Oct. 22, 1926, Culpina to Vargas, Culpina, Aug. 23, 1926.
90. CORR, Vargas to Culpina, Ingahuasi, Dec. 13, 1926.
91. Ibid., Oct. 22, 1926.
92. Ibid., June 8, 1928; inhabitants of Ingahuasi to Sr. Fabry, Ingahuasi, Feb. 19, 1928.
93. CORR, Vargas to Culpina, Ingahuasi, June 1, 1928.
94. CORR, folder "Asunto Simeón Torres," Culpina to Simeón Torres, Culpina, Oct. 7, 1929, Torres to Culpina, Ingahuasi, Oct. 7, 12, 1929, Torres to Culpina, Santa Elena, Dec. 13, 1929. Vargas retired in June 1929.
95. ANC, 1924: 19.
96. For evidence of emigration to Argentina, see JIVA, 1923: 1059, and 1926: 413. See also Cevallos Tovar, pp. 44–46.

CHAPTER SIX

1. For geographical descriptions of the Azero region, see Mather; Schmieder; and García Quintanilla, *Monografía Azero*. For a more recent description of the western portion of the province, which later became Hernando Siles province, see Acción Cultural Loyola, *Estudio Hernando Siles*, pp. 11–15.
2. For a useful summary of Chiriguano culture, see Métraux, "Chiriguano and Chané." The classic account is de Nino, *Etnografía*.
3. Métraux, "Ethnography." See also Karsten.
4. The literature on the origins of the Chiriguanos is voluminous. See particularly Métraux, "Les Migrations"; Métraux, "Chiriguano and Chané"; Nordenskiöld, "Guaraní Invasion"; and Susnik, *Dispersión*.
5. See Pinckert Justiniano, pp. 39–73; and Finot, pp. 295–300.
6. See Torres de Mendoza, pp. 323, 339; Saignes, "Frontière," pp. 54–58; and Mendieta S., p. 38.
7. Torres de Mendoza, p. 339.
8. See Mingo; Comajuncosa and Corrado, pp. 75–278; Angelis, 7: 97–166; Saignes, "Frontière"; Saignes, "Jesuites"; Finot, pp. 293–327; and Sanabria, *En busca*, pp. 225–41.
9. EC 1779: 238, fs. 12, 14, 23v, 33–33v, "Auto proveido pr esta Real Audiencia sobre que se pase a aberiguar qual aia sido el motivo delas Irrupciones delos Indios Barvaros."
10. NHM, 1901: 14, fs. 92v–93.
11. NHM, 1886: 77, 1892: 45, 1904: 10, 1905: 15, 1908: 2.
12. On the colonization of the Iguembe Valley, see Martarelli, p. 119; and Susnik, *Chiriguanos*, p. 231. Martarelli says that the settlers were mainly from Tarija, but I was unable to find any colonists who so

stated in the land-grant records. Some of the many who said they hailed from Ingre or Iguembe could have been from Tarija originally. Many land grants in the Ingre-Abatire area were owned by cristianos from Sauces and Sapirangui. On the alliances with local Chiriguanos and the counteralliance of local Indians with the Huacayeños, see NHM, 1885: 101, and 1886: 78.

13. Martarelli, p. 303. For an analysis of how the invasion of cattle affected the Chiriguano way of life, see Susnik, *Chiriguanos*, pp. 60, 63, 70. Gibson, pp. 280–81, notes a similar process in colonial central Mexico.

14. For the most detailed description of the spiritual conquest of Macharetí and Tiguipa, see Comajuncosa and Corrado, pp. 325–502.

15. Martarelli, pp. 151–56; Sanabria, *Apiaguaiqui*, pp. 90–93. Because of the disorganized state of the Monteagudo judicial archives, I was unable to find any documents pertaining to this case.

16. The text of this legislation is in Corvera, pp. 79–80.

17. Martarelli, p. 126. See Hennessy, p. 98, for a discussion of the term "hollow frontier." He gives it a slightly different meaning in applying the phrase to the São Paulo coffee frontier, but the basic idea is the same.

18. Martarelli, p. 301. The text of the 1877 law is in Corvera, pp. 86–87.

19. NHM, 1884–1916. Padilla's original grant is in NHM, 1885: 2; the others are NHM, 1885: 1, 98–100, 1886: 77, and 1902: 44.

20. *Límites*, p. xix. The pamphlet from which this quote is taken is in a collection dated 1879.

21. Martarelli, pp. 183–94. See also MC, 1916, p. 132.

22. Martarelli, p. 157; Sanabria, *Apiaguaiqui*, pp. 108–11.

23. See NHM, 1889: 54. See also Martarelli, pp. 224–45; and de Nino, *Prosecución*, pp. 65–66.

24. See Saignes, "Frontière," passim. On Tumpaismo, see Métraux, *Hommes dieux*.

25. An excellent account of the 1892 revolt, on which I relied heavily, is Sanabria's superb *Apiaguaiqui-Tumpa*.

26. *Sublevación*. For the 1893 conspiracy, see FP, Corregidor of Ingre to Azero Subprefect, Ingre, Dec. 21, 1893, Corregidor of Iguembe to Corregidor of Ingre, Iguembe, Dec. 24, 1893, Corregidor of Tapere to Azero Subprefect, Tapere, Dec. 25, 1893.

27. NHM, 1912: 4, 5, 1913: 2, 3; Giannecchini, p. 28; de Nino, *Guía*, p. 129.

28. IP, 1895, p. 23.

29. The quote is from Giannecchini, p. 146. For excerpts of the resolution of 1880, authorizing the colonization of Carandaití, see Corvera, pp. 92–93.

30. Giannecchini, p. 148.

31. IP, 1896, p. 44. For an overview of the reasons for a policy of exterminating rather than missionizing the Indians, see Service.

32. AJM, 1896: 1263. See also FP, M. M. Gómez to Prefect, Colonia de Meilageno, Dec. 13, 1895. In this letter, Gómez described how he and his colonists pursued a group of Indians for cattle rustling and killed 3 of their number, including a Toba chief and a woman.

33. Nordenskiöld, *Indianerleben*, pp. 304–8. See also Karsten, pp. 36–37. Karsten described this behavior as associated with magical notions that all foreigners brought mysterious disease spirits.

34. NHM, 1885: 1, f. 2.

35. NHM, 1901: 2, 1902: 22, f. 274v, 1906: 19, 1907: 3, 1908: 7, 1909: 4, 1915: 2.

36. NHM, 1908: 6, 1915: 2. IP, 1928, p. 170, suggests that the Indians remained in control of their land. Adolfo Montero, the subprefect, described the Indians in curiously highland Andean terms: "In the province there is only one property of community Indians (*comunarios*), in canton Sapirangui; their *ranchos* or *aillos* are named Rasete, Ayango, Matara, and Caraparirenda; the value of the land is calculated at 5,000 Bs; the amount of taxes paid [on the land] is unknown." See also AJM, 1924: nn.

37. See Corvera, pp. 167–72, for the complete text of the 1905 law. See Schurz, pp. 190–91, for a succinct analysis of this legislation. See also MC, 1925, p. 2.

38. For del Castillo's holdings, see NHM, 1909: 4, 6, 7, 1910: 3, 4, and 1913: 2, 4. For the Sánchez holdings, see NHM, 1909: 5, 8, 9, 1910: 1, 3, and 1915: 7. See also FP, Subprefect of Azero to Prefect, Monteagudo, Dec. 15, 1923. The subprefect, Julio Calvimontes, called the del Castillo family "the biggest cattle breeders and owners of immense zones of agricultural and pasture lands in Carandaití, Ihancaroinza [sic], and Camatindi" (p. 1).

39. See Langer and Jackson.

40. For a discussion of the effects of the 1905 law, see MC, 1909, p. xlix, 1911, p. 4, 1915, pp. 11–12, and 1925, p. 2. See also IP, 1914, p. xxxix; Schurz, pp. 190–92; and Prudencio, pp. 6–8.

41. MC, 1927, p. 116.

42. IP, 1918, p. 45; Argentina, *Anuario*, *1918–20*, p. 25, *1921–23*, 1: 28; Mendieta S., p. 58; Bolivia, *Comercio*, *1921*, p. 14. In 1927, each head was taxed between 25 Bs and 36 Bs, more than half the selling price in Argentina (MC, 1927, pp. 117–31).

43. Bolivia, *Comercio 1918*, pp. 56–58.

44. Ibid., p. 18. See also IP, 1918, p. 45; and A. Sajines G., pp. 350–81.

45. Mendieta S., p. 58.

46. Martarelli, pp. 120–21.

47. Bolivia, *Censo*, p. 74.

48. See, for example, ANM, 1880, f. 75, 1886, fs. 71–73, and 1901:

62; and AJM, 1902: 10; 1904: 1465. See also Mendieta S., p. 61; and Thouar, p. 249.

49. Mendieta S., p. 61.

50. ANM, Not. Cayetano Vargas, 1916: 48.

51. Mendieta S., p. 58.

52. Yamparaez merchants virtually monopolized the cattle trade to the highlands. See JIT, 1903: 64, 1909: 155, 1912: 180, 1918: nn, 1922: 51, 1924: 214, 246, 1927: 324, and 1929: 103.

53. The close ties between Padilla and Monteagudo are indicated by the many testaments showing that people from Monteagudo often maintained residences or stores in both towns. See, for example, ANM, 1882, f. 26, 1886, fs. 37–39, 1901, fs. 231–37, 1902: 2, 1918: 5, and 1927: 62.

54. Cardús, p. 242; de Nino, *Etnografía*, pp. 78–79.

55. MC, 1895, p. 144. However, Cardús had already complained about the negative effects of this migration in 1886.

56. MC, 1924, p. 62, 1925, p. 79.

57. MC, 1916, p. 126.

58. Bialet, p. 83. On p. 82 Bialet calls the Chiriguano "the king of the Indians in the valley of Ledezma."

59. Kaerger, *Landwirtschaft*, 1: 375.

60. Bialet, p. 78. See also Martarelli, p. 179.

61. See MC, 1909, p. xxxix, and 1914, p. 139; and AJM, 1907: 933.

62. de Nino, *Etnografía*, p. 305.

63. See MC, 1912, pp. 98, 111, and 1914, p. 139.

64. MC, 1915, pp. 17–19, 31–38.

65. The quote is from MC, 1924, p. 74. The debate on mission policy and Chiriguano emigration is reflected in the reports of the minister of colonization. See especially MC, 1916, p. 106, 1922, p. 69, and 1923, p. 68. The Franciscan campaign to halt the secularization of the missions had its most forceful spokesman in Bernardino de Nino. See his *Las tres misiones* and *Etnografía*, p. 79.

66. MC, 1909, pp. xl-xli. See also MC, 1907, pp. 18–19, and 1908, pp. 22–23.

67. See Nordenskiöld, *Indianerleben*, pp. 298–300. See also his *Indianer*. The history of the Bolivian rubber boom has yet to receive a definitive treatment. For an overview on this subject from the Santa Cruz perspective, see Sanabria, *En busca*, pp. 35–156.

68. MC, 1926, pp. 80–81, 1927, pp. 143–44. For incidents involving the murder and rape of Chiriguanos by Standard Oil workers, see FP, Juez Parroquial of Canton Yancaroinza to Fiscal of Azero, Nov. 6, 1923; and FP, M. Guereca to Prefect, Sucre, Jan. 9, 1924. They also beat members of the local elites. See FP, Azero Subprefect to Prefect, Monteagudo, July 15, 1927.

69. de Nino, *Etnografía*, p. 79.

70. The quote is from A. Sanjinés, *La reforma*, p. 277. The missionaries' arguments are to be found in Martarelli, pp. 177, 257; and de Nino, *Etnografía*, p. 79. Jofre's conclusions are in his *Informe*, pp. 97–98. An anonymous missionary who wrote a few months after the uprising, agreed. See his reasons in *Sublevación*, p. 3.

71. Bolivia, *Censo*, pp. 4, 5, 74, 75.

72. de Nino, *Etnografía*, p. 237.

73. Two excellent studies that discuss this phenomenon for the 1970's are Healy, pp. 146–49; and Acción Cultural Loyola, *Estudio Hernando Siles*, pp. 98–101. From my own fieldwork in 1981, it appears that this system is still in force in some of the most isolated areas along the Parapetí River.

74. Langer, "Franciscan Missions."

75. AJM, 1929: 500.

76. AJM, 1929: 78. Chiriguanos generally did not have last names. In legal papers they received a last name, most commonly Neófito, often abbreviated to N. Despite the word's religious connotation, both converts and non-converts were so identified in the documents.

77. The juggling of account books is still a common practice in certain parts of the region today. In 1981, in Upper Parapetí, just beyond Azero in Cordillera province, an hacendado accused the local schoolteacher of being a Communist because he was using the hacienda account books to teach the peons' children addition and subtraction. The landowner feared that once the children discovered his juggling of the accounts (as actually happened in one case), he would lose his valuable workers, for the peons would feel no compulsion to remain.

78. ANM, Not. Ramón Ledesma, 1919: 33, f. 94v. See also ANM, 1906, f. 5, and 1927: 48; and AJM, 1899: 481, 1913: 1155, 1917: 525, and 1919: 305.

79. IP, 1927, p. 103, "Estadística de la Provincia del Azero año 1927" (emphasis in the original). The report was composed by Ramón A. Cortés and José Manuel Padilla, two large landowners of the province. For similar sentiments, also see FP, Ramón Menduiña, "Informe de la Sub Prefectura de la Provincia de Azero," Monteagudo, Dec. 16, 1896, pp. 15–17.

80. AJM, 1913: 1155.

81. AJM, 1899: 481.

82. This strategy of obtaining Indian girls to attract male laborers was still common in the 1970's. See, for example, Acción Cultural Loyola, *Estudio Hernando Siles*, p. 96.

83. AJM, 1889: 549, f. 2.

84. AJM, 1893: 110. See also Payne and Wilson, p. 86; and AJM, 1920: 151.

85. On poor whites and mestizos also giving up their children, see, for example, ANM, 1899: 4, 1902: 18, and 1905: 4, fs. 160–61v. On

hacienda peons giving their children to their employers, see ANM, 1909: 3. Most "adoptions" were probably of the latter type, but it is impossible to tell from the wording of most documents.

86. ANM, 1927: 20.

87. See, for example, ANM, 1899: 4, 1902: 18, 24, and 1903: 18.

88. AJM, 1907: 728.

89. AJM, 1887: 173.

90. See, for example, AJM 1890: 859, 1891: 546, 1893: 110, and 1929: 9. In the only case I found in which a verdict was rendered, the Indians lost (AJM, 1917: 525).

91. AJM, 1903: 202.

92. See NHM, 1891: 29, 1895: 40, 44, 1897: 36, and 1901: 26. According to Kevin Healy, who has done extensive research in Azero, Tarabuqueños today work on Azero haciendas in return for corn and ají. But whether this phenomenon dates from the turn of the century is impossible to tell.

93. AJM, 1897: nn.

94. Ibid.

95. AJM, 1929: 9.

96. TD, "Borrador de empadronamientos: Azero 1906–1907," Sección Autos, Dr. José Orías, fincas "Pedernal," "Turupampa," n.p.

97. AJM, 1909: 39, 1909: nn.

98. See AJC, 1924: nn.; and IP, 1928, p. 170.

99. See MC, 1925, pp. 59–60, 1926, p. 65, 1927, pp. 130–31, and 1927, p. 103.

100. For the impact of the Depression on the Chilean nitrate industry, see Monteon. The effects of the Chilean tariff are described in Rutledge, "Plantations," p. 104.

101. There is an immense amount of literature on the Chaco War. Two of the best accounts are Zook; and R. Querejazu Calvo, *Masamaclay*. The accusation that the Chiriguanos aided the Paraguayans in the attack on Charagua is made in Querejazu, p. 421. An interesting monograph has been written about the Chiriguano-Guarayos by the Swiss anthropologists Georg and Friedl Grünberg.

102. Healy, passim.

CHAPTER SEVEN

1. See García Quintanilla, *Monografía Zudáñez*; and Acción Cultural Loyola, *Estudio Mojocoya*, pp. 13–20, and *Estudio Belisario Boeto*, pp. 81–104. I have taken Tomina province as it existed around 1900. In 1917, the cantons of San Pedro, Tarvita, and Pomabamba were split off of Tomina to become Azurduy province, and Tacopaya, Presto, Rodeo, Mojocoya, and Icla became Zudáñez province. In 1943, the canton of Pescado became Belisario Boeto province. In this chapter, I

use the old denomination of Tacopaya for the modern-day canton and town of Zudáñez.

2. Torres de Mendoza, p. 332.

3. Vásquez de Espinosa, p. 594.

4. See Torres de Mendoza, pp. 330, 338; P. Ramírez del Aguila, pp. 109–10; and Grieshaber, "Survival," pp. 59–61.

5. ANP, 1900: nn., "Diligencias de posesión y deslinde de la finca Nogales solicitado por Nicolas Santos." The document in the notarial file is a 1754 copy of a land grant confirmed in 1584. For the dimensions of a fanegada, see Real Academia Española, 3: 719–20. For a discussion of various measures in colonial Peru, see S. Ramirez, appendix 2.

6. ANB, "Matrícula . . . de Tomina (1877)," *Sopachuy.*

7. Thouar, p. 253.

8. García Quintanilla, *Monografía Zudáñez*, pp. 80–81; CR, Tomina 1897, *Icla*: 13.

9. Barnes von Marschall, p. 11; CR, Tomina 1902, *Mojocoya.*

10. See Havet, "Rational Domination," pp. 80–100. See also Havet, "Administrative Complexity," pp. 15–16; and Acción Cultural Loyola, *Estudio Belisario Boeto*, pp. 247–70 (Havet participated in this study as well).

11. ASNRA, Azurduy, Antonio López: 6387.

12. NHM, 1905: 3.

13. CR, Tomina 1902, *Pomabamba*: 436, 441.

14. Dalence, pp. 244–46. In this section, Dalence complains about cattle imports. Among the important cattle-producing areas he mentions as being hurt by these imports is Pomabamba.

15. Barnes von Marschall, p. 29; interview Esteban Arancibia, Tarabuco, Dec. 23, 1981. On the molasses trade, see, for example, ANP, 1880: 20, 1892: 13, 1902: 14, 1911: 4, 1915: 62, and Not. Félix Balderas 1922: 15.

16. IP, 1910, p. 34. No information is available on 19th-century cloth production, but it is clear from the prefect's report that this activity dated back to the colonial period.

17. CR, Tomina 1910, *Alcalá*; interview, Lic. Jorge Reyes, Sucre, June 29, 1985.

18. ARM, *Gesta Populi*, 1.13 (1922), p. 6.

19. de Nino, *Una página*, p. 182. The account on pp. 175–87 is extremely valuable for its rare descriptions of these small provincial towns at the turn of the century.

20. ANP, 1888, fs. 32v–33v.

21. ANP, Not. Isaac Velasco 1888: 22. For transactions involving Tarata real estate, see ANP, Not. Isaac Velasco 1885: 11, 1888: 4, 1888, fs. 225–29v, Not. Lázaro Plata 1887, fs. 184–86v, and Not. Félix Balderas 1909: 76, and 1923: 15. On the leatherworking trade in Cochabamba, see Rodríguez Ostria.

22. ANP, Not. Isaac Velasco 1883: 27, Not. Lázaro Plata 1890: 27, Not. Daniel Leaño 1894: 13, Not. Félix Balderas 1910: 69. Mariano Civera, notary in Padilla at the time of my research in 1985, was extremely helpful in explaining the reparto system.

23. ANP, Not. Lázaro Plata 1892: 13. The quote is on f. iv.

24. Ibid., 33. The quote is on f. iv. Sra. Espada's property, Cabracaca, is listed in the catastros as being worth 50 Bs in 1897 and 100 Bs in 1902, some of the lowest values for the canton in both cases. Total arable land, all without irrigation, did not exceed 2.5 ha., of which subsequent owners did not cultivate more than half (TD, Tomina 1897, *Villar*: 66, Tomina 1902, *Villar*: 72).

25. The important social component of this economic relationship is captured in the following statement made at a trial involving the return of some cattle: "Some time ago I provided two oxen ready for butchering [*bueyes de matanza*] to an individual named Isidoro Choque, *because of certain considerations of friendship*, so that he could return them to me in *novillos* [yearlings]; and, at the same time, I gave into his care a small steer" (emphasis mine), JIZ, 1911: 256, f. 1.

26. ANP, Not. Lázaro Plata 1885: 70.

27. *El Republicano* (Padilla), Nov. 1, 1902, p. 2, in JIZ, 1902: nn.

28. IP, 1928, pp. 121–44.

29. AR, "Rodeo Chico."

30. CR, Tomina 1897, Tomina 1902. Since one volume of the 1910 catastro is missing, the number of cattle in the province that year cannot be calculated.

31. See ANP, Not. Félix Balderas 1909: 152, 1913: 128, 1924: 76.

32. ANP, 1917: 42. The seller in this case was relatively well off. He sold 36 head of cattle, 5 mules, 3 horses, 5 tercios of corn, 70 quintales of salt, his house in San Pedro, and his fields in Padilla canton for 2,000 Bs. One clause stated (f. 76): "If upon my return from Argentina I am able to redeem the goods sold, it is a condition [of this contract] that the buyer give me preference in the resale, at no more than 5% more than the [original] purchase price."

33. Between 1896 and 1915, 35 children were given up to guardians; between 1916 and 1930, despite the shorter time span, there were 79 "adoptions." The number of cases is much lower than in Azero; whether this means that there were in fact fewer such transactions in Tomina is impossible to tell because a large (and undetermined) number of guardianships were recorded in the Padilla court records, not in the notary's office.

34. ANP, Not. Daniel Leaño 1902: 13, Not. José Manuel Miranda 1907: 80.

35. For example, Gavino Aquino, from Cochabamba, finally called it quits in 1919 and sold all his merchandise to a Padilla merchant for 4,500 Bs in anticipation of moving back to his hometown. See also ANM, 1902: 2; 1927: 62.

36. ANP, Not. Félix Balderas 1912: 88, 92, 1914: 7, 1915: 58, 1923: 34. The Morales and Bertram firm still operates throughout Bolivia under the name Casa Nicolas Juergen Schuett.

37. ANP, 1897: 32, Not. Daniel Leaño 1904: 8, Not. José Manuel Miranda 1906: 11, Not. Félix Balderas 1911: 50, 1922: 81, 1924: 3, Not. Félix Augustín Belaúnde 1929: 13, 17, 70, 1930: 39.

38. ANP, 1923: 94. Other important fairs were held in Huañoma (Yamparaez), Collpa, and Pirhuani (both northern Cinti). See also ANP, 1921: 26, and 1929: 16; and JIZ, 1922: 1040, 1926: 853, 1926: 360, and 1928: 1014.

39. ANP, Not. Daniel Leaño 1896: 75. Limabamba sold for 10,000 Bs, although the land-tax commission estimated its value at only 2,000 Bs in 1897. This exceedingly low valuation was probably a tribute to the Reyes family's political influence rather than a reflection of the estate's true value. The catastro's figure of 32 arrenderos in 1897 is also suspiciously low. There were, for example, numerous vaqueros on the property not listed in the catastro who had to pay the landowners in cattle. On the ties with Miranda, see ANM, 1918: 5.

40. Interview, Avelino and Lic. Jorge Reyes, Sucre, June 29, 1985.

41. Bolivia, *Censo*, p. 4.

42. CR, Tomina 1902, *Presto*: 47; TD, "Matrícula . . . de Tomina (1877)," *Presto*; Torres de Mendoza, p. 332.

43. See Carter et al., pp. 298–309; and Heyduk, "Huayrapampa," pp. 133–34. On smallholders, see JIZ, 1909: 734 (Mojocoya).

44. According to one former arrendero's lawyer, "Martin Muruchi gave back the arriendo in 1912, tired of working the whole year for Abasto without any remuneration, and of being forced to pay in cash all the unjust charges that he [Abasto] levied on him, to the point of almost finishing off his meager resources" (JIZ, 1912: 965). Julio M. Trigo, a neighboring hacendado and heir to part of the Arce fortune, accepted a number of workers who had escaped from Pasopaya (JIZ, 1911: 232, 243, 1912: 965, 79).

45. IP, 1926, p. xxxii.

46. DR, Sucre y su Cercado, 1888: 66, 67; DR, Tomina, 1900: 22; JIT, 1900: 52.

47. AER, "Libro Copiador de Hacienda 'Candelaria' de Junio 1924 . . . ," p. 82. CR, Tomina 1897, *Icla*: 51. The catastro listed the barley crop as 2,200 quintales of barley. My thanks to Elizabeth Rojas, who persevered in her search for documentation on La Candelaria.

48. See Heyduk, "Huayrapampa," pp. 61–67, for a more detailed description of these obligations. Much of the information in this section, especially the family history of the Rojas family, comes from interviews with the late Nicolas Rojas in July 1979 and subsequent conversations with his daughter, Elizabeth Rojas T. See also AER, "Libro Copiador," pp. 346–49.

49. AER, "Libro Copiador," pp. 122, 148–49, 216. Productivity was

low by the standards in the North Atlantic countries of the time. On La Candelaria in 1924–25, for example, wheat seed yields were 1 : 2 to 1 : 12; the average was 1 : 5.3. Barley averaged 1 : 3.9 (p. 122). For an excellent discussion of the impact of proportional versus fixed rents and the relationship to the "moral economy" of the peasant, see Scott, pp. 1–55.

50. AER, "Libro Copiador," p. 257. The project cost Rojas 13,188.35 Bs. It is impossible to tell from surviving documentation what kind of wages Rojas paid, but labor accounted for more than half his expenses.

51. AER, "Libro Copiador," pp. 72–79. For reports of the revolts, see IP, 1924, p. 5, and 1926, p. xxxii.

52. See Bolivia, *Censo*, p. 4. This count does not include the portions of Tacopaya and Icla not in the western highlands.

53. CR, Tomina 1902. Again, I did not include Tacopaya or Icla.

54. JIZ, 1928: 369, 1246.

55. On the Mojocoya labor system, see Barnes von Marschall, pp. 17–28. For examples of Mojocoya arriendo contracts, see JIZ, 1912: 42, and 1930: 12. For similar contracts elsewhere, see JIZ, 1899: 7 (Tacopaya); and ANP, Not. Lázaro Plata 1889, fs. 188–188v (Padilla), and Not. José Manuel Miranda 1901: 62 (Pescado).

56. JIZ, 1907: 734. My thanks to Víctor Hurtado M. and Guillermo Palma D., actuario and diligenciero, respectively, of the Zudáñez Juzgado de Instrucción, for explaining how these and other terms are used in Tomina.

57. Most rental agreements lasted between 2 and 8 years. For term rental agreements, see ANP, Not. Isaac Velasco 1886: 22, and Not. José Manuel Miranda 1901: 62; and JIZ, 1903: 445, 1912: 42, and 1930: 12. In some cases, the arrendero moved on without paying his debts. This did not happen only on Hacienda Pasopaya; see, for example, JIZ, 1912: 436. When landowners were unable to keep their workers, as in the case of Yotalilla in El Villar, the fields became "full of rocks and completely uncultivated because of the lack of workers, for [the property] has only two *arrenderos*" (ANP, José Manuel Miranda 1909: 63).

58. The purchase of a plot by an arrendero is recorded in JIZ, 1925: 730. For copies of Santa Cruz's testament, see JIZ, 1919: 121; and ANP, Not. Lázaro Plata 1882, fs. 176–79. On the willing of land to servants, see, for example, ANP, Not. Lázaro Plata 1882, fs. 160–62.

59. AR, "Rodeo Chico." All information dealing with Rodeo Chico, unless otherwise noted, is drawn from his source.

60. The most detailed contract between a vaquero and an hacendado is contained in ANP, 1923: 39.

61. The information on fiestas in Pescado comes from a former prominent landowner of the canton; interview, Alberto Monterde, Padilla, Jan. 20, 1982. For Andean ideas on work, see, for example, Vega, p. 157; and Isbell. Barnes von Marschall, pp. 83–85, reports that some forms of reciprocity continue in Mojocoya, but does not detail to

what extent or how divergent these arrangements are from the highlands. According to Acción Cultural Loyola, *Estudio Belisario Boeto,* p. 330, in Belisario Boeto province (formerly Pescado canton), "the *ayni* [relationship] is used relatively little." For a discussion of the remnants of Andean reciprocal work arrangements, see ibid., pp. 330–32.

62. ARM, *El Deber,* 4.12 (Aug. 24, 1919), p. 2.

63. IP, 1926, p. xlv.

64. In the late 1960's, when Che Guevara was operating in neighboring Vallegrande, the Bolivian army took over all of Padilla's governmental buildings, including the courthouse. According to witnesses, old records from the judicial archives were used as bedding and fuel by the soldiers; thus a significant portion of these valuable documents was lost.

65. See AJP, "Inventario de los espedientes criminales que el Actuario Roberto Rua ha entregado al igual Mariano Civera con asistencia del Fiscal del Partido Doctor José Luis Carvajal" and "1905: Juicios criminales."

66. IP, 1910, p. 7, 1915, p. 34, 1930, p. 100. See also ANP, 1920: 68, f. 48, where the landowner of Hacienda Pampas del Tigre (Pescado) asserts that he is unable to pay a debt because "the hacienda's [cattle herd] has disappeared owing to the constant robberies." On Tarvita, consult FP, Corregidor of Tarvita, May 17 and Oct. 26, 1929.

67. Hobsbawm, *Bandits.* Anyone studying banditry is indebted to this pathbreaking work. See also Hobsbawm, *Primitive Rebels.* Useful recent studies on banditry in Latin America are Orlove, "Position of Rustlers"; Taylor, "Sacarse de pobre"; and Slatta, *Bandidos.*

68. AJP, 1929: 139.

69. AJP, 1920: 68; JIZ, 1918: 160. In the first case, the landowner was a personal enemy of the corregidor; in the second, the accusers, who included many large landowners, asserted that the proprietor even robbed his own arrenderos.

70. See, for example, JIT, 1916: 22, 1926: 82, and 1928: 7; and JIZ, 1918: 160. See also, interview, Esteban Arancibia, Tarabuco, Dec. 23, 1981.

71. AJP, 1924: nn.

72. FP, Salvador Claros to Prefect, Villa Serrano, June 4, 1929. Information on lawyers from interview, Mariano Civera, Padilla, June 13, 1985.

73. Interview, Alberto Monterde, Padilla, Jan. 20, 1982.

74. Interview, Arcil Noyes, Villa Serrano, Jan. 19, 1982. At the time Sr. Noyes was subprefect of B. Boeto province.

75. AJP, 1903: 66.

76. FP Corregidor of Tarvita to Prefect, May 17, 1929.

77. See ARM, *El Deber,* 1915, no. 8.

78. JIZ, 1929: 146.

79. IP, 1914, pp. viii–x.

80. IP, 1915, pp. 33–34.
81. See IP, 1918, p. 15; 1919, p. 27; 1921, p. 20; 1922, p. 9; and 1923, p. 17.
82. See IP, 1925, p. 12; and AJM, 1904: 342.
83. Interview, Alberto Monterde, Padilla, Jan. 20, 1982.
84. AJP, 1926: 11.
85. JIZ, 1903: 445.
86. Interview, Arcil Noyes, Villa Serrano, Jan. 19, 1982.
87. IP, 1932, p. 110; Arze, *Guerra*.
88. IP, 1932, p. 114.

CHAPTER EIGHT

1. The literature on labor conditions during this period is extensive. See, for example, the several works by Tristan Platt in the Bibliography; and Bauer; Loveman; Gonzales; and Langer, "Debt Peonage."
2. Stinchcombe.
3. Skocpol.
4. This point, of course, forms part of Popkin's criticism of Scott's *The Moral Economy*.
5. This same point applies also to some Marxist scholars, who hope to see another socialist revolution in Latin America. See, for example, Huizer.
6. Foster.
7. Duncan and Markoff make a similar argument.
8. The eventual effectiveness of reform measures on Hacienda La Candelaria probably accounts for the high levels of distrust and social disorganization that Daniel Heyduk found in his study of the community after the Agrarian Reform ("Huayrapampa").
9. In his thoughtful article, Ronald Waterbury shows how important paternalism, among other things, could be in explaining the lack of revolutionary activity by the peasants of Oaxaca during the 1910 Mexican Revolution.
10. For an excellent study of the effects of the Depression on the Bolivian economy, see Whitehead, "El impacto."
11. IP, 1932, p. 9, annex, p. 50.
12. Monteon.
13. Rutledge, "Integration." For information on more recent Bolivian migration to northern Argentina, consult Whiteford.
14. For political conditions after the Chaco War, see Klein, *Parties*. Ucureña is studied in Dandler's dissertation. The struggle in the La Paz area is treated in Albó, *Achacachi*. On Potosí and Mojocoya, see Barnes von Marschall, pp. 38–43. On the incidents at Las Canchas and Caraparí, see Erasmus, "Land Reform," pp. 125–26. The information on Hacienda Payacota del Carmen is from ASNRA, Nor Cinti,

Payacota: 7120. On SAGIC, see LP, Price, Waterhouse, Peat and Co., "Informe y balance general al 31 de agosto de 1945," n.p.

15. For information on the Agrarian Reform and its effects, see Malloy, pp. 188–215; William E. Carter, in Malloy and Thorn, pp. 233–68; and Albó, *Bodas de plata*. A detailed analysis of the Agrarian Reform law is in Heath et al., pp. 30–62.

16. Erasmus, "Land Reform," p. 74.

17. McEwen.

18. Platt, *Estado boliviano*.

19. ASNRA, Oropeza, *Pocpo*: 3745.

20. On the breakdown of the fiesta system, see, for example, Erasmus, "Upper Limits."

21. Heyduk, "Hacienda System."

22. Erasmus, "Land Reform," p. 74.

23. Havet, "Administrative Complexity," p. 18. See also Acción Cultural Loyola, *Estudio Belisario Boeto* (Havet was a member of the research team for this study).

24. Erasmus, "Land Reform," p. 126. For a different and more accurate appraisal of this incident, see Healy, pp. 55–58.

25. Acción Cultural Loyola, *Estudio Hernando Siles*, pp. 26–30; Healy.

26. Healy, pp. 225–26.

Bibliography

On the entries for certain old Spanish publications that are difficult to locate, I have used the abbreviation BNB to indicate that the work is housed in the Biblioteca Nacional de Bolivia, Sucre.

ARCHIVAL SOURCES

Public Archives

Archivo and Biblioteca Nacional de Bolivia, Sucre:
  Expedientes Coloniales, 1779: 238, "Auto proveido por esta real Audiencia sobre que se pase a aberiguar qual aia sido el motivo delas Irrupciones delos Indios Bárvaros" (EC)
  Ministerio de Colonización, *Memorias,* selected years, 1895–1929 (MC)
  Prefectura de Chuquisaca, *Informes prefecturales de Chuquisaca,* selected years, 1888–1934 (IP)
  Tribunal Nacional de Cuentas, 1773, rev. 60, Chuquisaca, Tomina, "Tributos del Partido de Tomina"
Archivo General de Indias, Seville: Charcas 270, "Libro y relación sumaria que de orden del Exmo Señor duque de La Palata . . ."
Archivo Judicial de Camargo, 1880–1938 (AJC)
Archivo Judicial de Monteagudo, 1880–1930 (AJM)
Archivo Judicial de Padilla, 1880–1930 (AJP)
Archivo del Juzgado de Instrucción de Tarabuco, 1898–1930 (JIT)
Archivo del Juzgado de Instrucción de Villa Abecia, 1899–1930 (JIVA)
Archivo del Juzgado de Instrucción de Zudáñez, 1899–1930 (JIZ)
Archivo del Museo Etnográfico, Sucre
Archivo Notarial de Camargo, 1880–1930 (ANC)
Archivo Notarial de Monteagudo, 1880–1930 (ANM)
Archivo Notarial de Padilla, 1880–1930 (ANP)

Archivo Notarial de Villa Abecia, 1910–1930
Archivo Parroquial del Arzobispado de La Plata: Acchilla, Bautismos, 1696–1784; Presto, Bautismos, 1699–1709; San Lucas, Bautismos, 1673–99
Archivo Parroquial de Tarabuco, Libros de bautizos, 1715–45
Archivo del Servicio Nacional de Reforma Agraria, Sucre (ASNRA)
Archivos de la Corte Superior de Chuquisaca, Sucre:
    Derechos Reales (DR): Cinti, 1889–1902; Sucre y su Cercado, 1888–99; Tomina, 1889–1902
    Archivo Judicial de Sucre (AJS)
Biblioteca de la Universidad Mayor de San Andrés, La Paz, correspondence of Gregorio Pacheco, 1880–95 (GP)
Centro Bibliográfico Documental Histórico, Universidad Mayor, Real y Pontificia de San Francisco Xavier de Chuquisaca, Sucre:
    Fondo Prefectural:
        Correspondencia, 1880–1930   (FP)
        Notaría de Hacienda y Minas   (NHM): Escrituras mineras, 1907–30   (EM); Escrituras públicas, 1880–1930; Revisitas de tierras de orígen, 1891–1912; Tierras, 1907–9
        Tesoro Departamental   (TD): Catastros (CR), Azero (1900, 1906), Cinti, (1902, 1910), Oropeza (1923), Tomina (1897, 1902, 1910), Yamparaez (1881, 1907); "Libro de convenios entre proprietarios i colonos" (1907–8); Matrículas de indigenas, Tomina (1877), Yamparaez (1878)
        Protocolos Notariales: Not. Ezequiel Cabrera, 1887–92

Private Archives

Archivo Acción Cultural Loyola, Sucre
Archivo Juan José Dorado, Sucre
Archivo Hortensia Hernández, Sucre   (AHH)
Archivo Mario Linares, Sucre   (AML)
Archivo Rudy Miranda, Padilla   (ARM)
Archivo José Rodríguez, Sucre   (AR)
Archivo Elizabeth Rojas T., Sucre   (AER)
Archivo de la Sociedad Agrícola, Ganadera é Industrial de Cinti, La Paz (LP)
Archivo de la Sociedad Agrícola, Ganadera é Industrial de Cinti, San Pedro (SP): Correspondencia   (CORR)
Archivo Virgilio Toledo, Sucre
Archivo Marcelo Zamora, Sucre

PUBLISHED WORKS AND OTHER SOURCES

Abecia, Valentín. *Demografía i estadística: Movimiento de la población de la ciudad de Sucre capital de la república durante el año 1884.* Sucre, 1885.

———, ed. *Historia de Chuquisaca*. Sucre, 1939.
Acción Cultural Loyola. *Estudio socio-económico de la provincia Belisario Boeto, Chuquisaca*. Sucre, 1972.
———. *Estudio socio-económico de la provincia Hernando Siles*. 2d ed. Sucre, 1979.
———. *Estudio cultural socio-económico Mojocoya y Redención Pampa*. 2d ed. Sucre, 1979.
———. *Estudio socio-económico Provincia Oropeza*. 2d ed. 2 vols. Sucre, 1981.
Alarcón, J. Ricardo, ed. *Bolivia en su primer centenario de su independencia*. N.p., 1925.
Albarracín Millán, Juan. *El poder minero en la administración liberal*. La Paz, 1972.
Alberti, Giorgio, and Enrique Mayer, eds. *Reciprocidad é intercambio en los Andes peruanos*. Lima, 1974.
Albó, Javier. *Achacachi: Medio siglo de lucha campesina*. La Paz, 1979.
———. *¿Bodas de plata? O requiem por una reforma agraria*. La Paz, 1979.
Almaraz Paz, Sergio. *Petróleo en Bolivia*. La Paz, 1958.
Andrade, Claudio. "Sublevación Provincia Chayanta 1927." Unpublished manuscript, 1985.
Angelis, Pedro de. *Colección de obras y documentos relativos a la historia antigua y moderna de las provincias del Río de la Plata*. Buenos Aires, 1836.
Arce, Roberto. "'Los patriarcas de la plata' de Antonio Mitre," *Historia Boliviana*, 2.1 (1982), pp. 79–84.
Argentina. Dirección General de Estadística. *Anuario del comercio exterior de la República*. 1918–20, 1921–23.
———. *Comercio especial exterior*. 1873–1930.
Arzáns de Orsúa y Vela, Bartolomé. *Guerra y conflictos sociales (El caso rural boliviano en la campaña del Chaco)*. Cochabamba, 1987.
———. *Historia de la Villa Imperial de Potosí*, vol. 1. Providence, R.I., 1965.
Arze Cuadros, Eduardo. *La economía de Bolivia: Ordenamiento territorial y dominación externa*. La Paz, 1979.
Assadourian, Carlos Sempat. *El sistema de la economía colonial: Mercado interno, regiones, y espacio económico*. Lima, 1982.
Assadourian, Carlos Sempat, Heraclio Bonilla, Antonio Mitre, and Tristan Platt. *Minería y espacio económico en los Andes, siglos XVI–XX*. Lima, 1980.
Averanga Mollinedo, Asthenio. *Aspectos generales de la población boliviana*. La Paz, 1974.
Bakewell, Peter J. *Antonio López de Quiroga (Industrial minero del Potosí colonial)*. Potosí, 1973.
———. *Miners of the Red Mountain: Indian Labor in Potosí, 1545–1650*. Albuquerque, N.M., 1984.

————. *Silver Mining and Society in Colonial Mexico: Zacatecas, 1546–1700*. Cambridge, Eng., 1971.

Baptista, Mariano. *Obras completas*. 7 vols. La Paz, 1933.

Barnadas, Josep M. *Charcas: Orígenes de una sociedad colonial, 1535–1565*. La Paz, 1973.

Barnes von Marschall, Katherine. *Revolution and Land Reform in Chuquisaca and Potosí*. La Paz, 1970.

Barragán y Eyzaguirre, José María. *Reclamo de los compradores de terrenos del estado ante la Soberana Asamblea*. La Paz, 1871. BNB.

Basadre, Jorge, et al. *Reflexiones en torno de la guerra de 1879*. Lima, 1979.

Bauer, Arnold J. "Rural Workers in Spanish America: Problems of Peonage and Oppression," *Hispanic American Historical Review*, 59.1 (1979), pp. 34–63.

Benavides M., Julio. *Historia de la moneda en Bolivia*. La Paz, 1972.

Bertonio, Ludovico. *Vocabulario de la lengua aymara*. La Paz, 1956. Originally published in 1612.

Bialet y Massé, Juan. *El estado de las clases obreras argentinas a comienzos del siglo*. Córdoba, 1968. Originally published in 1904.

Bingham, Hiram. *Across South America: An Account of a Journey from Buenos Aires to Lima by Way of Potosí*. Boston, 1911.

Blanco, Pedro Aniceto. *Monografía de la industria minera en Bolivia*. La Paz, 1910.

Bolivia, Dirección General de Aduanas, Sección de Estadística Comercial. *Comercio especial de Bolivia*. Selected years, 1914–29.

————, Oficina de Inmigración, Estadística y Propaganda Geográfica. *Censo de la población de la Republica de Bolivia según el empadronamiento de 1 de septiembre de 1900*. 2d ed. 2 vols. Cochabamba, 1973.

Borah, Woodrow W. *Justice by Insurance: The General Indian Court of Colonial Mexico and the Legal Aides of the Half-Real*. Berkeley, Calif., 1983.

Brading, David. *Miners and Merchants in Bourbon Mexico, 1763–1810*. Cambridge, Eng., 1971.

Burr, Robert N. *By Reason or by Force: Chile and the Balancing of Power in South America, 1830–1905*. Berkeley, Calif., 1965.

Cabrera, Ladislao. *Memoria presentada a la Convención Nacional de 1880*. La Paz, 1880. BNB.

Cajías, Fernando. *La provincia de Atacama (1825–1842)*. La Paz, 1975.

Calancha, Antonio de la. *Corónica moralizadora del órden de San Agustín en el Perú*. Barcelona, 1639.

Calderón, Ignacio. *Memoria que el Ministro de Hacienda é Industria al H. Congreso Nacional de 1902*. La Paz, 1902. BNB.

Cardoso, Fernando Henrique, and Enzo Faletto. *Dependency and Development in Latin America*. Tr. Marjory M. Urquidi. Berkeley, Calif., 1979.

Cardús, José. *Las misiones franciscanas entre los infieles de Bolivia: Descripción del estado de ellos en 1883 y 1884 con una noticia sobre los caminos y tribus salvajes.* Barcelona, 1886.

Carmagnani, Marcello. *Estado y sociedad en América latina, 1850–1930.* Tr. P. R. Ferrer. Barcelona, 1984.

Carrasco, Manuel. *Simón I. Patiño, un prócer industrial.* Paris, 1960.

Carter, William E. *Aymara Communities and the Bolivian Agrarian Reform.* Gainesville, Fla., 1964.

Carter, William E., Mauricio Mamani, and Philip T. Parkerson. *Coca in Bolivia.* La Paz, 1980.

Cerutti, Mario. "Poder estatal, actividad económica y burguesía regional en el noreste de México (1855–1910)," *Siglo XIX,* 1.1 (Jan.–June 1986), pp. 67–134.

Cevallos Tovar, Daniel Ignacio. *Monografía de la Provincia de Cinti y estudio de sus posibilidades económicas, para establecer en centro determinado de su jurisdicción una agencia bancaria.* Potosí, 1942.

Chacón, Ramón. "John Kenneth Turner, *Barbarous Mexico,* and the Debate About Debt Peonage in Yucatán During the Porifirato," *Peasant Studies,* 13.2 (1986), pp. 97–119.

Chevalier, François. *Land and Society in Colonial Mexico: The Great Hacienda.* Tr. Alvin Eustis. Berkeley, Calif., 1963.

———. "Témoignages littéraires et disparités de croissance: L'expansion de la grande propriété dans le Haut-Pérou au XXe siècle." *Annales: Economies, Sociétés, Civilisations,* 21.4 (1966), pp. 815–31.

Cobb, Gwendolin. "Supply and Transportation for the Potosí Mines," *Hispanic American Historical Review,* 29.1 (1949), pp. 25–45.

Comajuncosa, Antonio, and Alejandro M. Corrado. *El colegio franciscano de Tarija y sus misiones.* Quaracchi, 1884.

Concolorcorvo [A. Carrio de la Bandera]. *El Lazarillo de ciegos caminantes desde Buenos Aires hasta Lima.* Madrid, 1959.

Condarco Morales, Ramiro. *Aniceto Arce, artífice de la extensión de la revolución industrial y forjador de la República de Bolivia.* La Paz, 1985.

———. *Historia del saber y la ciencia en Bolivia.* La Paz, 1978.

———. *Zárate, el "Temible" Willka: Historia de la rebelión indígena de 1899.* La Paz, 1966.

Contreras, Manuel E. "La mineria estañífera boliviana en la Primera Guerra Mundial," *Minería y economía en Bolivia.* La Paz, 1984.

Cook, David Noble, comp. *Tasa de la visita de Francisco de Toledo.* Lima, 1975.

Cortés Conde, Roberto. *The First Stages of Modernization in Spanish America.* New York, 1974.

Corvera Zenteno, Rómulo. *Legislación agraria bolivana, 1824–1926.* La Paz, 1926.

Costas Arguedas, José Felipe. *Folklore de Yamparaez.* Sucre, 1950.

Cotler, Julio. "Actuales pautas de cambio en la sociedad rural del

Perú," in José Matos Mar, comp., *Dominación y cambio en el Perú rural*. Lima, 1969.

Crespo, Alfonso. *Los Aramayo de Chichas: Tres generaciones de mineros bolivianos*. Barcelona, 1981.

Cushner, Nicolas P. *Lords of the Land: Sugar, Wine, and Jesuit Estates of Coastal Peru, 1600–1767*. Albany, N.Y., 1980.

Dalence, José Maria. *Bosquejo estadístico de Bolivia*. La Paz, 1975. Originally published in 1851.

Dandler, Jorge. "Politics of Leadership, Brokerage, and Patronage in the Campesino Movement of Cochabamba, Bolivia." Ph.D. dissertation, University of Wisconsin, 1971.

Davies, Keith A. *Landowners in Colonial Peru*. Austin, Tex., 1984.

Davis, Natalie Z. *Society and Culture in Early Modern France*. Stanford, Calif., 1965.

Démelas, Marie-Danièle. "Darwinismo a la criolla: El Darwinismo social en Bolivia, 1880–1910," *Historia Boliviana*, 1.2 (1981), pp. 55–82.

———. *Nationalisme sans nation?: La Bolivie aux XIXe–XXe siècles*. Paris, 1980.

de Nino, Bernardino. *Etnografía chiriguana*. La Paz, 1912.

———. *Guía al Chaco boliviano*. La Paz, 1913.

———. *Prosecución de la historia del Colegio de Potosí y sus misiones*. La Paz, 1918.

———. *Las tres misiones secularizadas de la Provincia de la Cordillera*. Tarata, 1916.

Dorado, José Vicente. *Proyecto de repartición de tierras y venta de ellos entre los indígenas*. Sucre, 1864. BNB.

D'Orbigny, Alcides. *Viaje a la America meridionial*, vol. 4. Tr. Alfredo Cepeda. Buenos Aires, 1945.

Duncan, Kenneth, and Ian Rutledge, eds. *Land and Labour in Latin America*, Cambridge, Eng., 1977.

Duncan, Silvio R., and John Markoff. "Civilization and Barbarism: Cattle Frontiers in Latin America," *Comparative Studies in Society and History*, 20.4 (1978), pp. 587–620.

Erasmus, Charles J. "Land Reform and Social Revolution in Southern Bolivia. The Valleys of Chuquisaca and Tarija," in Dwight B. Heath, Charles J. Erasmus, and Hans C. Buechler, eds., *Land Reform and Social Revolution in Bolivia*. New York, 1969.

———. "The Occurrence and Disappearance of Reciprocal Farm Labor in Latin America," in Dwight B. Heath and Richard N. Adams, eds., *Contemporary Cultures and Societies of Latin America: A Reader in the Social Anthropology of Middle and South America and the Caribbean*. New York, 1965.

———. "Upper Limits of Peasantry and Agrarian Reform," *Ethnology*, 6.3 (1967), pp. 349–80.

Espino M., Norberto. "Experiencia en Alcantarí." Sucre: Instituto

Boliviano de Tecnología Agropecuario/Laval University (Montreal, Canada), 1981. Mimeo.

Farriss, Nancy M. *Maya Society Under Colonial Rule: The Collective Enterprise of Survival*. Princeton, N.J., 1984.

Fernández Soliz, Jorge. *Tema: El petróleo*. La Paz, 1976.

Fifer, J. Valerie. *Bolivia: Land, Location and Politics Since 1825*. Cambridge, Eng., 1973.

———. "The Empire Builders: A History of the Bolivian Rubber Boom and the Rise of the House of Suárez," *Journal of Latin American Studies*, 2.2 (1970), pp. 113–46.

Finot, Enrique. *Historia de la conquista del oriente boliviano*. 2d ed. La Paz, 1978.

Flores-Galindo, Alberto. *Arequipa y el sur andino (siglos XVII–XX)*. Lima, 1977.

Flores Moncayo, Jose. *Derecho agrario boliviano*. La Paz, 1956.

———. *Legislación boliviana del indio*. La Paz, [1953?].

Florescano, Enrique. *Precios de maíz y crisis agrícolas en México, 1708–1810*. Mexico, D.F., 1969.

Foster, George M. *Culture and Conquest: America's Spanish Heritage*. Chicago, 1960.

Furtado, Celso. *Economic Development of Latin America: Historical Background and Contemporary Problems*. 2d ed. Tr. Suzette Macedo. Cambridge, Eng., 1976.

Gade, Daniel W. "Spatial Displacement of Latin American Seats of Government: From Sucre to La Paz as National Capital of Bolivia," *Revista Geografica*, 73 (1970), pp. 43–57.

García Quintanilla, Julio. *Monografía de la Provincia de Azero (Hoy Hernando Siles y Luis Calvo)*. Sucre, 1962.

———. *Monografía de la Provincia de Zudáñez*. Sucre, n.d.

Geddes, Charles F. *Patiño: Rey del estaño*. Tr. Walter Montenegro. Madrid, 1984.

Genovese, Eugene D. *Roll, Jordan, Roll: The World the Slaves Made*. New York, 1972.

Giannecchini, Doroteo. *Diario de la expedición exploradora boliviana al Alto Paraguay de 1886–1887*. S.M. de los Angeles (Asis), 1896.

Gibson, Charles. *The Aztecs Under Spanish Rule: A History of the Indians of the Valley of Mexico, 1519–1810*. Stanford, Calif., 1964.

Giménez Carrazana, Manuel. *El Banco Nacional de Bolivia en el centenario de su fundación*. La Paz, 1972.

Gisbert, Teresa, and José de Mesa. *Arquitectura andina 1530–1830: Historia y analisis*. La Paz, 1985.

Gómez, Walter. *La minería en el desarrollo económico de Bolivia, 1900–1970*. La Paz, 1978.

Gonzales, Michael J. "Capitalist Agriculture and Labor Contracting in Northern Peru, 1880–1905," *Journal of Latin American Studies*, 12 (1980), pp. 291–315.

Graham, Richard. *Britain and the Onset of Modernization in Brazil, 1850–1914.* Cambridge, Eng., 1968.

Grieshaber, Erwin P. "Export Expansion and Indian Land Sales in the Department of La Paz, Bolivia 1881–1920." Paper presented at the annual American Historical Association convention, Chicago, Ill., Dec. 29, 1986.

———. "Hacienda-Indian Community Relations and Indian Acculturation: An Historiographical Essay," *Latin American Research Review,* 14.2 (1979), pp. 107–28.

———. "Survival of Indian Communities in Nineteenth-Century Bolivia." Ph.D. dissertation, University of North Carolina, 1977.

Grünberg, Georg, and Friedl Grünberg. *Los chiriguanos: Guaraní occidentales del Chaco central paraguayo.* Asunción, 1975.

Guerrero, Andres. "Renta diferencial y vías de desolución de la hacienda precapitalista en el Ecuador," *Avances,* 1978, no. 2, pp. 71–94.

Gutman, Herbert G. *Work, Culture, and Society in Industrializing America: Essays in American Working-Class and Social History.* New York, 1976.

Guy, Donna J. *Argentine Sugar Politics: Tucumán and the Generation of Eighty.* Tempe, Ariz., 1980.

Halperin Donghi, Tulio. *The Aftermath of Revolution in Latin America.* Tr. Josephine de Bunsen. New York, 1973.

Handelman, Howard. *Struggle in the Andes: Peasant Political Mobilization in Peru.* Austin, Tex., 1975.

Hanke, Lewis. *The Imperial City of Potosí: An Unwritten Chapter in the History of Latin America.* The Hague, 1956.

Harris, Olivia. "El parentesco y la economía vertical en el Ayllu Laymi (Norte de Potosí)," *Avances,* 1978, no. 1, pp. 51–64.

Havet, José L. "Administrative Complexity and Agrarian Reform in Bolivia: Implications and Prospects," in University of Ottawa Institute for International Cooperation, *Discussion Papers.* Ottawa, 1980.

———. "Rational Domination: The Power Structure in a Bolivian Rural Zone." Ph.D. dissertation, University of Pittsburgh, 1978.

Healy, Kevin. *Caciques y patrones: Una experiencia de desarrollo rural en el sud de Bolivia.* Cochabamba, 1982.

Heath, Dwight B., and Richard N. Adams, eds. *Contemporary Cultures and Societies of Latin America: A Reader in the Social Anthropology of Middle and South America and the Caribbean.* New York, Random House, 1965.

Heath, Dwight B., Charles J. Erasmus, and Hans C. Buechler. *Land Reform and Social Revolution in Bolivia.* New York, 1969.

Hennessy, Alistair. *The Frontier in Latin American History.* Albuquerque, N.M., 1978.

Heyduk, Daniel. "The Hacienda System and Agrarian Reform in Highland Bolivia: A Re-evaluation," *Ethnology,* 13.1 (1974), pp. 71–82.

———. "Huayrapampa: Bolivian Highland Peasants and the New Social Order." Cornell Latin American Dissertation Series, 1971.

Hillman, John. "The Emergence of the Tin Industry in Bolivia," *Journal of Latin American Studies*, 16.2 (1984), pp. 403–37.

Hobsbawm, Eric J. *Bandits*. Rev. ed. New York, 1981.

——— *Primitive Rebels: Studies in Archaic Forms of Social Movement in the 19th and 20th Centuries*. Manchester, Eng., 1959.

Hu-DeHart, Evelyn. "Pacification of the Yaquis in the Late Porfiriato: Developments and Implications," *Hispanic American Historical Review*, 54.1 (1974), pp. 72–93.

———. *Yaqui Resistance and Survival: The Struggle for Land and Autonomy*. Madison, Wis., 1984.

Huizer, Gerrit. *The Revolutionary Potential of Peasants in Latin America*. Lexington, Mass., 1972.

International Bureau of American Republics. *Bolivia: Geographical Sketch, Natural Resources, Laws, Economic Condition, Actual Development, Prospects of Future Growth*. Washington, D.C., 1904.

Isbell, Billie Jean. "Parentesco andino y reciprocidad kuyaq: Los que nos aman," in Giorgio Alberti and Enrique Mayer, eds., *Reciprocidad é intercambio en los Andes peruanos*. Lima, 1974.

Jaimes, Julio L. *Cuadros y trabajos de la mesa estadística, dirección de Julio L. Jaimes*. La Paz, 1885.

Jáuregui Rosquellas, Alfredo. "Monografía de la capital de la república," in J. Ricardo Alarcón, ed., *Bolivia en el primer centenario de su independencia*. N.p., 1925.

———. *Sucre: Notas históricas, estadísticas y psicológicas de la capital de Bolivia*. 2 vols. Sucre, 1912.

Jenkins, J. Craig. "Why Do Peasants Rebel? Structural and Historical Theories of Modern Peasant Rebellions," *Journal of Sociology*, 88.3 (1982), pp. 487–514.

Jofre, Manuel O. *Colonias y misiones. Informe de la visita practicada por el Delegado de Supremo Gobierno, Doctor Manuel O. Jofre Hijo*. Tarija, 1895.

Joseph, Gilbert M. "From Castle War to Class War: The Historiography of Modern Yucatán (c. 1750–1940)," *Hispanic American Historical Review*, 65.1 (1985), pp. 111–34.

Kaerger, Karl. *Landwirtschaft und Kolonisation im Spanischen Amerika*. 2 vols. Leipzig, 1901.

Karsten, Rafael. "Indian Tribes of the Argentine and Bolivian Chaco," *Commentationes Humanarum Litterarum* (Societas Scientarum Fennica), 4.1 (1932).

Katz, Friedrich. "Labor Conditions on Haciendas in Porfirian Mexico: Some Trends and Tendencies," *Hispanic American Historical Review*, 54.1 (1974), pp. 1–47.

Keith, Robert G. *Conquest and Agrarian Change: The Emergence of the Hacienda System on the Peruvian Coast*. Cambridge, Eng., 1976.

Kirsch, Henry W. *Industrial Development in a Traditional Society.* Gainesville, Fla., 1977.

Klein, Herbert S. "American Oil Companies in Latin America: The Bolivian Experience," *Inter-American Economic Affairs*, 18.2 (1964), pp. 47–72.

———. *Bolivia: The Evolution of a Multi-Ethnic Society.* New York, 1982.

———. "The Creation of the Patiño Tin Empire," *Inter-American Economic Affairs*, 19.2 (1965), pp. 3–23.

———. *Parties and Political Change in Bolivia, 1880–1952.* Cambridge, Eng., 1971.

Langer, Erick D. "La comercialización de la cebada en los ayllus y las haciendas de Tarabuco (Chuquisaca) a comienzos del siglo XX," in Olivia Harris, Brooke Larson, and Enrique Tandeter, eds., *La participación indígena en los mercados surandinos: Estrategias y reproducción social siglos XVI a XX.* La Paz, 1987, pp. 583–601.

———. "Debt Peonage and Paternalism in Latin America," *Peasant Studies*, 13.2 (1986), pp. 121–27.

———. "Espacios coloniales y economías nacionales: Bolivia y el norte argentino 1810–1930," *Siglo XIX: Revista de Historia* (Monterrey, Mexico), 2.4 (1987), pp. 135–60.

———. "Franciscan Missions and Chiriguano Workers: Colonization, Acculturation, and Indian Labor in Southeastern Bolivia," *The Americas*, 42.1 (1987), pp. 305–22.

———. "Peasant Labor and Commercial Agriculture in Cinti, Bolivia." Paper presented at the tenth national meeting of the Latin American Studies Association. Washington, D.C., 1982.

Langer, Erick D., and Robert H. Jackson. "Colonial and Republican Missions Compared: The Cases of Alta California and Southeastern Bolivia," *Comparative Studies in Society and History*, 30.2 (1988), pp. 286–311.

Larson, Brooke. "Economic Decline and Social Change in an Agrarian Hinterland: Cochabamba (Bolivia) in the Late Colonial Period." Ph.D. dissertation, Columbia University, 1978.

———. "Rural Rhythms of Class Conflict in Eighteenth-Century Cochabamba," *Hispanic American Historical Review*, 60.3 (1980), pp. 407–30.

LeGrand, Catherine C. "Perspectives for the Historical Study of Rural Politics and the Colombian Case: An Overview," *Latin American Research Review*, 12.2 (1977), pp. 7–36.

Lehmann, David, ed. *Ecology and Exchange in the Andes.* Cambridge, Eng., 1982.

Lenz B., Tomás. "Población y desarrollo de Chuquisaca," *Revista del Instituto de Sociología Boliviana (ISBO)*, 1979, no. 10, pp. 82–97.

LeRoy Ladurie, Emmanuel. *Carnival in Romans.* Tr. Mary Feeny. New York, 1979.

Límites entre las Provincias del Azero y de Cordillera: varios documentos consernientes a la cuestión. Sucre, 1882.

Lofstrom, William Lee. "The Promise and Problem of Reform: Attempted Social and Economic Change in the First Years of Bolivian Independence." Cornell Latin American Dissertation Series, 1972.

López Avila, Miguel. *Sud Cinti (Historia y tradición).* La Paz, 1981.

Loredo, Rafael, ed. *Los repartos.* Lima, 1958.

Loveman, Brian. "Critique of Arnold J. Bauer's 'Rural Workers in Spanish America: Problems of Peonage and Oppression,'" *Hispanic American Historical Review,* 59.3 (1979), pp. 478–85.

Mallo, Nicanor, and Faustino Suárez. "Monografía contemporánea de Chuquisaca," in Valentin Abecia, ed., *Historia de Chuquisaca.* Sucre, 1939.

Mallon, Florencia. *The Defense of Community in Peru's Central Highlands: Peasant Struggle and Capitalist Transition, 1860–1940.* Princeton, N.J., 1983.

Malloy, James M. *Bolivia: The Uncompleted Revolution.* Pittsburgh, Pa., 1970.

Malloy, James M., and Richard S. Thorn. *Beyond the Revolution: Bolivia Since 1952.* Pittsburgh, Pa., 1971.

Mariaca Bilbao, Enrique. *Mito y realidad del petróleo boliviano.* La Paz, 1966.

Marsh, Margaret A. *Nuestros banqueros en Bolivia.* La Paz, 1980. Originally published in 1928.

Martarelli, Angélico. *El colegio franciscano de Potosí y sus misiones.* 2d ed. La Paz, 1918.

Martin, Cheryl E. *Rural Society in Colonial Morelos.* Albuquerque, N.M., 1985.

Martínez Alier, Juan. *Los huachilleros del Perú.* Lima, 1973.

Mather, Kirtley F. "Along the Andean Front in Southeastern Bolivia," *The Geographical Review,* 12.3 (1922), pp. 358–74.

McBride, George. *The Agrarian Indian Communities of Highland Bolivia.* New York, 1921.

McCreery, David. "Coffee and Class: The Structure of Development in Liberal Guatemala," *Hispanic American Historical Review,* 56.3 (1976), pp. 438–60.

———. "Debt Servitude in Rural Guatemala, 1876–1936," *Hispanic American Historical Review,* 63.4 (1983), pp. 735–59.

McEwen, William J. *Changing Rural Society: A Study of Communities in Bolivia.* New York, 1975.

McGreevy, William P. *An Economic History of Colombia, 1845–1930.* Cambridge, Eng., 1971.

Mendieta S., Manuel. *Tierra rica, pueblo pobre: Por nuestras fronteras.* Sucre, 1928.

Mendoza, Jaime. *Figuras del pasado: Gregorio Pacheco (rasgo biográficos).* Santiago, 1924.

Métraux, Alfred. "Chiriguano and Chané," in Julian H. Steward, ed., *Handbook of South American Indians*, vol. 3. Washington, D.C., 1948.

―――. "Ethnography of the Gran Chaco," in Julian H. Steward, ed., *Handbook of South American Indians*, vol. 1. Washington, D.C.

―――. *Les Hommes dieux chez les Chiriguano*. Tucumán, 1931.

―――. "Les Migrations historiques des Tupí-Guaraní," *Journal de la Société des Americanistes* (Paris), 19 (1927), pp. 1–30.

Migdal, Joel S. *Peasants, Politics, and Revolutions: Pressures Toward Political and Social Change in the Third World*. Princeton, N.J., 1974.

Mingo, Manuel de la Concepción. *Historia de las misiones franciscanas de Tarija entre Chiriguanos*. 2 vols. Tarija, 1981.

Mitre, Antonio. *El monedero de los Andes: Región económica y moneda boliviana en el siglo XIX*. La Paz, 1987.

―――. *Los patriarcas de la plata: Estructura socioeconómica de la minería boliviana en el siglo XIX*. Lima, 1981.

Monroy Cárdenas, Arturo. *Historia aduanera de Bolivia y tratados comerciales con los paises vecinos 1825–1958*. La Paz, 1959.

Monteon, Michael. *Chile in the Nitrate Era: The Revolution of Economic Dependence*. Madison, Wis., 1982.

Montgomery, David. "Gutman's Nineteenth-Century America," *Labor History*, 19 (1978), pp. 416–29.

Mörner, Magnus. "The Spanish American Hacienda: A Survey of Recent Research and Debate," *Hispanic American Historical Review*, 53.2 (1973), pp. 183–216.

Mujía, Ricardo. *Bolivia-Paraguay: Epoca colonial*. La Paz, n.d.

Murra, John V. *Formaciones económicas y políticas del mundo andino*. Lima, 1975.

Nordensköld, Erland. "The Guaraní Invasion of the Inca Empire in the Sixteenth Century: An Historical Indian Migration," *Geographical Review*, 4 (1917), pp. 103–21.

―――. *Indianer und Weisse in Nordostbolivien*. Stuttgart, 1922.

―――. *Indianerleben: El Gran Chaco (Südamerika)*. Leipzig, 1912.

Oakes, James. *The Ruling Race: A History of American Slaveholders*. New York, 1982.

O'Brien, Thomas F. "The Antofagasta Company: A Case Study of Peripheral Capitalism," *Hispanic American Historical Review*, 60.1 (1980), pp. 1–31.

―――. "Chilean Elites and Foreign Investors: Chilean Nitrate Policy, 1880–1882," *Journal of Latin American Studies*, 11.1 (1979), pp. 101–20.

Orlove, Benjamin S. "The Position of Rustlers in Regional Society: Social Banditry in the Andes," in Benjamin S. Orlove and Glynn Custred, eds., *Land and Power in Latin America*. New York, 1978.

————. "Reciprocidad, desigualdad y dominación," in Giorgio Alberti and Enrique Mayer, eds., *Reciprocidad é intercambio en los Andes peruanos*. Lima, 1974.

Ovando Sanz, Jorge Alejandro. *El tributo indígena de las finanzas bolivianas del siglo XIX*. La Paz, 1985.

Paige, Jeffery M. *Agrarian Revolution: Social Movements and Export Agriculture in the Underdeveloped World*. New York, 1975.

Payne, Will, and Charles T. W. Wilson. *Missionary Pioneering in Bolivia, with Some Account of Work in Argentina*. London, n.d.

Pearse, Andrew. *The Latin American Peasant*. London, 1975.

Peñaloza, Luis. *Historia económica de Bolivia*. 2 vols. La Paz, 1946.

Peñaloza Cordero, Luis. *Nueva historia económica de Bolivia*. 5 vols. La Paz, 1981–85.

Pentland, Joseph Barclay. *Informe sobre Bolivia*. Tr. Jack Aitken Soux. Potosí, 1975.

Piel, Jean. *Capitalisme agraire au Pérou: L'essor du neo-latifundisme dans le Pérou républicain*. Paris, 1983.

————. "The Place of the Peasantry in the National Life of Peru in the Nineteenth Century," *Past and Present*, 46 (1970), pp. 108–33.

Pinckert Justinano, Guillermo. *La guerra chiriguana*. Santa Cruz, Bolivia, 1978.

Platt, Tristan. "Acerca del sistema tributario pre-toledano en el Alto Perú," *Avances*, 1978, no. 1, pp. 33–46.

————. "Conciencia andina y conciencia proletaria: Qhuyaruna y ayllu en el norte de Potosí," *HISLA: Revista latinoamericana de historia económica y social*, 2 (1983), pp. 47–73.

————. "Dos visiones de la relación ayllu/estado: La resistencia de los indios de Chayanta a la revisita general (1882–1885)," *Historia Boliviana*, 2.1 (1982), pp. 33–46.

————. *Espejos y maíz: Temas de la estructura simbólica andina*. La Paz, 1976.

————. *Estado boliviano y ayllu andino: Tierra y tributo en el norte de Potosí*. Lima, 1982.

————. *Estado tributario y librecambio en Potosí (Siglo XIX): Mercado indígena, proyecto proteccionista y lucha de ideologías monetarias*. La Paz, 1986.

————. "Liberalism and Ethnocide in the Southern Andes," *History Workshop*, 17 (Spring 1984), pp. 3–18.

————. "The Role of the Andean *Ayllu* in the Reproduction of the Petty Commodity Regime in North Potosí (Bolivia)," in David Lehmann, ed., *Ecology and Exchange in the Andes*. Cambridge, Eng., 1982.

————. "Symétries en miroir. Le concept *yanantin* chez les Macha de Bolivie," *Annales: Economies, Sociétés, Civilisations*, 33.5–6 (1978), pp. 1082–1084.

256   *Bibliography*

Popkin, Samuel L. *The Rational Peasant: The Political Economy of Rural Society in Vietnam.* Berkeley, Calif., 1979.
Prudencio, Juan Francisco. *El fracaso de la obra colonizadora en Bolivia: La cuestión del Chaco.* Sucre, 1927.
Querejazu, Jorge. *Apuntes para una historia económica de Chuquisaca.* Sucre, 1977.
Querejazu Calvo, Roberto. *Guano, salitre y sangre: Historia de la Guerra del Pacífico.* Cochabamba, 1979.
———. *Llallagua: Historia de una montaña.* 2d ed. La Paz, 1978.
———. *Masamaclay: Historia política, diplomática y militar de la guerra del Chaco.* 3d ed. La Paz, 1975.
Ramirez, Susan E. *Provincial Patriarchs: Land Tenure and the Economics of Power in Colonial Peru.* Albuquerque, N.M., 1986.
Ramírez del Aguila, Pedro. *Noticias políticas de Indias (1639).* Transcribed by Jaime Urioste Arana. Sucre, 1978.
Ramírez Ramírez, Juan. *Cinti, tierra de labor en decadencia.* Potosí, 1935.
———. "Historia de la Hacienda El Patronato." Unpublished manuscript, n.d.
———. "Monografía de Cinti." Unpublished manuscript, 1975.
Real Academia Española. *Diccionario de la lengua castellana.* Madrid, 1732.
Reyeros, Rafael. *El ponguaje.* La Paz, 1949.
Rivera, José E. "El Banco Nacional de Bolivia," in J. Ricardo Alarcón, ed., *Bolivia en su primer centenario de su independencia.* N.p., 1925.
Rivera C., Silvia. "La expansión del latifundio en el altiplano boliviano: Elementos para la caracterización de una oligarquía regional," *Avances,* 1978, no. 2, pp. 95–118.
———. *'Oprimidos pero no vencidos': Luchas del campesinado aymara y qhechua 1900–1980.* La Paz, 1986.
Robinson Wright, Maria. *Bolivia: The Central Highway of South America, a Land of Rich Resources and Varied Interest.* Philadelphia, 1907.
Roca, José Luis. *Fisonomía del regionalismo boliviano.* La Paz, 1980.
Rock, David. *Argentina in the Twentieth Century.* London, 1975.
Rodríguez Ostria, Gustavo. "Analisis histórico del proceso de constitución de la región," *Los Tiempos,* Sept. 14, 1985, p. 5.
Rojas, Gabriel de. "Memoria de los repartimientos de las Charcas enviada por el capitán Gabriel de Rojas," in Rafael Loredo, ed., *Los repartos.* Lima, 1958.
Rossells, Beatriz. "Ideologías sobre la mujer en el siglo XIX en las revistas bolivianas." Unpublished manuscript, n.d., in my possession.
Rück, Ernesto O. *Biografía de don Avelino Aramayo.* Potosí, 1891.
Rutledge, Ian. "The Integration of the Highland Peasantry into the Sugar Cane Economy of Northern Argentina, 1930–43," in Kenneth

Duncan and Ian Rutledge, eds., *Land and Labour in Latin America.* Cambridge, Eng., 1977.

————. "Plantations and Peasants in Northern Argentina: The Sugar Cane Industry of Salta and Jujuy, 1930–1943," in David Rock, ed., *Argentina in the Twentieth Century.* London, 1975.

Saignes, Thierry. "Une 'Frontière fossile': La Cordillère Chiriguano au XIII siècle." Ph.D. dissertation, Ecole des Hautes Etudes (Paris), 1974.

————. "Jésuites et Franciscains face aux Chiriguano: Les ambiguités de la réduction missionnaire," in *Eglise et politique en Amérique hispanique.* Bordeaux, 1984.

Sanabria Fernández, Hernando. *Apiaguaiqui-Tumpa: Biografía del pueblo chiriguano y de su último caudillo.* La Paz, 1972.

————. *En busca de Eldorado: La colonización del oriente boliviano.* 2d ed. La Paz, 1973.

Sánchez Albornoz, Nicolas. *Indios y tributos en el Alto Perú.* Lima, 1978.

Sanjines G., Alfredo. *La reforma agraria en Bolivia.* La Paz, 1932.

Sanjines U., Bernardino. "Ventas de las tierras de comunidad [1871]," *Illimani*, 1976, no. 8–9, pp. 51–76.

Santiváñez, José María. "Revindicación de los terrenos de comunidad [1871]," *Illimani*, 1976, no. 8–9, pp. 99–138.

————. "Revindicación de los terrenos de comunidad ó sea refutación del folleto titulado 'Legitimidad de las compras de tierras realengas' [1871]," *Illimani*, 1976, no. 8–9, pp. 151–82.

Schmieder, Oscar. "The East Bolivian Andes South of the Rio Grande or Guapay," *University of California Publications in Geography,* 2.5 (Nov. 10, 1926), pp. 85–210.

Schoop, Wolfgang. *Ciudades bolivianas.* La Paz, 1981.

Schurz, W. L. *Bolivia: A Commercial and Industrial Handbook.* Washington, D.C., 1921.

Scott, James C. *The Moral Economy of the Peasant: Rebellion and Subsistence in Southeast Asia.* New Haven, Conn., 1976.

Service, Elman R. "Indian-European Relations in Colonial Latin America," *American Anthropologist,* 62.3 (1955), pp. 411–25.

Singelmann, Peter. "The Closing Triangle: Critical Notes on a Model for Peasant Mobilization in Latin America," *Comparative Studies in Society and History,* 17.4 (1975), pp. 389–409.

Skocpol, Theda. "What Makes Peasants Revolutionary?," in Robert P. Weller and Scott E. Guggenheim, eds., *Power and Protest in the Countryside: Studies of Rural Unrest in Asia, Europe, and Latin America.* Durham, N.C., 1982.

Slatta, Richard W. "Rural Criminality and Social Conflict in Nineteenth-Century Buenos Aires Province," *Hispanic American Historical Review,* 60.3 (1980), pp. 450–72.

————, ed. *Bandidos: The Varieties of Latin American Banditry.* Westport, Conn., 1987.

Solares Arroyo, Rodolfo. *Una causa sagrada: Chuquisaca se muere.* Sucre, 1917.

Solicitud presentada al Supremo Gobierno por los compradores de tierras de comunidad. La Paz, 1873.

Stern, Steve J. *Peru's Indian Peoples and the Challenge of Spanish Conquest: Huamanga to 1640.* Madison, Wis., 1982.

———. "The Social Significance of Judicial Institutions in an Exploitative Society: Huamanga, Peru, 1570–1640," in George A. Collier, Renato I. Rosaldo, and John D. Wirth, eds., *The Inca and Aztec States 1400–1800: Anthropology and History.* New York, 1982.

Stinchcombe, Arthur L. "Agricultural Enterprise and Rural Class Relations," *Journal of Sociology,* 67.3 (1961), pp. 65–76.

Sublevación de los indios chiriguanos en las Provincias de Azero y Cordillera pertenecientes a los departamentos de Sucre y Santa Cruz de la República de Bolivia. Potosí, 1892. By an anonymous "misionero."

Susnik, Bratislava. *Chiriguanos,* vol. 1. Asunción, 1968.

———. *Dispersión Tupí-Guaraní prehistórica.* Asunción, 1975.

Taylor, William B. *Drinking, Homicide, and Rebellion in Colonial Mexican Villages.* Stanford, Calif., 1979.

———. *Landlord and Peasant in Colonial Oaxaca.* Stanford, Calif., 1972.

———. "Sacarse de pobre: El bandolerismo en la Nueva Galicia 1794–1821," *Revista Jalisco,* 2.1–2 (1981), pp. 34–45.

Temple, Edmond. *Travels in Various Parts of Peru,* vol. 2. London, 1830.

Thompson, E. P. "The Moral Economy of the English Crowd in the Eighteenth Century," *Past and Present,* no. 50 (1971), pp. 76–136.

Thorp, Rosemary, and Geoffrey Bertram. *Peru 1890–1977: Growth and Policy in an Open Economy.* New York, 1978.

Thouar, A. *Explorations dans l'Amérique de Sud.* Paris, 1891.

Tilly, Charles. *From Mobilization to Revolution.* Reading, Mass., 1978.

Torres de Mendoza, Luis, ed. *Colección de documentos inéditos relativos al descubrimiento, conquista y organización de las antiguas posesiones españolas de América y Oceania sacados de los archivos del reino y muy especialmente del de Indias,* vol. 9. Madrid, 1868.

Ulpana Vicente, Filemon. *Yachayninchej: El saber agrícola campesino de San Lucas.* Sucre, 1981.

Vargas, Pedro. *Indicaciones económicas para la reforma del sistema tributario de Bolivia.* Potosí, 1864. BNB.

Vásquez de Espinosa, Antonio. *Compendio y descripción de las Indias Occidentales.* Washington, D.C., 1948.

Vega, Garcilaso de la. *The Incas: The Royal Commentaries of the Inca Garcilaso de la Vega.* Tr. Maria Jolas. Ed. Alain Gheerbrant. New York, 1961.

Wachtel, Nathan. *The Vision of the Vanquished: The Spanish Conquest Through Indian Eyes, 1530–1570.* Tr. Ben and Sian Reynolds. New York, 1983.

Walle, Paul. *La Bolivie et ses mines.* Paris, n.d.

Wasserman, Mark. *Capitalists, Caciques, and Revolution: The Native Elite and Foreign Enterprise in Chihuahua, Mexico, 1854–1911.* Chapel Hill, N.C., 1984.

Waterbury, Ronald. "Nonrevolutionary Peasants: Oaxaca Compared to Morelos in the Mexican Revolution," *Comparative Studies in Society and History*, 17.4 (1975), pp. 410–42.

Whiteford, Scott. *Workers from the North: Plantations, Bolivian Labor, and the City in Northwest Argentina.* Austin, Tex., 1981.

Whitehead, Lawrence. "El impacto de la gran depresión en Bolivia," *Desarrollo Económico*, 12.45 (1972), pp. 49–80.

———. "The Vineyards of Cinti Canyon, Bolivia." Unpublished manuscript, 1970, in my possession.

Index

In this Index an "f" after a number indicates a separate reference on the next page, and an "ff" indicates separate references on the next two pages; "passim" is used for clusters of references in close but not consecutive sequence.

Library of Congress Cataloging-in-Publication Data

Langer, Erick Detlef.
  Economic change and rural resistance in southern Bolivia,
1880–1930 / Erick D. Langer.
      p.   cm.
  Bibliography: p.
  Includes index.
  ISBN 0-8047-1491-6 (alk. paper)
    1. Chuquisaca (Bolivia)—Economic conditions.   2. Chuquisaca
(Bolivia)—Rural conditions.   3. Social change—Bolivia—Chuquisaca—
History—20th century.   4. Social change—Bolivia—Chuquisaca—
History—19th century.   5. Economic development—Social aspects—
Case studies.   I. Title.
HC183.C48L36 1989   88-31117
303.4'0984'24—dc19   CIP